who knew?

cooking essentials

365 make ahead meals

who knew?

cooking essentials

365 make ahead meals

CASTLE POINT PUBLISHING

Bruce Lubin & Jeanne Bossolina Lubin

Cover concept: Richard Pasquarelli
Interior layout and design: Quadrum Solutions Pvt. Ltd.

Castle Point Publishing
58 Ninth Street
Hoboken, NJ 07030
www.castlepointpub.com

ISBN: 978-0-9832376-0-0

Printed and bound in the United States of America

10 9 8 7 6 5 4 3 2 1

Please note: The authors have compiled the information contained herein from a variety of sources, and neither the authors, publisher, manufacturer, nor distributor can assume responsibility for the effectiveness of the recipes or tips herein. Caution is urged when using any of the solutions, recipes, or tips in this book. Castle Point Publishing shall have no liability for damages (whether direct, indirect, consequential or otherwise) arising from the use, attempted use, misuse, or application of any of the solutions, recipes, or tips described in this book.

Dedication

For Jack, Terrence, and Aidan, for eating (most) of the food we put in front of them, even the "experiments."

Acknowledgments

We're grateful to our families, friends, and fans for providing us with their favorite family recipes and allowing us to print them here—we couldn't have done it without you! Thanks to Joy Mangano and Brian Scevola, whose support we are forever grateful for; Beth Blackburn and Maureen Lordon, for keeping our engines running; Joanie Rudolph and Andrea Cajuste, our logistics and shipping goddesses; and Jennifer Boudinot, Lupe Velasquez, and the entire staff of Castle Point Publishing.

Table of Contents

Who Knew? Cooking Essentials

Two-Meal Soups And Stews

Easy Casseroles

Introduction

As many of our readers know, we've been compiling household tips for almost twenty years. As we pulled together our many tips on cooking, we found ourselves reminiscing about our favorite family recipes, and looking forward to using our newfound knowledge to make them even easier.

We wanted to bring these recipes (along with their accompanying tips) to you, but we also wanted our *Who Knew? Cooking Essentials* library to be more than just some delicious recipes. We wanted to give you ingredients that were inexpensive, meals that would be easy to make even if you had little or no cooking knowledge, and enough recipes to guarantee you'd always be able to find one you could make with ingredients you have on-hand.

We challenged ourselves to cook a different meal every night of the year, based on what we found on sale that week at the grocery store: soup, beans, and other canned items play a large role, as do prepared foods like spaghetti sauce and ramen noodles. We asked our friends with children (the more kids the better) what recipes they had success with—"What foods to you make that your kids always eat?" and "What's your 'go-to' dinner?"

We wanted to make cookbooks that reflect the way people really eat. If you enjoy complicated recipes that contain only the finest ingredients, there are plenty of cookbooks out there for you. This cookbook is an everyday, hard-working cookbook that will give you fast, simple recipes for common ingredients.

We wanted our cookbooks to be more than that, too! If you do have time to do a little cooking, we've included 12 "Light Switch" recipes that give you low-fat versions of many of the ingredients you'll find in our cookbooks—from cream of mushroom soup to Velveeta cheese. Because you'll be making them from scratch, they'll also be cheaper than their store-bought counterparts—giving you yet another way to save. And if you don't have the time (like so many of us), you can simply buy the already-prepared versions at the store.

This book, *365 Make-Ahead Meals*, makes meal-planning easy by giving you hundreds of recipes you can make over the weekend (or whenever you have time) for your entire week. It also includes hearty soups that will last you at least two meals, and quick slow-cooker recipes that you can start in the morning and eat when you get home from work. Whether you're looking for a casserole recipe to freeze for when you need it, a delicious dish to keep in the fridge for later in the week, or an easy meal that will last your family several days, you'll find it here.

We hope you enjoy our recipes as much as you've enjoyed our tips! And while you're waiting for the timer to ding, don't forget to visit us at WhoKnewTips.com and let us know *your* favorite recipe or cooking tip. We might just add it to our next book!

Light Switch Recipes

The recipes on the following pages are low-fat, inexpensive substitutes for many foods you find at the grocery store, in your cabinets, and in the pages of this book. Use them interchangeably with their store-bought counterparts, or use them when you see the "Light Switch" sidebars throughout the book.

1 Healthy Chicken Broth

Chicken broth is so easy to make, we start a pot of it every time we're having a whole chicken. Just put your scraps in the pot along with a few vegetables, and you'll have low-fat alternative to the canned stuff that's practically free!

4–5	**pounds of chicken parts, including necks, backs, and meaty bones**
1	**large onion, quartered**
2	**large carrots, peeled and halved**
4	**stalks celery, leafy tops intact, halved**
2	**cloves garlic**
1	**bay leaf**
½	**tablespoon whole black peppercorns**
4	**quarts cold water**

1. Place all ingredients in large soup pot. Cook on high until boiling, then reduce heat to low and cook, stirring occasionally, for 3 hours.
2. Pour broth through a strainer, saving the liquid only. Place in refrigerator until cool and fat congeals at top.
3. Skim fat; store broth in refrigerator or freezer until ready to use.

Yields approximately 3 quarts.
1¾ cups = 1 (15 ounce) can

 Who Knew?

Don't worry about peeling the onion before you put it in the soup pot—the onion skin will give your soup a richer brown color.

2 Healthy Beef Broth

Cheap beef parts are not usually as easy to come by at the butcher's as cheap chicken parts, but if you've just prepared a roast or your family has just devoured some short ribs, save the bones to make this super cheap broth. Or ask at the deli counter for what they have available!

2 **pounds meaty beef soup bones (beef shanks or short ribs)**
1 **medium onion, quartered**
2 **carrots, peeled, quartered**
2 **celery ribs with leaves, halved**
¼ **cup warm water**
6 **cups cold water**
2 **bay leaves**
1 **garlic cloves**
4 **whole peppercorns**
1 **teaspoon dried thyme or oregano**

1. Preheat oven to 450°.
2. Place soup bones in roasting pan. Bake uncovered for 30 minutes. Add onion, carrots, and celery and bake for additional 30 minutes.
3. Transfer to large soup pot. Add warm water to roasting pan and stir to loosen browned material at bottom of pan. Transfer water and juices to soup pot.
4. Add cold water, bay leaves, garlic, peppercorns, and thyme or oregano. Cook on high heat until boiling, then reduce heat to low and simmer for 4 hours.
5. Pour broth through a strainer, saving the liquid only. Place in refrigerator until cool and fat congeals at top.
3. Skim fat; store broth in refrigerator or freezer until ready to use.

Yields approximately 1 quart.
1¾ cup = 1 (15 ounce) can

3 Low-Fat Cream of Chicken Soup Base

This recipe makes 9 soup can–sized portions of condensed soup to use as a base in casseroles and other dishes. To eat as a meal, simply add an additional 1¼ cups water in step 2.

2 **cups nonfat dry milk powder**
¾ **cup cornstarch**
¼ **cup reduced sodium chicken bouillon granules**
¼ **teaspoon onion powder**
½ **teaspoon ground thyme**
½ **teaspoon dried basil**
⅛ **teaspoon black pepper**

1. Combine milk powder, cornstarch, chicken bouillon, onion powder, thyme, basil, and black pepper and mix until blended. Keep in an airtight container until ready to use.
2. To make 1 can's worth of condensed soup, combine ⅓ cup of mixture and 1¼ cups water in saucepan. Cook, stirring, until mixture thickens.

Yields 11¼ cups.
1¼ cup = 1 (10 ounce) can condensed soup

4 Low-Fat Cream of Celery Soup Base

This easy recipe makes 2 soup can–sized portions of condensed soup to use as a base in casseroles and other dishes. To eat as a meal, simply add an additional 2½ cups water to this recipe.

2½ **cups chopped celery**
1 **tablespoon butter or margarine**
2 **tablespoons flour**
½ **cup vegetable stock**
1½ **cups 1% or 2% milk**
1 **teaspoon celery salt or table salt**
¼ **teaspoon black pepper**

1. Place celery in microwave-safe container and heat on HIGH, covered, until celery is tender 2–3 minutes.
2. Melt butter in saucepan over medium heat. Add flour and mix well to form a roux.
3. Add celery and remaining ingredients and cook over medium heat, stirring constantly, until mixture thickens, about 7 minutes.
4. Pour into blender and blend until smooth.
5. Store in airtight container in refrigerator until ready to use.

Yields 2 cups.
1¼ cup = 1 (10 ounce) can condensed soup

5 Low-Fat Four-Cheese Blend

Low-fat cheese blends are great for their waistline-saving properties, but often sacrifice taste. This four-cheese blend uses a mixture of reduced-fat cheese and cheeses that are naturally low in fat to give you fewer calories with a richer taste. You'll also save a bundle by grating the cheese yourself!

1 **cup grated low-fat sharp Cheddar cheese**
1 **cup grated jalapeno Cheddar cheese**
1 **cup part-skim mozzarella cheese**
1 **cup grated smoked Gouda cheese**

1. Combine grated cheese and toss to mix thoroughly. Store refrigerated in airtight container until ready to use.

Yields 4 cups.
2 cups = 1 (8 ounce) package shredded cheese

 Who Knew?

Want to know the easiest way to clean a cheese grater? Before you begin grating, spray it with vegetable oil, which will make it less sticky. Afterward, rub the crusty heel from a stale loaf of French bread over the grater, and your clean-up is finished!

6 Melty Cheese Sauce

No cheese sauce can really compare to the creamy, melty quality of Velveeta cheese—but maybe that's a good thing, because we'd have to have a laboratory in our home! This cheese sauce at least comes close, and it's richer in flavor. Use low-fat cheese and it will save you a lot of calories.

2 tablespoons butter or margarine
2 tablespoons flour
2 cups skim milk
1 teaspoon white wine or lemon juice
2 cups grated Cheddar cheese (use reduced-fat if desired)
1 teaspoon salt

1. Melt butter in saucepan over medium heat. Add flour and mix well to form a roux.
2. Add milk and wine or lemon juice and cook, stirring constantly, until sauce thickens, about 7–10 minutes. Make sure sauce does not boil.
3. Remove from heat; add Cheddar cheese and salt and mix until cheese is melted. If necessary, warm over low heat to melt cheese.
4. Let cool to room temperature and store in airtight container in refrigerator until ready to use.

Yields approximately 3 cups.
1½ cups = 1 (8 ounce) package Velveeta, melted

 Who Knew?

Most reduced-fat Cheddar will take longer to melt than regular Cheddar, so make sure to grate it finely. You may also want to add it gradually while stirring constantly over low heat.

7 Super Healthy Salsa

Once you've tried this fresh salsa, you may never go back to canned! This recipe is for medium salsa, but make it as mild or as spicy as you wish by adjusting the amount of jalapeno pepper.

4–5 medium to large tomatoes
½ of 1 jalapeno pepper
½ of 1 medium red onion, chopped
1 clove garlic, chopped
¼ cup chopped fresh cilantro
¼ teaspoon salt
⅛ teaspoon black pepper

1. Chop tomatoes in bite-sized chunks. Place in bowl and add remainder of ingredients.
2. If a less-chunky salsa is desired, remove half of tomato mixture and puree in blender until smooth. Add back in.
3. Keep in airtight container in refrigerator until ready to use.

Yields 2–4 cups.
2 cups = 1 (16 ounce) jar salsa

8 Low-Fat Sour Cream Substitute

¾ cup low-fat cottage cheese
¼ cup non-fat plain yogurt
2 tablespoons skim milk
2 tablespoons lemon juice

1. Add ingredients to blender or food processor and blend until smooth.
2. Refrigerate for at least 4 hours before serving.

Yields approximately 1 cup.
1 cup = 1 (8 ounce) carton sour cream

 Who Knew?

Add seasonings like minced garlic, freshly ground black pepper, or chopped scallions to make flavored sour cream for dips or special garnishes.

9 Low-Fat Alfredo Sauce

It's hard to make a cream-based sauce low fat, but this recipe gets a little help from some reduced fat cream cheese.

2 tablespoons butter or margarine
1 garlic clove, minced
2½ tablespoons flour
2 cups skim milk
½ of 1 (8 ounce) package light cream cheese, softened
½ cup grated Parmesan cheese
½ teaspoon salt
¼ teaspoon black pepper

1. Melt butter or margarine is saucepan over medium heat. Add garlic and cook, stirring, until garlic begins to turn translucent, about 1 minute.
2. Add flour and mix well to form roux.
3. Add milk and cook, stirring constantly, over medium-high heat. When mixture begins to bubble, reduce heat to low and continue stirring constantly until mixture thickens, about 5 minutes.
4. Add cream cheese, Parmesan cheese, salt, and pepper. Stir until cheese melts.
5. Store in airtight container in refrigerator.

Yields approximately 3 cups.
1¾ cups = approximately 1 (16 ounce) jar Alfredo sauce

10 Homemade Spaghetti Sauce

This recipe uses carrots rather than sugar to neutralize the acidity of the tomatoes.

¼ cup olive oil
2 medium yellow onions, finely chopped
4 garlic cloves, minced
1 tablespoon tomato paste
2 (32 ounce) cans crushed tomatoes
½ cup vegetable broth or water
2 carrots, peeled and grated
1 tablespoon dried oregano
1 tablespoon Italian seasoning
1 teaspoon salt
½ teaspoon black pepper
½ teaspoon crushed red pepper flakes (optional)

1. Heat oil in large saucepan over medium-high heat. When hot, add onions. Cook, stirring, until onions just begin to turn translucent, about 5 minutes. Add garlic and tomato paste and continue to cook, stirring, until tomato paste begins to brown.
2. Add tomatoes, broth, carrots, oregano, Italian seasoning, and salt and mix well. Heat until bubbling, then reduce heat to low and simmer, stirring occasionally, for 1 hour.
3. Add black pepper and red pepper flakes (if desired).

Yields approximately 6 cups.
1¾ cups = approximately 1 (16 ounce) jar spaghetti sauce

11 Italian Salad Dressing Mix

This mix is a delicious, homemade substitute for a packet of Italian dressing. It also gives you the ability to omit the sugar or salt according to your diet.

1 teaspoon carrot, grated, then finely chopped
1 teaspoon red bell pepper, finely minced
2 teaspoons sugar
¾ teaspoon lemon pepper
¼ teaspoon dried parsley flakes
¼ teaspoon garlic powder
⅛ teaspoon onion powder
⅛ teaspoon ground oregano
1 teaspoon salt
⅛ teaspoon black pepper

1. Preheat oven to 250°.
2. Place carrot and bell pepper on baking ban and heat in oven until dry, but not brown, about 45–60 minutes.
3. Combine dried carrot and bell pepper with the other ingredients in small bowl; mix well. Store in airtight container.
4. To make into dressing, mix with ¼ cup vinegar, then slowly add ½ cup oil and mix until well blended.

Yields approximately 2 tablespoons.
2 tablespoons = 1 (1 ounce) packet Italian dressing mix

12 Low-Fat Meatballs

Use these meatballs instead of the frozen variety or on top of spaghetti and in soup. We use bread crumbs in our version to lower the fat content.

2 **pounds lean ground beef**
1 **cup breadcrumbs**
1 **medium onion, chopped**
2 **eggs**
1 **tablespoon dried oregano**
2 **cloves garlic, minced**
1 **teaspoon salt, divided**
½ **teaspoon black pepper**
1 **tablespoon vegetable or canola oil**

1. Combine beef, breadcrumbs, onion, eggs, oregano, garlic, salt, and pepper in bowl. Mix well and form into meatballs about 1¼ inches in diameter.
2. Heat oil in large skillet over medium-high heat. When hot, add meatballs and cook, turning and flipping occasionally, until meatballs are brown on all sides. Remove to paper towels and let drain.

Yields approximately 18 ounces.
18 ounces = 1 package frozen meatballs

 Who Knew?

Here's the famous tip that inspired our upside-down egg logo: Always store your eggs upside down! This centers the yolk and makes them last longer. It's also much better to keep your eggs in their original carton than placing them in the "egg section" of your refrigerator door. This allows their temperature to be more constant and keeps them from absorbing odors.

Make Now, Refrigerate For Later!

Every Sunday, we spend at least part of our afternoon in the kitchen, where we prepare meals that will last us a week! And while the casseroles and two-meal soups you'll find later in this book give you large dishes that will last you several days, the quick and easy meals in this chapter give you lots of options for simple, delicious dinners that will make sure your weekly menu isn't too homogenous. And they won't take up a lot of room in your fridge!

1 Parmesan Chicken Breasts

6 boneless, skinless chicken breast halves
1½ cups dry breadcrumbs
½ cup grated Parmesan cheese
1 teaspoon dried basil
½ teaspoon garlic powder
1 (8 ounce) carton sour cream

1. Preheat oven to 325°.
2. Flatten chicken to ½-inch thickness.
3. Combine breadcrumbs, cheese, basil, and garlic powder in shallow dish.
4. Dip chicken in sour cream, then coat with crumb mixture. Place in sprayed, 10 x 15-inch baking dish, making sure chicken breasts do not touch.
5. Bake until golden brown, about 50–60 minutes.

SERVES 6.

 Who Knew? Light Switch

To make this recipe lower in fat, substitute 1 cup of our Low-Fat Sour Cream Substitute (Light Switch #8) for the carton of sour cream.

2 Sunny Chicken

This sweet and tangy dish will brighten up any plate.

4 boneless, skinless chicken breast halves
1½ teaspoons curry powder
1 teaspoon salt
½ teaspoon black pepper
1½ cups orange juice
1 tablespoon brown sugar
1 cup uncooked rice
1 teaspoon mustard

1. Rub chicken breasts with curry powder, salt, and pepper.
2. Combine orange juice, brown sugar, rice, and mustard in large skillet and mix well.
3. Place chicken breasts on top of rice mixture and bring to a boil. Reduce heat, cover, and simmer for 30 minutes.
4. Remove from heat and let stand, covered, until all liquid absorbs into rice, about 10 minutes.

SERVES 4.

3 Italian Chicken and Rice

1 tablespoon olive oil
3 boneless, skinless chicken breast halves, cut into strips
1 (14 ounce) can chicken broth
1 teaspoon Italian seasoning
¾ cup rice
  Water, as necessary
¼ cup grated Parmesan cheese

1. Heat oil over medium heat in large skillet. When hot, add chicken strips. Cook, stirring, until chicken is cooked through, about 10 minutes. Set aside chicken.
2. Add broth and rice to skillet, and heat to boil. Cover and simmer over low heat for 25 minutes. (Add water if necessary.)
3. Stir in cheese, and return chicken to pan. Cover and cook until done, about 5 minutes.

SERVES 6.

4 Dijon Skillet Chicken

¼ cup ranch salad dressing
1 tablespoon Dijon-style mustard
2 tablespoons butter
4 boneless, skinless chicken breast halves
3 tablespoons white wine or chicken broth

1. Combine salad dressing and mustard in salad bowl and set aside.
2. Melt butter in large skillet over medium heat. Add chicken and cook, flipping occasionally, until chicken is brown on both sides, about 10–15 minutes.
3. Add wine or broth and simmer for additional 20 minutes, flipping once.
4. Whisk in mustard mixture and cook, stirring constantly, until it blends and is heated through.
5. Serve over rice or egg noodles.

SERVES 4.

 Who Knew?

Have leftover rice after eating this dish? Rice can be stored in fridge for a longer amount of time if you store a slice of toast on top of it. The toast will absorb excess moisture and keep the rice fluffy and fresh.

5 Super Cheese Chicken

1 (10 ounce) can cream of chicken soup
1 cup regular brown rice
1½ cups water
¼ teaspoon salt
¼ teaspoon black pepper, divided
4–6 boneless, skinless chicken breast halves
1 (8 ounce) package shredded Colby-Jack cheese

1. Preheat oven to 350°.
2. Combine soup, rice, water, salt, and half pepper in bowl.
3. Transfer rice-soup mixture to 9 x 13-inch baking dish.
4. Sprinkle chicken with remaining pepper and place in baking dish with rice-soup mixture.
5. Cover and bake for 50 minutes. Uncover, sprinkle cheese over chicken, and serve.

SERVES 6.

 Who Knew? Light Switch

To make this recipe lower in fat, substitute 1¼ cup of our Low-Fat Cream of Chicken Soup Base (Light Switch #3) for the can of cream of chicken soup, and 2 cups of our Low-Fat Four-Cheese Blend (Light Switch #5) for the package of Colby-Jack cheese.

6 Chicken Scarborough Fair

We named this chicken dish after its tasty seasonings: parsley, sage, rosemary, and thyme!

6 boneless, skinless chicken breast halves
½ cup (1 stick) butter, softened, divided
¼ teaspoon salt
⅛ teaspoon black pepper
3 slices mozzarella cheese
1 egg
1 tablespoon water
½ cup flour
1 cup seasoned breadcrumbs
2 tablespoons chopped parsley
¼ teaspoon dried sage
¼ teaspoon rosemary
¼ teaspoon thyme
½ cup dry white wine

1. Flatten chicken to ¼-inch thickness.
2. Top each with salt, pepper, and 1 slice cheese. Roll up with cheese in center. Tuck in ends.
3. Beat egg with water. Coat chicken lightly with flour, dip in egg mixture, and roll in breadcrumbs. Arrange rolls seam-side down in sprayed, 7 x 11-inch baking dish. Refrigerate for 1 hour.
4. When ready to bake, preheat oven to 350°. Remove chicken rolls from refrigerator.
5. Melt remaining butter in saucepan, and stir in parsley, sage, rosemary, and thyme. Pour ½ mixture over chicken.
6. Cover rolls and bake for 30 minutes, basting with remaining butter mixture halfway through cooking time.
7. Remove from oven and pour wine over chicken. Bake, uncovered, for additional 20 minutes, basting with pan juices once during cooking.

SERVES 6.

7 Chicken Super Supper

5 boneless, skinless chicken
  breast halves
5 slices onion
5 potatoes, peeled, quartered
1 (10 ounce) can cream of celery soup
¼ cup water

1. Preheat oven to 325°.
2. Place chicken breasts in sprayed, 9 x 13-inch baking dish. Top chicken with onion slices and place potatoes around chicken.
3. Heat soup with water in saucepan over medium heat for 5 minutes.
4. Pour soup over chicken and vegetables. Cover and bake for 1 hour 10 minutes.

SERVES 5.

 Who Knew? Light Switch

To make this dish lower in fat, substitute 1¼ cups of our Low-Fat Cream of Celery Soup Base (Light Switch #4) for the can of soup.

8 Chicken with White Wine Sauce

¼ cup (½ stick) butter
4 large boneless, skinless chicken
  breast halves
1 cup diced celery
½ cup seeded, diced green or red
  bell pepper
½ cup minced onion
1½ cups white wine

1. Melt butter in large skillet over medium-high heat, and brown chicken on all sides, about 5 minutes per side.
2. Remove chicken and set aside.
3. Sauté celery, bell pepper, and onion in saucepan until tender, about 5–8 minutes. Pour in wine and stir.
4. Return chicken to skillet, cover, and cook over medium heat until juices run clear, about 15 minutes. While cooking, baste with pan juices several times.

SERVES 4.

 Who Knew?

Old white wine can be used for more than just cooking! Use white wine to wipe down your shower doors and bathroom title. Its low alcohol content makes it perfect for soap scum, while remaining non-toxic.

9 Orange-Spiced Chicken

This Indian-inspired chicken dish is great over brown rice.

- ²/₃ **cup flour**
- 1 **teaspoon salt**
- ½ **teaspoon black pepper**
- ½ **teaspoon dried basil**
- ¼ **teaspoon leaf tarragon**
- 2–3 **tablespoons olive oil**
- 6 **boneless, skinless, chicken breast halves**
- 1 **(6 ounce) can frozen orange juice concentrate, thawed**
- ¼ **cup water**
- ½ **cup white wine vinegar**
- ²/₃ **cup packed brown sugar**

1. Preheat oven to 350°.
2. Mix flour, salt, pepper, basil, and tarragon in resealable plastic bag.
3. Pour oil into large skillet and heat.
4. Coat chicken in flour mixture, then cook in skillet until both sides are browned.
5. Mix orange juice, water, vinegar, and brown sugar in small bowl.
6. Place browned chicken in sprayed, 9 x 13-inch baking dish. Cover with orange juice mixture and bake for 1 hour.
7. Serve chicken and orange sauce over rice.

SERVES 6.

10 Better Breaded Chicken

Using corn flakes in this recipe rather than bread crumbs not only gives the chicken a satisfying crunch, it also makes them lower in fat!

- 2 **cups buttermilk**
- 2 **tablespoons Dijon-style mustard**
- 2 **teaspoons garlic powder**
- 1 **teaspoon cayenne pepper**
- 6 **boneless, skinless chicken breast halves**
- 3 **cups crushed corn flakes**
- 2 **tablespoons olive oil**

1. Combine buttermilk, mustard, garlic powder, and cayenne pepper in large bowl; mix well.
2. Place chicken pieces in bowl and turn to coat well. Place in refrigerator for 2 hours or overnight.
3. When ready to bake, preheat oven to 400°.
4. Line large baking pan with foil and spray with cooking oil.
5. In large, shallow bowl, drizzle olive oil over crumbs and toss until coated well.
6. Remove 1 piece chicken at a time from marinade and dredge in crumb mixture, pressing crumbs onto all sides of chicken.
7. Place chicken in baking pan. Do not let sides touch. Bake for 35–40 minutes.

SERVES 6.

11 Chicken Diablo

Cumin, one of our favorite spices, gives this chicken a rich, smoky flavor.

6 boneless, skinless chicken
   breast halves
1 (8 ounce) package cream
   cheese, softened
1 (16 ounce) jar salsa
2 teaspoons ground cumin
1 bunch fresh scallions with
   tops, chopped

1. Preheat oven to 350°.
2. Pound chicken breasts to flatten.
3. Beat cream cheese in bowl until smooth; add salsa, cumin, and onions.
4. Place heaping spoonful of cream cheese mixture on each chicken breast. There will be leftover mixture for later.
5. Roll up each breast so cream cheese mixture is wrapped in center.
6. Place chicken rolls seam-side down in sprayed, 7 x 11-inch baking dish. Spoon remaining cream cheese mixture over rolls.
7. Cover and bake for 30 minutes. Uncover and continue baking until chicken rolls are light brown.

SERVES 6.

 Who Knew? Light Switch

To save money and make this recipe even healthier, substitute 2 cups of our Super Healthy Salsa (Light Switch #7) for the jar of salsa.

12 Grilled Tequila Chicken

½ cup lime juice
¼ cup tequila
1½ teaspoons chili powder
1½ teaspoons minced garlic
 1 teaspoon seeded jalapeno pepper,
   very finely chopped
 6 boneless chicken breast halves
¼ teaspoon salt
⅛ teaspoon black pepper

1. Combine lime juice, tequila, chili powder, garlic, and jalapeno pepper in large resealable plastic bag.
2. Add chicken breasts, seal bag, and turn to coat. Refrigerate for 10 hours or overnight.
3. Remove breasts from marinade and sprinkle with salt and pepper. Discard marinade.
4. Grill chicken breasts skin-side down for 5–7 minutes. Turn over and grill until cooked through, about 10 minutes.
5. Remove to platter, cover, and let stand for 5 minutes before serving.

SERVES 6.

13 Salsa-Grilled Chicken

4–5 boneless, skinless chicken
     breast halves
1 (16 ounce) jar thick-and-chunky
     salsa, divided
¼ cup soy sauce
1 tablespoon Dijon-style mustard

1. Pound chicken to about ½-inch thick.
2. Combine half of salsa, soy sauce, and mustard in large bowl. Add chicken to bowl, coat with marinade, and marinate for 2–3 hours in refrigerator.
3. Grill over hot coals, flipping as needed, until juices run clear. Top with remaining salsa.

SERVES 4–5.

 Who Knew? Light Switch

To save money and make this recipe even tastier, use 1 cup of our Super Healthy Salsa (Light Switch #7) rather than jarred salsa for the garnish.

14 Grilled Lime-Salsa Campsite Chicken

Even if you don't have a campfire (or a charcoal grill), this recipe tastes delicious using a propane or countertop grill.

¼ cup olive oil
1 (10 ounce) jar green chili salsa
1½ tablespoons lime juice
½ teaspoon sugar
1 tablespoon minced garlic
1 teaspoon ground cumin
½ teaspoon oregano
6 boneless, skinless chicken
     breast halves

1. Combine oil, salsa, lime juice, sugar, garlic, cumin, and oregano in bowl and mix well. Add chicken breasts and marinate for 3–4 hours.
2. Cook over hot coals, turning occasionally, until juices run clear, about 10–15 minutes.

SERVES 6.

 Who Knew?

Mincing garlic is usually a sticky mess, but it doesn't have to be! Just sprinkle the garlic with a few drops of olive oil beforehand. The oil will prevent the garlic from sticking to your hands or the knife.

15 Almond Chicken

We love the tiny taste of bourbon in this dish! Don't worry, the alcohol cooks off, so it's safe for the kids, too!

3 tablespoons butter
4 boneless, skinless chicken breast halves
1 (6 ounce) can frozen orange juice concentrate, thawed
½ teaspoon salt
¼ teaspoon black pepper
2 tablespoons bourbon
½ cup chopped, salted almonds, toasted

1. Melt butter in skillet. Add chicken and cook over medium heat, flipping once, until brown on both sides, about 10 minutes. Reduce heat to low.
2. Add orange juice, salt, and pepper. Cover and cook over medium heat for 25 minutes. Spoon sauce over chicken twice while it cooks. Remove chicken to serving platter and keep warm.
3. Add bourbon to sauce in skillet and cook, stirring occasionally, for 10 minutes.
4. Pour mixture over chicken and serve over rice. Sprinkle with almonds.

SERVES 4.

 Who Knew?

One of the easiest—and certainly one of the most fun—ways to toast nuts is in a popcorn air popper. Place the almonds for this recipe into the popper and plug it in for 60 seconds. The nuts will be perfectly browned on all sides!

---

16 Fruited Chicken

6 large boneless, skinless chicken breast halves
½ cup (1 stick) butter, melted
⅔ cup flour
½ teaspoon salt
¼ teaspoon black pepper
¼ teaspoon paprika
1 (15 ounce) can chunky fruit cocktail with juice

1. Preheat oven to 350°.
2. Dip chicken in butter, then in flour. Place in sprayed, 9 x 13-inch baking dish. Sprinkle with salt, pepper, and paprika.
3. Bake for 45 minutes.
4. Pour fruit and half juice over chicken. Bake for additional 20 minutes.

SERVES 6.

17 Sassy Chicken Over Tex-Mex Corn

2 teaspoons garlic powder
1 teaspoon ground cumin
²/₃ cup flour
1½ teaspoons salt
4 boneless, skinless chicken breast halves
1 tablespoon olive oil
2 tablespoons water
1 (10 ounce) can chicken broth
1½ cups hot salsa
1 (11 ounce) can Mexicorn
1 cup rice, cooked

1. Combine garlic powder, cumin, flour, and salt in shallow bowl.
2. Cut chicken breasts in half lengthwise. Then dip in flour mixture, coating all sides.
3. Pour oil in heavy skillet over medium-high heat. Brown each chicken breast on both sides (about 2 minutes per side), reduce heat, and add water to skillet.
4. Cover and simmer for 15 minutes. Transfer chicken to foil-lined baking pan and place in oven at 250° to keep warm.
5. Using the same skillet, combine broth, salsa, and corn and cook for 10 minutes. Stir in rice until well mixed.
6. To serve, spoon corn mixture on platter and place chicken breasts over corn.

SERVES 4.

 Who Knew? Light Switch

To save money and make this recipe even healthier, substitute 1¼ cups of our Healthy Chicken Broth (Light Switch #1) for the can of chicken broth, and 2 cups of our Super Healthy Salsa (Light Switch #7) for the jar of salsa.

---

18 Chili-Chicken Roll-Ups

8 boneless, skinless chicken breast halves
1 teaspoon salt
½ teaspoon black pepper
2 (4 ounce) cans diced green chilies
1 (8 ounce) package shredded Cheddar cheese
½ cup (1 stick) butter, melted
2 cups crushed tortilla chips

1. Place each chicken breast on wax paper and flatten to about ¼-inch thickness with rolling pin or mallet. Sprinkle with salt and pepper.
2. Place ⅛ of green chilies and ⅛ of cheese evenly in center of each chicken breast. Carefully roll each chicken breast so no chilies or cheese seep out, and secure with toothpicks.
3. Place chicken rolls in small baking dish, and refrigerate or freeze.
4. When ready to bake, thaw chicken rolls and preheat oven to 350°.
5. Dip each chicken roll in melted butter, then in crushed tortilla chips.
6. Bake until heated through, about 25–30 minutes.

SERVES 8.

19 Lupe's Fiesta Chicken

We owe lots of thanks to our assistant, Lupe, for making our business run! We also owe her for this delicious chicken recipe!

½ cup (1 stick) butter
5–6 boneless, skinless chicken breast halves
2 cups finely crushed cheese crackers
2 tablespoons taco seasoning mix
1 bunch scallions with tops, chopped
1 tablespoon flour
1 teaspoon chicken bouillon
1 cup milk
1 (8 ounce) package shredded Monterey Jack cheese
1 (4 ounce) can chopped green chilies, drained

1. Preheat oven to 350°.
2. Melt butter in 9 x 13-inch baking dish and set aside.
3. Pound chicken breasts to ¼-inch thick.
4. Combine cracker crumbs and taco seasoning in bowl and mix well. Dredge chicken in mixture and make sure crumbs stick to chicken.
5. Place chicken breasts in baking dish with butter. Remove 3 tablespoons melted butter from dish and place in saucepan.
6. Add scallions and cook, stirring over medium-high heat, until tender, about 4 minutes.
7. Reduce heat to low and add flour; mix well to form paste. Add chicken bouillon and milk. Cook, stirring constantly, until mixture thickens, about 10 minutes. Add cheese and green chilies and stir until cheese melts.
8. Pour mixture over chicken in baking dish and bake for 55 minutes.

SERVES 8.

 Who Knew? Light Switch

To make this recipe lower in fat, substitute 2 cups of our Low-Fat Four-Cheese Blend (Light Switch #5) for the package of Monterey Jack cheese.

20 Chip Chicken

This simple chicken recipe is one of our favorites, and goes perfectly with one of kids' favorite "foods"—ketchup.

2 cups crushed potato chips
¼ teaspoon garlic powder
5–6 boneless, skinless chicken breast halves
½ cup (1 stick) butter, melted

1. Preheat oven to 350°.
2. Combine potato chips and garlic powder in bowl and mix well.
3. Dip chicken breasts in butter and roll in potato chip mixture.
4. Place in sprayed, shallow baking dish and bake for 55 minutes.

SERVES 6.

21 Chicken Crunch

Here's another recipe that uses super-healthy corn flakes as a low-fat breading.

4–6 boneless, skinless chicken breast halves
½ cup Italian salad dressing
½ cup sour cream
2½ cups crushed corn flakes

1. Place chicken in resealable plastic bag; add salad dressing and sour cream. Seal and refrigerate 1 hour. Remove chicken from marinade and discard marinade.
2. When ready to bake, preheat oven to 375°.
3. Dredge chicken in corn flakes, and place in sprayed, 9 x 13-inch baking dish.
4. Bake for 45 minutes.

SERVES 4–6.

 ## Who Knew? Light Switch

We love making this marinade with our Low-Fat Sour Cream Substitute (Light Switch #8) and our Italian Salad Dressing Mix (Light Switch #11).

22 Lemon Dill Chicken

3 tablespoons butter
5–6 boneless, skinless chicken breast halves
2 cups water
½ teaspoon salt
2 teaspoons dried dill weed
1 tablespoon lemon juice
¼ teaspoon black pepper

1. Melt butter in skillet over medium-high heat. Place chicken breast halves in skillet and cook over medium-high heat until brown on both sides, about 3–5 minutes per side.
2. Stir water, salt, and dill weed into skillet; bring to a boil.
3. Reduce heat to low, cover, and simmer, stirring occasionally, until chicken is cooked through, about 25–30 minutes.
4. Add lemon juice and pepper and cook for 5 minutes more.
5. Serve over white or brown rice.

SERVES 6.

23 Springy Chicken

4–5 boneless, skinless chicken
     breast halves
  1 tablespoon oregano
  ¾ teaspoon garlic powder
  ½ cup (1 stick) butter, melted

1. Rub chicken with oregano and garlic powder and marinate in refrigerator for 3–4 hours.
2. When ready to bake, preheat oven to 325°.
3. Place chicken in sprayed, 9 x 13-inch baking dish and pour melted butter on top.
4. Cover and bake for 1 hour.

SERVES 5.

 Who Knew?

Don't worry if you're missing a spice other ingredient you as prepare tonight's dinner. Just head over to RecipeTips.com, where you'll find all sorts of substitutions (and healthier options) so you can keep your meal on schedule!

---

24 Sweet Pepper Chicken

6–8 boneless, skinless chicken
     breast halves
  2 tablespoons vegetable or
     canola oil
  ⅓ cup cornstarch
  ⅔ cup sugar
  ½ cup packed brown sugar
  1 teaspoon chicken bouillon
     granules
  1 (15 ounce) can pineapple
     chunks with juice
1½ cups orange juice
  ½ cup vinegar
  ¼ cup ketchup
  2 tablespoons soy sauce
  ¼ teaspoon ground ginger
  1 red bell pepper, seeded,
     thinly sliced

1. Preheat oven to 325°.
2. Place chicken breast halves in skillet with oil and cook over medium-high heat until brown on both sides, about 3 minutes per side. Place in sprayed, 10 x 15-inch baking dish.
3. Combine cornstarch, sugar, brown sugar, and bouillon granules in large saucepan and mix well.
4. Drain pineapple and set aside juice. Add pineapple juice, orange juice, vinegar, ketchup, soy sauce, and ginger to cornstarch mixture and mix well.
5. Cook on high heat, stirring constantly, until mixture thickens. Pour sauce over chicken breasts.
6. Bake for 45 minutes.
7. Remove from oven, add pineapple chunks and bell pepper, and bake for additional 15 minutes.

SERVES 8–10.

25 Baked Chicken Poupon

Here's another great way to use Dijon mustard to perfectly season a chicken breast.

2 tablespoons Dijon-style mustard
2 tablespoons olive oil
1 teaspoon garlic powder
½ teaspoon Italian seasoning
4 boneless, skinless chicken breast halves

1. Preheat oven to 375°.
2. Combine mustard, oil, garlic powder, and seasoning in resealable plastic bag. Add chicken breasts and marinate for 15 minutes.
3. Place chicken in sprayed, 9 x 13-inch baking pan.
4. Bake for 35 minutes.

SERVES 4.

26 Curry-Glazed Chicken

3 tablespoons butter
⅓ cup honey
2 tablespoons Dijon-style mustard
1½ teaspoons curry powder
4 boneless, skinless chicken breast halves

1. Preheat oven to 375°.
2. Melt butter in 9 x 13-inch baking pan.
3. Mix honey, mustard, and curry powder in pan with butter.
4. Add chicken to pan and turn until chicken is coated with butter mixture.
5. Bake for 50 minutes, basting twice with liquid in pan. Serve over rice.

SERVES 4.

 Who Knew?

Before using a measuring cup to measure out sticky liquid like honey, coat the inside with vegetable oil or nonstick cooking spray. The liquid will pour out easily.

27 Snazzy Chicken

4 boneless, skinless chicken breast halves
1 teaspoon salt
½ teaspoon black pepper
¼ cup lime juice
1 (1 ounce) packet Italian salad dressing mix
¼ cup (½ stick) butter, melted

1. Preheat oven to 325°.
2. Sprinkle chicken with salt and pepper, and place in sprayed, 7 x 11-inch baking dish.
3. Mix lime juice, salad dressing, and melted butter in bowl, and pour over chicken.
4. Cover and bake for 1 hour. Uncover for last 15 minutes of cooking time.

SERVES 4.

 Who Knew? Light Switch

To save money, try using our Italian Salad Dressing Mix (Light Switch #11) rather than using the store-bought version.

---

28 Sesame Chicken

Sesame seeds are often added as a garnish on buns, bagels, and other bread products, but they also have a rich, nutty flavor all to themselves. You'll love the taste of them in this dish!

½ cup flour
½ teaspoon chili powder
¼ teaspoon paprika
½ teaspoon onion salt
½ teaspoon celery salt
1 teaspoon lemon pepper
1 teaspoon garlic powder
8 boneless, skinless chicken breast halves
½ cup (1 stick) butter, melted
1 cup sesame seeds, lightly toasted

1. Preheat oven to 350°.
2. Thoroughly mix flour, chili powder, paprika, onion salt, celery salt, lemon pepper, and garlic powder in bowl.
3. Roll chicken breasts in flour mixture until all flour mixture is used.
4. Dip floured chicken in butter and roll in sesame seeds.
5. Place chicken breasts in sprayed, 10 x 15-inch baking dish. Pour any extra butter in baking dish with chicken.
6. Bake for 1 hour.

SERVES 8.

29 Crispy Nutty Chicken

Once you taste this scrumptious chicken coated in corn flakes and peanuts, you'll never want to go back to breadcrumbs again!

1/3 **cup finely chopped dry-roasted peanuts**
1 **cup corn flake crumbs**
1/2 **cup ranch-style, buttermilk salad dressing**
6 **boneless, skinless chicken breast halves**

1. Preheat oven to 350°.
2. Combine peanuts and corn flake crumbs on wax paper.
3. Pour dressing into pie pan. Dip each chicken breast in dressing and roll in crumb mixture to coat.
4. Arrange chicken in sprayed, 9 x 13-inch baking dish. Bake until light brown, about 50 minutes.

SERVES 6.

30 Cilantro Chicken Breasts

6 **boneless, skinless chicken breast halves**
1½ **teaspoon salt, divided**
1 **teaspoon black pepper**
3 **teaspoons finely chopped cilantro, divided**
1¼ **teaspoons ground cumin, divided**
2 **cups breadcrumbs**
1 **tablespoon olive oil**
3 **tablespoons butter**
¼ **cup flour**
2 **cups milk**
1/3 **cup dry white wine**
1 **(8 ounce) package shredded Monterey Jack cheese**

1. Preheat oven to 350°.
2. Pound chicken breast halves to ¼-inch thick with mallet or rolling pin.
3. Mix salt, pepper, 2 teaspoons cilantro, and 1 teaspoon cumin. Sprinkle seasonings over chicken cutlets. Dip cutlets in breadcrumbs.
4. Heat oil in large skillet and brown chicken on both sides. Remove to sprayed, 9 x 13-inch baking dish.
5. Melt butter in saucepan. Blend in flour, ½ teaspoon salt, 1 teaspoon cilantro, and ¼ teaspoon cumin. Add milk, stirring constantly, and cook until sauce thickens.
6. Remove from heat and stir in wine. Pour sauce over chicken.
7. Cover and bake for 45 minutes. Remove from oven, sprinkle cheese on top of each piece of chicken, and return to oven for 5 minutes.

SERVES 6.

 Who Knew?

The easiest way to "chop" the cilantro for this recipe is to use a clean pair of kitchen scissors!

31 Cola Chicken

The cola in this unique recipe doesn't have to be fizzy, so it's a great way to use up soda that has gone flat!

4–6 boneless, skinless chicken breast halves
1 teaspoon salt
½ teaspoon black pepper
1 cup ketchup
1 cup cola
2 tablespoons Worcestershire sauce

1. Preheat oven to 350°.
2. Place chicken in sprayed, 9 x 13-inch baking dish, and sprinkle with salt and pepper.
3. Mix ketchup, cola, and Worcestershire sauce in bowl and pour over chicken.
4. Cover and bake for 50 minutes.

SERVES 6.

32 Creamy Chicken Divine

6 boneless, skinless chicken breast halves
1 (10 ounce) can cream of chicken soup
1 (3 ounce) package cream cheese
1 (8 ounce) carton sour cream
½ teaspoon lemon pepper

1. Preheat oven to 300°.
2. Place chicken breasts in shallow, 9 x 13-inch baking dish.
3. Combine soup, cream cheese, and sour cream in saucepan. Heat on low just until cream cheese melts and ingredients mix well.
4. Pour soup mixture over chicken breasts and sprinkle with lemon pepper. Cover and bake for 1 hour.
5. Uncover and bake for additional 15 minutes. Serve over rice.

SERVES 6.

 Who Knew? Light Switch

To make this recipe lower in fat, substitute 1¼ cup of our Low-Fat Cream of Chicken Soup Base (Light Switch #3) for the can of cream of chicken soup, and 1 cup of our Low-Fat Sour Cream Substitute (Light Switch #8) for the carton of sour cream.

33 Lemon-Herb Chicken

6 boneless, skinless chicken breast halves
1 cup (2 sticks) butter, melted, divided
1 cup flour
¼ cup lemon juice
½ teaspoon lemon pepper
½ teaspoon garlic powder
2 tablespoons brown sugar
½ teaspoon oregano
½ teaspoon crushed rosemary
1 teaspoon lemon peel
½ teaspoon salt
¼ cup hot water

1. Preheat oven to 350°.
2. Dip each chicken breast in butter, then in flour, and place in sprayed, 9 x 13-inch baking dish. Set aside remaining butter.
3. Cover and bake for 30 minutes.
4. While chicken is cooking, combine lemon juice, lemon pepper, garlic powder, brown sugar, oregano, rosemary, and lemon peel in a mixing bowl. Add remaining butter, salt, and water and mix well.
5. After chicken cooks for 30 minutes, uncover and pour sauce over chicken. Bake for additional 25 minutes and serve over white rice.

SERVES 6.

 ## Who Knew?

Grate more lemon peel than you need and mix it with sugar in a food processor for some delicious "lemon sugar," which is perfect for the tops of cookies and cakes, and the rims of cocktail glasses!

---

34 Baked and Breaded Chicken

This simple recipe is one of our favorite ways to prepare chicken on the fly!

1½ cups biscuit mix
⅔ cup grated Parmesan cheese
6 boneless, skinless chicken breast halves
½ cup (1 stick) butter, melted

1. Preheat oven to 325°.
2. Combine biscuit mix and cheese in shallow bowl.
3. Dip chicken in butter, then in biscuit-cheese mixture.
4. Place in sprayed, 9 x 13-inch baking dish. Bake until light brown, about 1 hour.

SERVES 6–8.

35 Montezuma Celebration Chicken

6 boneless, skinless chicken
   breast halves
1 green bell pepper, seeded, cut
   in rings
1 (16 ounce) jar hot salsa
2/3 cup packed brown sugar
1 tablespoon mustard
1/2 teaspoon salt

1. Preheat oven to 350°.
2. Place chicken breasts in sprayed, 9 x 13-inch baking dish without breasts touching each other. Cover with bell pepper rings. Combine salsa, brown sugar, mustard, and salt in bowl and spoon over each piece of chicken.
3. Cover and bake for 35–40 minutes. Uncover and continue baking for additional 10–15 minutes to let chicken breasts brown slightly.

SERVES 6.

 Who Knew? Light Switch

To save money and make this recipe even healthier, substitute 2 cups of our Super Healthy Salsa (Light Switch #7) for the jar of salsa. Add a pinch of cayenne pepper for kick.

36 Oven-Fried Chicken

2/3 cup fine dry breadcrumbs
1/3 cup grated Parmesan cheese
1/2 teaspoon garlic salt
1/2 cup Italian salad dressing
6 boneless, skinless chicken
   breast halves

1. Preheat oven to 350°.
2. Combine breadcrumbs, cheese, and garlic salt in shallow bowl. Pour salad dressing in separate shallow bowl. Dip chicken in dressing and dredge in crumb mixture.
3. Place chicken in 9 x 13-inch sprayed baking pan.
4. Bake for 50 minutes.

SERVES 6.

 Who Knew? Light Switch

To save money and make this dish even more delicious, try using our Italian Salad Dressing Mix (Light Switch #11)!

37 Bacon-Wrapped Chicken

If you're like us, you get excited about a dish as soon as you hear "bacon-wrapped"! Onion and chive cream cheese makes this meal even better.

6 boneless, skinless chicken breast halves
1 (8 ounce) package onion and chive cream cheese
1 tablespoon butter
¼ teaspoon salt
6 slices bacon

1. Preheat oven to 375°.
2. Flatten chicken to ½-inch thickness. Spread 3 tablespoons cream cheese over each piece.
3. Dab each chicken breast with butter, and sprinkle on salt. Roll up each piece and wrap with 1 bacon slice. Secure with toothpick.
4. Place chicken rolls seam-side down in sprayed, 9 x 13-inch baking dish. Bake until juices run clear, about 40–45 minutes.
5. To brown, broil 6 inches from heat until bacon is crisp, about 3 minutes.

SERVES 6.

38 Family-Secret Chicken and Noodles

¼ cup (½ stick) butter
½ cup flour
½ teaspoon basil
½ teaspoon parsley
½ teaspoon salt
2 cups milk
1 (4 ounce) can sliced mushrooms, drained
1 (10 ounce) can cream of mushroom soup
1 (2 ounce) jar diced pimentos
6 cups chopped rotisserie chicken
1 (14 ounce) can chicken broth
1 (16 ounce) package medium egg noodles
1 cup shredded Cheddar or American cheese

1. Melt butter in saucepan over medium heat and add flour, basil, parsley, and salt. Add milk slowly and stir constantly until thick.
2. Add mushrooms, mushroom soup, pimentos, diced chicken, and chicken broth.
3. Cook noodles according to package directions. Drain.
4. Mix noodles with sauce, stirring gently.
5. Pour mixture into 10 x 15-inch baking dish. Sprinkle with cheese, cover, and refrigerate until baking time.
6. When ready to bake, preheat oven to 350°.
7. Bake until it heats thoroughly, from 20–30 minutes.

SERVES 8–10.

39 Apricot-Ginger Chicken

2 teaspoons ground ginger
½ cup Italian dressing
4 boneless, skinless chicken
   breast halves
⅔ cup apricot preserves

1. Combine ginger and Italian dressing; place in large resealable plastic bag.
2. Add chicken to bag. Marinate in refrigerator overnight, turning occasionally.
3. When ready to bake, preheat oven to 350°.
4. Remove chicken from refrigerator and reserve ¼ cup marinade. Place chicken in shallow baking dish. Bake, covered, for 35 minutes.
5. Pour reserved marinade in saucepan, bring to boil over medium-high heat, and cook, stirring, for 1 minute. Remove from heat and stir in apricot preserves.
6. Brush chicken with marinade mixture and return to oven for additional 10 minutes.

SERVES 4.

 Who Knew? Light Switch

To save money and make this recipe even tastier, try using our Italian Salad Dressing Mix (Light Switch #11)!

40 Chicken and Wild Rice

For a thicker sauce in this dish, spoon 3 tablespoons sauce into small bowl and stir in 2 tablespoons flour. Mix well and add back to rest of sauce. Heat over low heat, stirring constantly until sauce thickens.

1 (6 ounce) package long-grain and
   wild rice mix
4–5 boneless, skinless chicken
   breast halves
1 tablespoon olive oil
2 cans French onion soup
¾ cup water
1 red bell pepper, seeded, julienned
1 green bell pepper, seeded, julienned

1. Cook rice according to package directions in saucepan. Keep warm.
2. Brown chicken breasts on both sides with oil in over medium-high heat, about 3 minutes per side.
3. Add soup, water, and bell peppers. Reduce heat to medium-low. Cover and cook for 15 minutes.
4. To serve, place rice on serving platter with chicken breasts on top. Transfer onion soup sauce into a gravy boat, and pour over chicken and rice when ready to eat.

SERVES 5.

41 Quick and Tasty Baked Chicken

This is an easy dish to stick in the oven while you're also baking a casserole!

4 boneless, skinless chicken
   breast halves
1 (10 ounce) can Italian tomato soup
2 tablespoons Worcestershire sauce
1 teaspoon garlic powder
1½ tablespoons packed brown sugar

1. Preheat oven to 350°.
2. Place chicken breasts in sprayed, 7 x 11-inch baking dish.
3. Combine tomato soup, Worcestershire sauce, garlic, and brown sugar in small bowl and mix well. Spoon over chicken.
4. Bake for 1 hour.

SERVES 4.

 ## Who Knew?

If you only have "regular" tomato soup, simply add a teaspoon of oregano and/or basil to this recipe.

42 Jalapeno Chicken

The sour cream and white wine balance out the spiciness of this festive dish.

5–6 boneless, skinless chicken
   breast halves
¼ cup olive oil
¼ cup white wine
1 (1 pint) carton sour cream
1 tablespoon flour
1 clove garlic, minced
½ teaspoon salt
¼ teaspoon black pepper
½ teaspoon ground cumin
1 (7 ounce) can whole
   jalapeno peppers
1 (12 ounce) package shredded
   Monterey Jack cheese
1 onion, sliced in rounds

1. Preheat oven to 325°.
2. Cook chicken on with oil in skillet over medium-high heat, flipping once, until both sides are brown, about 3 minutes per side. Place in 9 x 13-inch baking dish.
3. Combine wine, sour cream, flour, garlic, salt, pepper, cumin, and jalapeno peppers in blender. Blend until smooth to make sauce.
4. Pour sauce over chicken breasts, sprinkle with cheese, and top with onion rings.
5. Cover and bake for 1 hour.

SERVES 6.

 ## Who Knew?

The seeds and membranes are the hottest parts of jalapenos, so if you want to make this dish extra hot, leave some of the seeds in.

43 Party Chicken Breasts

We barely remember what happened at the legendary party that inspired the name of this chicken dish, but we can tell you dinner was delicious!

6 boneless, skinless chicken breast halves
6 strips bacon
1 (2.5 ounce) jar dried beef
1 (10 ounce) can cream of chicken soup
1 (8 ounce) carton sour cream

1. Preheat oven to 325°.
2. Wrap each chicken breast with 1 strip bacon and secure with toothpicks.
3. Place dried beef in bottom of sprayed, 9 x 13-inch baking pan and top with chicken.
4. In saucepan, heat soup and sour cream over medium heat until heated through. Pour over chicken.
5. Bake for 1 hour.

SERVES 6–8.

 Who Knew? Light Switch

To make this recipe lower in fat, substitute 1¼ cup of our Low-Fat Cream of Chicken Soup Base (Light Switch #3) for the can of cream of chicken soup, and 1 cup of our Low-Fat Sour Cream Substitute (Light Switch #8) for the carton of sour cream.

44 Peachy Chicken

½ cup Italian dressing
2 teaspoons ground ginger
4 boneless, skinless chicken breast halves
⅓ cup peach preserves

1. Combine Italian dressing and ginger in large resealable plastic bag. Place chicken in plastic bag and turn several times to coat chicken.
2. Marinate in refrigerator for 4 hours or overnight, turning occasionally.
3. When ready to cook, remove chicken and reserve ⅓ cup marinade. Discard remaining marinade.
4. Pour reserved marinade in small saucepan and bring to a boil; heat for 1 minute. Remove from heat, stir in peach preserves, and set aside.
5. Broil chicken until juices run clear, about 10 minutes on each side. Brush with peach marinade for the last 5 minutes of cooking.

SERVES 4.

 Who Knew? Light Switch

To save money, try using our Italian Salad Dressing Mix (Light Switch #11)!

45 Pineapple-Teriyaki Chicken

You'll fall in love with the sweet taste of pineapple mixed with the teriyaki sauce in this delectable dinner.

6 boneless, skinless chicken breast halves
½ red onion, sliced
1 green bell pepper, seeded, sliced
1 cup teriyaki marinade
1 (15 ounce) can pineapple rings with juice

1. Preheat oven to 350°.
2. Place chicken in sprayed, 9 x 13-inch baking dish and arrange vegetables over chicken.
3. Mix teriyaki marinade with juice from canned pineapple. Pour over vegetables and chicken.
4. Bake for 35 minutes. Spoon juices over chicken once during baking.
5. Place pineapple rings on top of chicken and return to oven for additional 10 minutes.

SERVES 6.

46 Mandarin Chicken

1 (11 ounce) can mandarin oranges, drained
1 (6 ounce) can frozen orange juice concentrate
1 tablespoon lemon juice
²/₃ cup water
1 tablespoon cornstarch
4 boneless, skinless chicken breast halves
2 tablespoons garlic-and-herb seasoning
2 tablespoons butter
Water, as necessary

1. Combine oranges, orange juice concentrate, lemon juice, water, and cornstarch in saucepan. Cook on medium heat, stirring constantly, until mixture thickens. Set aside.
2. Sprinkle chicken breasts with seasoning and place in skillet with butter. Cook until brown on each side, about 7 minutes per side.
3. Lower heat and spoon orange juice mixture over chicken. Cover and simmer for 20 minutes, adding a little water if sauce gets too thick.

SERVES 4.

 ## Who Knew?

Who needs a spoon rest when you're at the stove cooking? Just rest your spoon on a piece of bread, which will catch all the juices and bits of food. Toss the bread when you're done cooking and clean-up is a cinch!

47 Sunday Chicken

Of all the meals we make for the week on Sundays, this one often gets eaten first.

5–6 boneless, skinless chicken
     breast halves
½ cup sour cream
¼ cup soy sauce
1 (10 ounce) can French onion soup

1. Preheat oven to 350°.
2. Place chicken in sprayed, 9 x 13-inch baking dish.
3. Combine sour cream, soy sauce, and soup in saucepan and heat over medium heat, mixing well. Pour over chicken breasts.
4. Cover and bake for 55 minutes.

SERVES 6.

 Who Knew? Light Switch

To make this recipe lower in fat, use our Low-Fat Sour Cream Substitute (Light Switch #8).

48 Reuben Chicken

4 boneless, skinless chicken
     breast halves
4 slices Swiss cheese
1 (15 ounce) can sauerkraut, drained
1 (8 ounce) bottle catalina
     salad dressing

1. Preheat oven to 350°.
2. Arrange chicken breasts in sprayed, 7 x 11-inch baking pan.
3. Place 1 slice cheese on top of each chicken breast and spread sauerkraut on top. Cover with dressing.
4. Cover and bake for 30 minutes. Uncover and continue baking for additional 15 minutes.

SERVES 4.

Who Knew?

You should always store cooked foods above uncooked meat in your fridge. This minimizes the risk of food poisoning caused by drips from uncooked meat and other foods.

49 Rosemary Chicken

½ cup flour
1 tablespoon dried rosemary, divided
½ cup Italian salad dressing
4–5 boneless, skinless chicken breast halves

1. Preheat oven to 350°.
2. Combine flour and half rosemary in bowl. Pour Italian dressing in separate shallow bowl.
3. Dip chicken breasts in dressing, then dredge in flour mixture. Place in sprayed, 9 x 13-inch baking dish.
4. Bake for 40 minutes.
5. Remove from oven and sprinkle remaining rosemary over chicken. Bake for additional 10 minutes.

SERVES 4.

 ☀️ Who Knew? Light Switch

To save money and make this dish even more delicious, try using our Italian Salad Dressing Mix (Light Switch #11)!

50 Saucy Chicken Breasts

White wine Worcestershire sauce will add a pleasing color and flavor to this chicken dish.

1½ cups mayonnaise
½ cup cider vinegar
¼ cup lemon juice
⅓ cup sugar
3 tablespoons white wine Worcestershire marinade for chicken
5 boneless, skinless chicken breast halves
2 teaspoons black pepper

1. Combine mayonnaise, vinegar, lemon juice, sugar, and Worcestershire sauce in saucepan. Mix well with whisk until mixture is smooth.
2. Pour half mixture into resealable plastic bag with chicken breasts and marinate for 4–6 hours. Move chicken around a couple of times to make sure the breasts are coated.
3. When ready to cook, preheat oven to 350°. Place chicken breasts in sprayed, 9 x 13-inch baking pan, making sure they don't touch.
4. Pour remaining half of marinade over chicken. Sprinkle pepper on top.
5. Bake for 50–60 minutes. If chicken breasts are not slightly brown, place under broiler for additional 3–4 minutes, but watch closely. Cook until juices run clear or sauce is just light brown. Do *not* let sauce between chicken breasts get brown.

SERVES 6.

51 Ranch Chicken

6 boneless, skinless chicken breast halves
1 (1 ounce) packet ranch buttermilk salad dressing mix
1 cup buttermilk
½ cup mayonnaise
2–3 cups crushed corn flakes

1. Preheat oven to 350°.
2. Pat chicken pieces dry and place on paper towels.
3. Combine ranch dressing mix, buttermilk, and mayonnaise in shallow bowl and mix well.
4. Dip chicken pieces in dressing and cover well. Roll each piece in corn flakes and coat all sides well.
5. Place chicken pieces in sprayed, 9 x 13-inch baking dish. Make sure they do not touch each other. Bake for 1 hour.

SERVES 6–8.

 Who Knew?

Want to cook once and eat twice? Next time you're preparing boneless, skinless chicken breasts, make a few extra, toss in a freezer bag with some Caesar dressing, and refrigerate. Tomorrow night, warm them in the microwave, toss over salad greens, shave a little Parmesan cheese on top, and dinner is ready!

52 Ritzy Chicken

You'll be surprised what a different taste the sour cream gives this melt-in-your mouth chicken dish.

⅓ (12 ounce) box round buttery crackers, crushed
¼ teaspoon black pepper
6 boneless, skinless chicken breast halves
1 (8 ounce) carton sour cream

1. Preheat oven to 350°.
2. Combine cracker crumbs and pepper in dish or pie plate.
3. Dip chicken in sour cream, then roll in cracker crumbs.
4. Place chicken in sprayed, 9 x 13-inch baking dish.
5. Bake for 55 minutes.

SERVES 6.

 Who Knew? Light Switch

To make this recipe lower in fat, substitute 1 cup of our Low-Fat Sour Cream Substitute (Light Switch #8) for the carton of sour cream.

53 Chicken Supreme

6 boneless, skinless chicken
  breast halves
¼ cup (½ stick) butter
½ teaspoon salt
  Dash of black pepper
1 (10 ounce) can cream of
  chicken soup
¾ cup chicken broth
1 (8.5 ounce) can sliced water
  chestnuts, drained
1 (4 ounce) can sliced mushrooms,
  drained
2 tablespoons seeded, chopped
  green bell peppers
¼ teaspoon dried, crushed
  thyme leaves

1. Preheat oven to 350°.
2. Brown chicken breasts on all sides with butter in skillet over medium-high heat, about 5 minutes on each side.
3. Arrange in 9 x 13-inch baking pan. Sprinkle with salt and pepper.
4. Add soup to remaining butter in skillet, and slowly stir in broth. Add water chestnuts, mushrooms, bell peppers, and thyme leaves. Heat to boil.
5. Pour soup mixture over chicken. Cover and bake for 45 minutes. Uncover and bake for additional 15 minutes.

SERVES 6.

 Who Knew? Light Switch

To make this recipe lower in fat, substitute 1¼ cup of our Low-Fat Cream of Chicken Soup Base (Light Switch #3) for the can of cream of chicken soup.

54 Cranberry Chicken

Stock up on cranberry sauce once it goes on sale after the holidays. Save it until the memories of family feasts are almost gone, then make this delicious cranberry-seasoned chicken dish.

1 (6 ounce) jar sweet-and-sour sauce
1 (1 ounce) packet onion soup mix
1 (16 ounce) can whole
  cranberry sauce
6 boneless, skinless chicken
  breast halves

1. Preheat oven to 325°.
2. Combine sweet-and-sour sauce, onion soup mix, and cranberry sauce in bowl.
3. Place chicken breasts in sprayed, 9 x 13-inch, shallow baking dish. Pour cranberry mixture over chicken breasts.
4. Cover and bake for 30 minutes. Uncover and bake for additional 25 minutes.

SERVES 6–8.

55 Encore Chicken

1 tablespoon vegetable or canola oil
6 boneless, skinless chicken breast halves
1 (16 ounce) jar thick-and-chunky salsa
1 cup packed light brown sugar
1 tablespoon Dijon-style mustard
½ teaspoon salt

1. Preheat oven to 325°.
2. Heat oil over medium-high heat in large skillet. When hot, add chicken breasts and cook until browned, about 2 minutes per side. Place in sprayed, 9 x 13-inch baking dish.
3. Combine salsa, brown sugar, mustard, and salt in bowl. Pour over chicken.
4. Cover and bake for 45 minutes. Serve over brown rice.

SERVES 6.

 Who Knew? Light Switch

To save money and make this recipe lower in fat, substitute 2 cups of our Super Healthy Salsa (Light Switch #7) for the jar of salsa.

56 Pop's Pleasing Pasta

1 (14 ounce) package frozen, cooked, breaded chicken cutlets, thawed
1 (28 ounce) jar spaghetti sauce, divided
2 (5 ounce) packages grated Parmesan cheese, divided
1 (8 ounce) package thin spaghetti, cooked

1. Preheat oven to 400°.
2. Place cutlets in sprayed, 9 x 13-inch baking dish. Top each with about ¼ cup spaghetti sauce and 1 heaping tablespoon Parmesan cheese. Bake for 15 minutes.
3. Place cooked spaghetti on serving platter and top with chicken cutlets. Sprinkle remaining cheese over cutlets.
4. Heat remaining spaghetti sauce and serve with chicken and spaghetti.

SERVES 6.

 Who Knew? Light Switch

To make this recipe lower in fat, substitute 2¾ cups of our Homemade Spaghetti Sauce (Light Switch #10) for the jar of spaghetti sauce.

57 Simply Seasoned Chicken

Here's another recipe that uses ranch dressing mix to make simple, delicious chicken.

½ cup Parmesan cheese
1½ cups crushed buttery crackers
1 (1 ounce) packet ranch-style salad dressing mix
2 pounds chicken drumsticks
½ cup (1 stick) butter, melted

1. Preheat oven to 350°.
2. Combine cheese, corn flakes, and salad dressing mix in bowl.
3. Wash and dry chicken drumsticks. Dip in melted butter and dredge in cracker mixture.
4. Bake until golden brown, about 50 minutes.

SERVES 8.

58 Prairie Spring Chicken

2 pounds chicken thighs
1 tablespoon olive oil
¾ cup chili sauce
¾ cup packed brown sugar
1 (1 ounce) packet onion soup mix
1/8 teaspoon cayenne pepper
½ cup water

1. Preheat oven to 325°.
2. Cook chicken with oil in skillet over medium-high heat until brown on both sides, about 2–3 minutes per side. Place in sprayed, 9 x 13-inch baking dish.
3. Combine chili sauce, brown sugar, dry soup mix, cayenne pepper, and water in bowl and pour over chicken.
4. Cover and bake for 20 minutes. Uncover and bake for additional 15 minutes. Serve over rice.

SERVES 8.

 Who Knew?

If your rice sticks together when you cook it, next time add a teaspoon of lemon juice to the water when boiling. Your sticky problem will be gone!

59 Four-Legged Chicken

8 chicken thighs
8 chicken legs
¾ cup honey
½ cup mustard
½ cup (1 stick) butter, melted
1 teaspoon salt
1 teaspoon curry powder
2 teaspoons chopped cilantro

1. Preheat oven to 350°.
2. Arrange all chicken pieces in sprayed, 10 x 15-inch baking dish.
3. Mix honey, mustard, butter, salt, curry powder, and cilantro in bowl. Spread evenly over chicken pieces.
4. Bake for 30 minutes.
5. Remove from oven and baste chicken with pan juices. Return to oven and bake until chicken is golden brown, about 30 minutes.

SERVES 8.

60 Southern-Stuffed Peppers

This is a delicious recipe for chicken livers, a flavorful, inexpensive, and often overlooked part of the chicken.

6 large green peppers
½ pound chicken livers, chopped
6 slices bacon, chopped
1 cup chopped onion
1 cup sliced celery
1 clove garlic, crushed
1 teaspoon salt
1 (4 ounce) can sliced mushrooms
2 cups cooked rice

1. Preheat oven to 375°.
2. Wash peppers, slice off stem end, and remove seeds. Cook peppers 5 minutes in small amount of boiling, salted water. Remove from water and drain.
3. Cook chicken livers, bacon, onion, celery, garlic, and salt in medium saucepan over medium heat until vegetables are tender, about 8–10 minutes. Add mushrooms and rice; mix well.
4. Arrange peppers on sprayed baking pan. Stuff peppers with chicken liver mixture. If you plan to eat later, seal pan and freeze; to serve, thaw and add ½-inch water to pan before baking.
5. Cover and bake for 20–25 minutes.

SERVES 6.

 Who Knew?

Try using a sprayed muffin pan instead of a baking pan for this recipe. It will help the stuffed peppers hold their shape, and make sure they don't tip over when you take them out of the oven.

61 Onion-Sweet Chicken

Eat one chicken now, and save the other for later! This recipe makes whole chickens even cheaper (and more delicious) than buying them pre-cooked at the grocery store.

2 whole chickens, quartered
1 (12 ounce) jar grape jelly
1 (8 ounce) bottle catalina salad dressing
1 (1 ounce) packet onion soup mix
½ teaspoon black pepper

1. Preheat oven to 350°.
2. Place chicken quarters in sprayed, 10 x 15-inch baking dish. Combine jelly, salad dressing, soup mix, and pepper in bowl. Blend well and pour over chicken.
3. Cover and bake for 1 hour. Uncover and continue cooking for additional 10 minutes to brown.

SERVES 6–8.

62 Sunshine Chicken

1 chicken, quartered
2 tablespoons olive oil
1 cup flour
1 cup barbecue sauce
½ cup orange juice

1. Preheat oven to 350°.
2. Place chicken in bowl of flour and coat well.
3. Cook chicken in oil in skillet over medium-high heat until brown on all sides, about 6–8 minutes. Place in sprayed, 9 x 13-inch baking pan.
4. Combine barbecue sauce and orange juice in bowl. Pour over chicken.
5. Cover and bake for 45 minutes. Uncover, spoon sauce over chicken, and bake for additional 20 minutes.

SERVES 4.

 Who Knew?

If you like to channel surf while cooking, place your remote control in a plastic bag or plastic wrap. The buttons will still be visible, and the control will stay clean.

63 Tangy Chicken

1 (2 pound) broiler-fryer chicken, cut up
3 tablespoons butter
½ cup steak sauce
½ cup water

1. Preheat oven to 350°.
2. Cook chicken pieces with butter in skillet over medium heat until brown on all sides, about 10–12 minutes. Place in sprayed, 9 x 13-inch baking pan.
3. Combine steak sauce and water and pour over chicken.
4. Cover and bake for 35 minutes. Uncover and continue baking until juices run clear and chicken browns, about 10 minutes.

SERVES 6.

64 Chicken Cacciatore

You don't need to use the oven to make a whole chicken! This stovetop supper is perfect for when the oven's full.

1 (2½ pound) frying chicken
3 tablespoons salt
2 tablespoons black pepper
1 tablespoon olive oil
2 onions, sliced
1 (15 ounce) can stewed tomatoes
1 (8 ounce) can tomato sauce
1 teaspoon dried oregano
2 teaspoons capers

1. Quarter chicken and sprinkle with salt and pepper.
2. Place in large skillet with oil on medium-high heat. Add sliced onions, then cook until chicken is browned, about 3 minutes on each side. Heat 10 minutes more, flipping halfway through.
3. Add stewed tomatoes, tomato sauce, oregano, and celery seed. Bring mixture to a boil, then reduce heat to low and simmer for 20 minutes.
4. Serve over hot pasta.

SERVES 6.

 Who Knew?

Reusable plastic containers are perfect for keeping leftovers, but tomato sauce will often stain clear plastic. To keep this from happening, simply spray the container with non-stick cooking spray (or vegetable oil) before storing tomato-based dishes like this one.

65 Roasted Chicken and Vegetables

This simple recipe gives you an easy way to prepare miscellaneous chicken parts that you may find on sale!

3 pounds chicken parts
1 cup lemon pepper marinade, divided
1 (16 ounce) package frozen mixed vegetables, thawed
¼ cup olive oil
½ teaspoon salt

1. Preheat oven to 375°.
2. Arrange chicken skin-side down in sprayed baking pan. Pour ⅔ cup marinade over chicken.
3. Bake for 30 minutes. Turn chicken over and baste with remaining ⅓ cup marinade.
4. Toss vegetables with oil and salt. Arrange vegetables around chicken and cover with foil. Return pan to oven and bake for additional 30 minutes.

SERVES 8.

66 Rosemary Roasted Chicken

1 whole roaster chicken
2 tablespoons olive oil
½ teaspoon salt
¼ teaspoon black pepper
2 cloves garlic, minced
2 teaspoons rosemary

1. Preheat oven to 450°. Rinse chicken under tap and pat dry.
2. Combine oil, salt, pepper, garlic, and rosemary. Mix well.
3. Truss chicken by pulling legs across the cavity and tying together with trussing twine or dental floss. Lift up skin of chicken and rub oil mixture underneath skin using basting brush.
4. Cook, uncovered, in roasting pan until cooked through, about 50 minutes. Let sit 15 minutes before carving.

SERVES 8.

67 Honey-Mustard Turkey Breast

½ cup maple syrup
1 cup honey
1 teaspoon dry mustard
¼ cup red wine vinegar
1 (4 pound) bone-in turkey breast

1. Combine syrup, honey, mustard, and vinegar in saucepan and bring to a boil.
2. Reduce heat and simmer until glaze is thick, about 20 minutes. Reserve 1 cup.
3. Place turkey breast in roasting pan and pour remaining glaze over turkey. Bake until cooked through, about 1½ –2 hours.
4. Slice turkey and serve with heated, reserved glaze. Let sit 15 minutes.

SERVES 8.

68 Herb-Roasted Turkey

2 tablespoons poultry seasoning
2 teaspoons paprika
2 teaspoons garlic powder
½ teaspoon ground nutmeg
2 tablespoons salt
1 teaspoon black pepper
1 (12 pound) turkey, thawed
1 large onion, cut in wedges
2 tablespoons oil
1½ cup water, divided
1 (1 ounce) packet turkey gravy mix
3 tablespoons flour
1 cup pan drippings or canned turkey broth

1. Preheat oven to 325°.
2. Combine poultry seasonings, paprika, garlic powder, nutmeg, salt, and pepper in small bowl.
3. Rinse turkey under cold water and pat dry. Place onion wedges in turkey cavity and rub about half of rub mixture inside.
4. Place turkey breast-side up on shallow roasting pan lined with heavy foil. Spread oil over outside of turkey. Sprinkle remaining rub mixture over turkey. Add ½ cup water to roasting pan.
5. Cover loosely with heavy foil and bake until meat thermometer inserted in breast reaches 175°, about 3 hours 30 minutes. Let stand for 15 minutes before carving. Reserve pan juices for gravy.
6. Combine gravy mix and flour in saucepan. Slowly stir in pan drippings and remaining water, stirring constantly.
7. Bring to a boil, then reduce heat and stir constantly until mixture thickens.

SERVES 16–20.

69 Turkey Croquettes

If you don't have any leftover turkey to use for this recipe, ask for a slab of unsliced turkey at your market's deli counter.

1½ cups cooked, chopped turkey
1 (10 ounce) can cream of chicken soup
1 cup stuffing mix
2 eggs
1 tablespoon minced onion
1 cup flour
Vegetable or canola oil

1. Combine turkey, soup, stuffing mix, eggs, and onion in bowl and refrigerate for several hours.
2. Divide mixture and shape into patties or balls.
3. Dredge croquettes in flour and fry in vegetable or canola oil until brown, about 1–2 minutes.

SERVES 6.

 Who Knew? Light Switch

To make this recipe lower in fat, substitute 1¼ cup of our Low-Fat Cream of Chicken Soup Base (Light Switch #3) for the can of cream of chicken soup.

70 Grilled Caribbean Turkey

These turkey tenderloins have a wonderful sweet-and-spicy Caribbean flavor. If you can't find raspberry-chipotle sauce, you can just use regular chipotle sauce with a little raspberry or other jam added in.

2 tablespoons jerk seasoning
1½–2 pounds turkey tenderloins
1 tablespoon fresh, chopped rosemary
1½ cups raspberry-chipotle sauce, divided

1. Rub jerk seasoning evenly over tenderloins.
2. Sprinkle with rosemary and press seasonings into meat. Cover and refrigerate for 1–2 hours.
3. Grill tenderloins with lid closed over medium-high heat for 5–10 minutes on each side.
4. Baste with half raspberry-chipotle sauce. Let tenderloins stand for 10 minutes before slicing.
5. Serve with remaining raspberry-chipotle sauce. Serve over mashed potatoes or rice.

SERVES 6.

71 Hot Bunwiches

8 hamburger buns
24 slices deli turkey (about 1 pound)
16 slices deli ham (about ¾ pound)
8 slices Swiss cheese
8 slices American cheese

1. Lay out all 8 buns and place slices of turkey, ham, Swiss cheese, and American cheese on bottom buns. Place top bun over American cheese.
2. Wrap each bunwich individually in foil and place in freezer. Remove from freezer 2–3 hours before serving.
3. When ready to heat, preheat oven to 325°.
4. Heat for 30 minutes and serve hot.

SERVES 8.

 Who Knew?

When buying the sliced meats and cheeses for this recipe, make sure to check both the refrigerated section of your grocery store and at the deli counter. Deals on freshly cut meats are sometimes cheaper than their pre-packaged counterparts.

72 Simply Delicious Cornish Game Hens

For the most part, Cornish game hens are a rare treat in our house. But if you happen to find them on sale, here's a simple, delicious way to prepare them.

4 (2 pound) Cornish game hens
¼ cup olive oil
2 teaspoons paprika
2 tablespoons black pepper
1 tablespoon salt

1. Preheat oven to 350°.
2. Wash and dry hens and place in sprayed baking pan. Rub hens with oil.
3. Sprinkle paprika, pepper, and salt over each.
4. Bake until juices run clear, about 1 hour 30 minutes–2 hours.

SERVES 4.

 Who Knew?

Poultry must be thoroughly cleaned inside and out before cooking, in order to remove any residue that may be left from the slaughtering process. If you detect a slight "off" odor when you open the package, rinse the bird under cool water, then submerge in a solution of water plus 1 tablespoon lemon juice or vinegar and 1 teaspoon salt per cup of water. Then refrigerate 1–4 hours before cooking.

73 All-the-Trimmings Corned Beef

1 (4–5 pound) corned beef brisket
  Water
4 large potatoes, peeled, chopped
6 carrots, peeled, chopped
4 medium onions, chopped
1 head cabbage
  Salt and pepper to taste

1. Place corned beef in roasting pan and add water until just covered. Bring to a boil over high heat, then reduce heat and simmer for 3 hours. Add more water if necessary.
2. Add potatoes, carrots, and onions. Cut cabbage into eighths and lay over top of other vegetables.
3. Bring to a boil, then reduce heat and cook until vegetables are done, about 30–40 minutes.
4. Let sit 10–15 minutes, then slice across grain to serve. Add salt and pepper to taste.

SERVES 8–10.

74 Cabbage Rolls Along

This is a wonderful family recipe and a super way to get kids to eat oh-so-nutritious cabbage.

1 large head cabbage, cored
1½ pounds lean ground beef
1 egg, beaten
3 tablespoons ketchup
⅓ cup seasoned breadcrumbs
2 tablespoons dried minced onion flakes
1 teaspoon salt
2 (15 ounce) cans Italian stewed tomatoes
¼ cup cornstarch
3 tablespoons brown sugar
2 tablespoons Worcestershire sauce

1. Preheat oven to 325°.
2. Place head of cabbage in large soup pot of boiling water. Let sit until outer leaves are tender, about 10 minutes. Drain well. Rinse in cold water and remove 10 large outer leaves, or pairs of 2 smaller leaves put together. Set aside.
3. Slice or shred remaining cabbage. Place in sprayed, 9 x 13-inch baking dish.
4. Combine ground beef, egg, ketchup, breadcrumbs, onion flakes, and salt in large bowl and mix well.
5. Pack together about ½ cup meat mixture and place on one cabbage leaf. Remove thin vein from leaf and fold in sides to enclose filling. Pierce with toothpick to secure. Repeat with each leaf, then place over shredded cabbage.
6. Place stewed tomatoes in large saucepan. Combine cornstarch, brown sugar, and Worcestershire sauce in bowl and spoon mixture into tomatoes. Cook on high heat, stirring constantly, until mixtures thickens.
7. Pour over cabbage rolls. Cover and bake for 1 hour.

SERVES 10.

 Who Knew?

Has your brown sugar become hard? Simply add a couple of apple slices to the bag and clamp or tape it shut. The brown sugar will soften within a few days (just make sure to remove the apple)! If you don't have the time to wait, place is a microwave-safe dish and microwave, covered, on HIGH until it softens, about 30–60 minutes.

75 Easy Winter Warmer

This is a delicious spaghetti sauce on noodles and a great substitute for cream.

1 (12 ounce) package medium
   egg noodles
½ tablespoon vegetable or canola oil
3 tablespoons butter
1½ pounds lean ground beef
1 (10 ounce) package chopped
   onions and peppers, thawed
1 (28 ounce) jar spaghetti
   sauce, divided
1 (12 ounce) package shredded
   mozzarella cheese

1. Preheat oven to 350°.
2. Cook noodles according to package directions in pot of boiling water with oil and salt. Drain thoroughly, then add butter, stirring until butter melts.
3. Brown beef and onions and peppers in skillet and drain thoroughly.
4. Pour half spaghetti sauce in sprayed, 9 x 13-inch baking dish. Layer half noodles, half beef and half cheese. Repeat for second layer.
5. Cover and bake until dish is hot, about 30 minutes.

SERVES 6–8.

76 Ravioli and More

1 pound lean ground beef
1 teaspoon garlic powder
½ teaspoon salt
½ teaspoon black pepper
1 large onion, chopped
2 zucchini squash, grated
¼ cup (½ stick) butter
1 (28 ounce) jar spaghetti sauce
1 (25 ounce) package ravioli with
   portobello mushrooms, cooked
1 (12 ounce) package shredded
   mozzarella cheese

1. Preheat oven to 350°.
2. Brown ground beef in large skillet over medium heat until no longer pink; drain. Add garlic powder, salt, and pepper. Set aside.
3. Cook onion and zucchini in butter in skillet over medium-high heat just until tender-crisp, about 4 minutes. Stir in spaghetti sauce.
4. Spread ½ cup sauce in sprayed, 9 x 13-inch baking dish.
5. Layer half of ravioli, half of remaining sauce, half of beef, and half of cheese. Repeat with remaining ravioli, sauce, and beef.
6. Cover and bake for 35 minutes.
7. Sprinkle remaining cheese on top. Let stand for 10 minutes before serving.

SERVES 6–8.

Who Knew? Light Switch

To make this recipe lower in fat, substitute 2¾ cups of our Homemade Spaghetti Sauce (Light Switch #10) for the jar of spaghetti sauce.

77 Kids' Favorite Dinner

1 **pound lean ground beef**
1 **(10 ounce) can chili with beans**
1 **(15 ounce) can baked beans**
½ **cup salsa**
¼ **teaspoon salt**
2 **cups biscuit mix**
2 **tablespoons butter, softened**
⅔ **cup milk**
¾ **cup American cheese, cut into small pieces**

1. Preheat oven to 400°.
2. Cook ground beef in skillet over medium heat, stirring often, until light brown. Drain.
3. Add chili, baked beans, salsa, and salt. Heat, stirring often, just until mixture is hot. Spoon into sprayed, 7 x 11-inch glass baking dish.
4. Combine biscuit mix, butter, and milk. Stir until a soft dough forms. Place tablespoons of dough around edges of casserole.
5. Bake until dough is golden brown, about 20–24 minutes. Sprinkle cheese over top, then bake until cheese melts, about 1 minute.

SERVES 6.

 Who Knew? Light Switch

To make this recipe lower in fat, use our Super Healthy Salsa (Light Switch #6), margarine, and reduced-fat American cheese.

78 Shepherd's Pie

1 **pound lean ground beef**
1 **(1 ounce) packet taco seasoning mix**
¾ **cup water**
1 **cup shredded Cheddar cheese**
1 **(8 ounce) can whole kernel corn, drained**
2 **cups cooked instant mashed potatoes**

1. Preheat oven to 350°.
2. Cook beef in skillet, stirring occasionally, over medium heat until brown, about 10 minutes. Drain.
3. Add taco seasoning and water. Cook for an additional 6 minutes.
4. Spoon beef mixture into 8-inch baking pan. Sprinkle cheese on top. Sprinkle corn on top of cheese, and spread mashed potatoes over corn.
5. Bake until top is golden, about 25 minutes.

SERVES 5.

79 Taco Bueno Bake

Spanish rice mixes can be turned into much more than a side dish. This delicious dinner is so simple, you'll find yourself stacking up on rice mixes every time they're on sale!

2 (8 ounce) packages Spanish rice mix
2 pounds ground beef
1½ cups taco sauce
1 (8 ounce) package shredded Mexican four-cheese blend, divided

1. Preheat oven to 350°.
2. Prepare Spanish rice according to package directions.
3. Heat ground beef in skillet over medium heat, stirring occasionally, until no longer pink, about 8–12 minutes. Drain.
4. Add taco sauce, rice, and half cheese. Spoon mixture into sprayed, 3-quart baking dish.
5. Cover and bake for 35 minutes. Uncover and sprinkle remaining cheese on top; return to oven for 5 minutes.

SERVES 8.

 Who Knew? Light Switch

To make this recipe lower in fat, substitute 2 cups of our Low-Fat Four-Cheese Blend (Light Switch #5) for the package of Mexican four-cheese blend.

 Who Knew?

Need a little help budgeting your trips to the supermarket? Many chains now offer prepaid gift cards. Buy one for yourself and think of it as a portable checking account: Put money on the card, then "withdraw" from it every time you shop. With a dedicated grocery "account," you'll find it's easier to keep a tighter rein on your spending.

80 Cheesy Stuffed Bell Peppers

This is one of the rare occasions in which bell peppers are the star attractions at the dinner table—and they're so delicious, you'll want to stuff 'em all the time!

6 red, green, yellow, or orange
   bell peppers
1½ pounds ground beef
½ cup chopped onion
¾ cup cooked rice
1 egg
2 (15 ounce) cans Italian stewed
   tomatoes, divided
½ teaspoon garlic powder
1 tablespoon Worcestershire sauce
½ teaspoon salt
½ teaspoon black pepper
1 (8 ounce) package shredded
   Cheddar cheese, divided

1. Preheat oven to 350°.
2. Cut off tops of bell peppers and remove seeds and membranes. Place in roasting pan with salted water and boil for 10 minutes. (They will be only partially cooked.) Drain and set aside to cool.
3. Cook ground beef and onion in skillet over medium heat, stirring occasionally, until beef is browned and onions are tender, about 7 minutes. Drain.
4. Add rice, egg, 1 can tomatoes, garlic powder, Worcestershire sauce, salt, and pepper. Simmer for 5 minutes. Remove from heat and add 1 cup cheese; mix well.
5. Stuff peppers with meat mixture and set upright in sprayed baking dish.
6. Pour remaining can of tomatoes over and around peppers.
7. Bake for 25 minutes.
8. Remove from oven, sprinkle remaining cheese on top, and return to oven until cheese melts, about 10 minutes.

SERVES 6.

 Who Knew?

If you can't get the pepper to stand upright, trim the bottoms, a small sliver at a time, until they have a more even base.

81 Easy Beef and Rice Supper

1 (6 ounce) package long-grain and wild rice mix
1½ pounds lean ground beef
1 onion, chopped
1 small green bell pepper, seeded, chopped
1 (10 ounce) can tomatoes and green chilies
1 (10 ounce) can tomato soup
⅛ teaspoon black pepper
1 cup shredded Mexican four-cheese blend

1. Preheat oven to 350°.
2. Cook rice mix according to package directions; set aside.
3. Cook beef, onion, and bell pepper in skillet over medium heat until beef is browned and vegetables are tender, about 8 minutes. Drain.
4. Stir in tomatoes and green chilies, soup, pepper, and cooked rice mixture. Spoon into sprayed baking dish.
5. Cover and bake for 30 minutes.
6. Sprinkle cheese over dish and bake uncovered just until cheese melts, about 5–10 minutes.

SERVES 4.

 ## Who Knew? Light Switch

To make this recipe lower in fat, use our Low-Fat Four-Cheese Blend (Light Switch #5) instead of the Mexican four-cheese blend.

 ## Who Knew?

Do you become a blubbering mess when you try to chop onions? Keep the tears away by keeping your onions in your refrigerator's crisper drawer. At the colder temperature, they'll release less of the chemical that makes you cry.

82 Best Pot Roast Dinner

1 (4 pound) boneless rump roast
3 tablespoons plus ½ teaspoon salt, divided
2 tablespoons plus ½ teaspoon black pepper, divided
2 tablespoons garlic powder
2¼ cups water, divided, plus more if needed
6 potatoes, peeled, quartered
8 carrots, peeled, quartered
3 onions, peeled, quartered
3 tablespoons cornstarch

1. Preheat oven to 375°.
2. Set roast in roasting pan with lid and sprinkle with 3 tablespoons salt, 2 tablespoons pepper, and garlic powder. Add 1½ cups water.
3. Cover and bake for 30 minutes.
4. Turn heat down to 325° and bake until roast is fork tender, about 2 hours–2 hours 30 minutes. Add water if needed.
5. Add potatoes, carrots, and onions. Cook for additional 35–40 minutes.
6. Lift roast out of roasting pan and place on serving platter.
7. Place potatoes, carrots, and onions around roast.
8. Combine cornstarch and ¾ cup water in bowl. Add to juices left in roasting pan. Add ½ teaspoon each of salt and pepper and stir to make gravy.
9. Place pan on stove and cook on high, stirring constantly, until gravy thickens. Serve in gravy boat with roast and vegetables.

SERVES 8–10.

83 Seasoned-Beef Tenderloin

3 tablespoons Dijon-style mustard
2 tablespoons horseradish
1 (3 pound) center-cut beef tenderloin
½ cup seasoned breadcrumbs

1. Combine mustard and horseradish in bowl and spread over beef tenderloin.
2. Spread breadcrumbs onto mustard-horseradish mixture and wrap beef in foil. Refrigerate for at least 12 hours.
3. When ready to bake, preheat oven to 375°.
4. Remove wrap and place beef on sprayed broiler pan. Bake for 30 minutes.
5. Let tenderloin stand for 15 minutes before slicing.

SERVES 8–10.

84 Skillet Sirloin

This is one of the easiest-and most delicious-ways to prepare beef sirloin.

2 teaspoons vegetable or canola oil
2 teaspoons minced garlic
½ teaspoon cayenne pepper
2 tablespoons soy sauce
2 tablespoons honey
1 pound beef sirloin, thinly sliced

1. Combine oil, garlic, cayenne pepper, soy sauce, and honey. Place in resealable plastic bag.
2. Add sliced beef, seal bag, and shake. Refrigerate for 30 minutes.
3. Place beef mixture in large sprayed skillet over medium-high heat. Cook until beef reaches desired doneness without overcooking, about 5–6 minutes. If desired, serve with vegetables over rice.

SERVES 6.

 Who Knew?

It's easier to thinly slice meat if it's partially frozen. Leave the beef for this recipe in the freezer for about 10 minutes before you slice it.

85 Steak and Potatoes

2 pounds round steak
⅓ cup flour
⅓ cup vegetable or canola oil
5 peeled potatoes, diced
¼ teaspoon salt
⅛ teaspoon black pepper
¼ cup chopped onions
½ cup water
1 (10 ounce) can cream of mushroom soup

1. Preheat oven to 350°.
2. Cut steak into serving-size pieces and coat in flour. Brown with oil in heavy skillet; drain. Place steak in sprayed, 9 x 13-inch baking dish.
3. Sprinkle potatoes with salt and pepper. Place over steak. Cover potatoes with onions.
4. Add water to mushroom soup and pour over top of dish.
5. Cover and bake for 1 hour 30 minutes.

SERVES 8.

86 Italian Steak Extraordinary

1½ pounds beef round steak
¼ teaspoon salt
1 teaspoon black pepper
½ cup flour
2 tablespoons vegetable or canola oil
1 (14 ounce) jar spaghetti sauce
1 (10 ounce) can chopped tomatoes and green chilies
1 (10 ounce) package frozen Italian green beans, thawed
1 bunch fresh scallions, thinly sliced

1. Preheat oven to 350°.
2. Cut steak into 6 serving-size pieces, and sprinkle with salt and pepper.
3. Pour flour into resealable plastic bag. Add steak pieces and shake until steak is covered with flour.
4. Brown steak pieces in canola oil in large skillet over medium-high heat, turning over once, about 2 minutes per side.
5. Place steak pieces in sprayed, 9 x 13-inch glass baking dish. Pour spaghetti sauce and tomatoes and green chilies over steak.
6. Cover and bake for 45 minutes.
7. Place green beans in sauce around beef. Cover and continue baking until beef is cooked through, about 30 minutes.
8. Before serving, sprinkle fresh scallions over steak.

SERVES 6–8.

87 Marinated and Grilled London Broil

Trying to get your husband to make dinner? Tell him he can use the grill, and point him toward this recipe.

1 (12 ounce) can cola
1 (10 ounce) bottle teriyaki sauce
1 teaspoon black pepper
1 (3 pound) London broil (top round roast)

1. Combine cola, teriyaki sauce, and black pepper in large resealable plastic bag.
2. Add London broil, seal, and marinate in refrigerator for 24 hours, turning occasionally.
3. Remove London broil from marinade and discard marinade. Grill covered for 14 minutes on each side.
4. Let stand for 10 minutes before slicing diagonally across grain to serve.

SERVES 8.

 ## Who Knew?

To make your grill even hotter, place a large sheet of aluminum foil on top of it for 10 minutes before you start grilling. This is a great way to achieve those impressive grill marks on your meat!

88 Grilled Garlic-Herb Tenderloin

Charcoal grills may be a little more work, but they sure make food taste good! This home-style pork dish requires a charcoal grill and marinade brush.

2 (1 pound) pork tenderloins
1 (12 ounce) bottle roasted garlic-herb marinade, divided
1 (8 ounce) package medium egg noodles
¼ cup (½ stick) butter

1. Butterfly pork lengthwise, being careful not to cut all the way through. Press open to flatten. Place in large resealable plastic bag.
2. Pour ¾ cup marinade into bag and close top securely. Marinate for 25 minutes, turning several times.
3. Grill for 8 minutes, with pork 4–5 inches from hot coals.
4. Turn pork over and brush with additional marinade. Cook for another 8 minutes.
5. Cook noodles according to package directions. Drain. Add butter and coat well. When ready to serve, place pork chops over noodles.

SERVES 8.

89 Praiseworthy Pork Tenderloin

⅓ cup ketchup
¼ cup packed brown sugar
1 tablespoon dry white wine
1 tablespoon soy sauce
¼ teaspoon ground mustard
1 teaspoon minced garlic
2 (1 pound) pork tenderloins

1. Combine ketchup, brown sugar, wine, soy sauce, mustard, and garlic in bowl. Mix well. Pour in shallow bowl or plastic dish.
2. Place tenderloins in ketchup–brown sugar mixture and turn to coat. Cover and refrigerate for at least 1 hour, but no longer than 8 hours.
3. When ready to bake, preheat oven to 425°.
4. Using slotted spoon, place pork in shallow roasting pan and roast uncovered for 29–30 minutes. Discard marinade.
5. Slice tenderloins and serve over pasta or rice.

SERVES 6.

 Who Knew?

The best place to store your brown sugar is in the freezer. The lower temperature will ensure it won't clump up.

90 Sweet Peach Pork Tenderloin

3 tablespoons Dijon-style mustard
1 tablespoon soy sauce
1 (12 ounce) jar peach preserves
2 (1 pound) pork tenderloins
¼ teaspoon salt
⅛ teaspoon black pepper

1. Preheat oven to 325°.
2. Combine mustard, soy sauce, and peach preserves in saucepan. Heat and stir just until mixture blends.
3. Place tenderloins in sprayed baking pan and spoon peach mixture over top.
4. Sprinkle salt and pepper over tenderloins.
5. Cover pan with foil and bake for 1 hour.
6. Remove from oven and let stand for 10 minutes before slicing.

SERVES 8.

91 Orange Pork Chops

1 teaspoon salt
½ teaspoon black pepper
6 (½ inch) boneless pork chops
2 tablespoons vegetable or canola oil
1⅓ cups instant rice
1 cup orange juice
¼ teaspoon ground ginger
1 (10 ounce) can chicken with rice soup
½ cup chopped walnuts

1. Preheat oven to 350°.
2. Sprinkle salt and pepper over pork chops. Brown with oil in skillet over medium-high heat, about 2–3 minutes on each side.
3. Sprinkle rice into sprayed, 7 x 11-inch baking dish.
4. Add orange juice. Then arrange pork chops over rice.
5. Add ginger to soup can, stirring right in can. Pour soup over pork chops.
6. Sprinkle walnuts on top.
7. Cover and bake for 25 minutes.
8. Uncover and bake until rice is tender, about 10 minutes.

SERVES 6.

 ### Who Knew?

Never use quick-cooking rice in a dish that will be frozen, as it becomes mushy when reheated. Make sure to only refrigerate this one (not freeze!) for later.

92 Italian-Style Pork Chops

If this meal is hearty enough to feed our family of growing boys, it will feed anyone!

6 (¾-inch thick) bone-in pork chops
1½ teaspoon salt, divided
1 teaspoon black pepper, divided
1 tablespoon vegetable or canola oil
2 green bell peppers
1 (15 ounce) can tomato sauce
1 (15 ounce) can Italian stewed
    tomatoes with liquid
1 cup water
½ of 1 onion, chopped
1 teaspoon Italian seasoning
1 clove garlic, minced
1 tablespoon Worcestershire sauce
½ cup brown rice

1. Preheat oven to 350°.
2. Sprinkle pork chops with 1 teaspoon salt and ½ teaspoon pepper. In hot oil, brown chops on both sides over medium-high heat, about 2–3 minutes per side. Remove chops from skillet, drain, and set aside.
3. Cut top off 1 bell pepper and remove seeds. Cut 6 thick rings and set aside. Seed remaining bell pepper and roughly chop.
4. Combine chopped bell pepper, tomato sauce, stewed tomatoes, water, onion, Italian seasoning, garlic, Worcestershire sauce, and remaining salt and pepper in bowl. Mix well.
5. Spread rice evenly in lightly sprayed, 9 x 13-inch baking dish. Slowly pour tomato mixture over rice.
6. Arrange pork chops over rice mixture and top each with 1 bell pepper ring.
7. Cover and bake until rice is tender, about 1 hour.

SERVES 6.

93 Onion-Smothered Pork Chops

6 (½-inch thick) pork chops
1 tablespoon vegetable or canola oil
2 tablespoons butter
1 medium onion, chopped
1 (10 ounce) can cream of
    onion soup
½ cup water

1. Preheat oven to 325°.
2. Cook pork chops on each side with oil in skillet over medium-high heat until brown, about 4 minutes per side. Reduce heat to low and simmer for 5 minutes per side. Place chops in shallow baking pan.
3. Add butter to skillet and cook onion, stirring, until onion is tender. (Pan juices will turn onion brown.)
4. Add onion soup and water and stir well. Pour mixture over pork chops.
5. Cover and bake for 40 minutes. Serve over rice.

SERVES 6.

94 Pork Chops and Apples

Apples are a traditional accompaniment to pork chops, and we've added raisins and pecans to this recipe for a touch of even more sweetness.

6 (¾ inch thick) bone-in pork chops
¼ cup (½ stick) butter, divided
6 cups croutons
1 cup green apples, peeled, chopped
½ cup chopped celery
½ cup golden raisins
½ cup chopped pecans
½ cup water
2 teaspoons crushed, dried sage
1 teaspoon salt
1 tablespoon Dijon-style mustard

1. Preheat oven to 325°.
2. Brown pork chops on both sides with 2 tablespoons butter in large skillet over medium-high heat, about 2 minutes per side. Set aside.
3. In same skillet, melt remaining butter and stir in croutons, apples, celery, raisins, pecans, water, sage, and salt. Mix well.
4. Place crouton mixture into sprayed, 7 x 11-inch baking dish. Top with pork chops.
5. Spread thin layer of mustard over each pork chop.
6. Cover and bake for 40 minutes. Uncover and bake for additional 10 minutes.

SERVES 6.

 Who Knew?

To crush the sage for this recipe, simply rub the dried sage between your fingers until it turns into a powder.

95 Apricot Pork Chops

1 (15 ounce) can apricot halves with juice
8 (½ inch thick) boneless pork chops
3 tablespoons butter
⅓ cup chopped celery
1 yellow bell pepper, seeded, chopped
2½ cups instant rice
¾ cup water
1 teaspoon chicken bouillon granules
⅓ cup golden raisins
½ teaspoon ground ginger
½ teaspoon salt
½ cup slivered almonds

1. Preheat oven to 350°.
2. Place apricots in food processor, cover, and process until smooth. Set aside.
3. Brown pork chops on both sides with butter in large skillet over medium-high heat, about 3–5 minutes per side. Reduce heat to low and simmer, covered, for 10 minutes. Remove pork chops to heated plate.
4. In same skillet, sauté celery and bell pepper. Add rice, water, bouillon granules, raisins, ginger, salt, and apricot puree; bring to a boil.
5. Remove from heat and stir in almonds. Spoon into 9 x 13-inch baking dish.
6. Place pork chops on top of rice mixture.
7. Cover and bake for 20 minutes.

SERVES 8.

96 Pork Chops Topped with Zucchini

2 ribs celery, sliced
½ cup chopped onion
2 tablespoons butter
3 cups chopped zucchini
3 cups white bread cubes, toasted
1 egg
1 teaspoon poultry seasoning
1 (10 ounce) can chicken broth, divided
6 boneless pork chops

1. Preheat oven to 325°.
2. Sauté celery and onion with butter in skillet over medium-high heat until tender, about 4 minutes.
3. Combine celery-onion mixture, zucchini, bread cubes, egg, poultry seasoning, and half of chicken broth in bowl. Mix well. Cover and refrigerate.
4. Arrange pork chops in sprayed, 9 x 13-inch glass baking dish. Drizzle remaining broth over pork chops.
5. Bake uncovered for 30–35 minutes.
6. Top with a large spoonful zucchini–bread cube mixture. Cover and bake for additional 20 minutes.

SERVES 6.

97 Easy Baked Chops

This pork chop recipe is so easy, even our teenager can prepare it!

1 tablespoon vegetable oil
4 (½–1 inch thick) pork chops
1–2 tablespoons onion soup mix
2 tablespoons French salad dressing
¼ cup water

1. Preheat oven to 350°.
2. Heat oil over medium-high heat in skillet. When hot, add pork chops and brown on each side, about 3–5 minutes per side. Sprinkle soup mix over top.
3. Combine salad dressing and water in small bowl, then pour over top.
4. Cover and bake for 1 hour.

SERVES 4.

 Who Knew?

You should always keep vegetable oil around, and not just for cooking. You can also use it instead of WD-40 to silence squeaky hinges, and even to lube up a stuck zipper!

98 German-Style Ribs and Kraut

3–4 pounds baby back pork ribs or country-style pork ribs, trimmed
½ teaspoon black pepper
1 cup water
3 potatoes, peeled, cubed or sliced
1 (32 ounce) jar refrigerated sauerkraut, drained
¼ cup pine nuts, toasted

1. In large, sprayed pan, cook ribs over medium-high heat until browned on all sides, about 2 minutes per side.
2. Add pepper and water. Bring to a boil, then reduce heat to low and simmer until ribs are very tender, about 2 hours.
3. Add potatoes and continue to cook on low heat for 20 minutes. Add sauerkraut and continue cooking until potatoes are tender.
4. Sprinkle pine nuts on ribs and kraut just before serving.

SERVES 6–8.

 Who Knew?

To toast pine nuts, place them in skillet on medium heat, stirring constantly until golden brown. You can also put them on a baking sheet and cook at 300° for 5–10 minutes.

99 Oven-Roasted Baby Backs

⅓ cup orange juice
⅓ cup soy sauce
1 teaspoon ground cumin
½ cup packed brown sugar
2–3 pounds baby back pork ribs

1. Combine orange juice, soy sauce, cumin, and brown sugar in large, resealable plastic bag. Shake or mash bag to blend thoroughly and to dissolve brown sugar.
2. Cut ribs into individual ribs, add to bag, and marinate for 1–2 hours.
3. When ready to bake, preheat oven to 325°.
4. Transfer ribs and marinade to shallow baking pan and arrange in one layer. Ribs should not touch.
5. Bake for 45 minutes. Remove from oven, turn ribs with tongs, and continue roasting for an additional 1 hour.

SERVES 5–7

 Who Knew?

When picking out the best rack of ribs, go for some that have an even dispersal of fat throughout the rack. This will ensure even cooking.

100 Peach-Glazed Ham

If you prefer a glazed ham, here is a sweetly delicious glaze that has a kick of mustard.

1 (5 pound) boneless ham
1 (16 ounce) jar peach preserves
3 tablespoons Dijon-style mustard
¼ cup packed brown sugar

1. Preheat oven to 350°.
2. Place ham in large roasting pan. Wrap foil over top and seal edges around pan opening. Bake for 3 hours.
3. Combine preserves, mustard, and brown sugar in bowl and mix well.
4. Remove ham from oven and drain any liquid. Brush with half of preserve-sugar mixture and return to oven for 30 minutes.
5. Heat remaining preserve-sugar mixture in saucepan over medium heat until warm. Serve ham with heated mixture.

SERVES 8.

101 Cheesy-Broccoli Soufflé

1 (3 ounce) package cream cheese
6 large eggs, slightly beaten
1 cup half and half
¾ cup biscuit mix
1 (10 ounce) package frozen, chopped broccoli, thawed
1 (8 ounce) package shredded mozzarella cheese
1 cup small curd cottage cheese
1 cup cooked, cubed ham
½ teaspoon salt

1. Preheat oven to 350°.
2. Beat cream cheese in bowl until fairly smooth.
3. Add eggs, half and half, and biscuit mix, mixing well. Stir in broccoli, mozzarella cheese, cottage cheese, ham, and salt.
4. Pour mixture into sprayed, 2½-quart glass baking dish. Bake until knife inserted in center comes out clean, about 55 minutes. Let stand for 10 minutes before serving.

SERVES 6–8.

 Who Knew?

It's easier to grate Swiss, Cheddar, mozzarella and other softer cheeses if you place them in the freezer for 10–15 minutes before grating.

102 Falling Off a Log Baked Ham

This recipe really is as easy as falling off a log, and when we serve it, people always rave about it! Best of all, you'll find this is often one of the cheapest cuts of meat in your grocery store!

1 (4–5 pound) shank or butt-portion ham

1. Preheat oven to 350°.
2. Place ham in large roasting pan. Wrap foil over top and seal edges around pan opening.
3. Bake for 3 hours–3 hours 30 minutes.
4. Let sit 15 minutes before slicing to serve.

SERVES 8.

 ## Who Knew?

While you're waiting to slice the ham, put that used aluminum foil to good use by sharpening your kitchen scissors! Simply fold the foil 3 or 4 times, then cut through it several times with your scissors.

---

103 Old-Fashioned Ham Loaf with Horseradish Sauce

3 eggs
3 pounds lean ground ham
3 cups fresh fine breadcrumbs
2 teaspoons brown sugar
3 teaspoons horseradish, divided
½ pint whipping cream
¼ teaspoon salt

1. Preheat oven to 350°.
2. Slightly beat eggs in large bowl.
3. Stir in ground ham, mixing thoroughly.
4. Add breadcrumbs, brown sugar, and 2 teaspoons horseradish. Stir to mix well.
5. Shape into loaf and place in sprayed baking dish.
6. Bake for 1 hour 30 minutes.
7. Mix 1 teaspoon horseradish, whipping cream, and salt in bowl and refrigerate. Allow sauce to reach room temperature before serving, about 20 minutes.
8. Remove loaf from oven, let stand for 5 minutes before slicing. Serve with sauce.

SERVES 6–8.

104 Pork-Stuffed Eggplant

1 large eggplant
2½ teaspoons salt, divided
¾ pound ground pork
½ pound pork sausage
1 egg
½ cup seasoned breadcrumbs
½ cup grated Romano cheese
1 tablespoon dried onion flakes
2 teaspoons dried oregano
½ teaspoon black pepper
1 (15 ounce) can stewed tomatoes
1 (8 ounce) can tomato sauce

1. Preheat oven to 350°.
2. Cut off eggplant stem and cut eggplant in half lengthwise. Scoop out and reserve center, leaving a ½-inch shell. Cube reserved eggplant and sprinkle shell and cubes with 2 teaspoons salt. Let sit in colander or drying rack; salt will draw out excess water.
3. Microwave shell halves on HIGH until tender, about 2–5 minutes, turning halfway through if your microwave does not have a turntable.
4. Cook cubed eggplant in saucepan with boiling water for 6 minutes. Drain well and set aside.
5. Cook ground pork and sausage in skillet over medium heat until no longer pink, about 8–12 minutes; drain.
6. Add eggplant, egg, breadcrumbs, cheese, onion flakes, oregano, ½ teaspoon salt, and pepper. Mix well.
7. Fill eggplant shells with pork mixture and place in sprayed, 7 x 11-inch baking dish.
8. Pour stewed tomatoes and tomato sauce over eggplant.
9. Cover and bake for 30 minutes.

SERVES 4–6.

105 Zesty Ziti

Don't tell anyone what the secret ingredient is! Ketchup is a great ingredient to add a bit of sweetness and some seasonings to your sauce.

1 (16 ounce) package ziti pasta
1 pound Italian sausage links, cut into ½-inch pieces
1 onion, coarsely chopped
1 green bell pepper, seeded, sliced
1 tablespoon vegetable or canola oil
1 (15 ounce) can diced tomatoes
1 (15 ounce) can Italian stewed tomatoes
2 tablespoons ketchup
1 cup shredded mozzarella cheese

1. Preheat oven to 350°.
2. Cook ziti according to package directions. Drain.
3. Cook sausage, onion, and bell pepper in oil in large skillet over medium heat. Drain.
4. Add diced tomatoes, stewed tomatoes, and ketchup. Mix well.
5. Stir in pasta and cheese.
6. Spoon into sprayed, 3-quart baking dish. Cover and bake for 20 minutes.

SERVES 6.

106 Italian Stuffed Peppers

4 large bell peppers
1 pound bulk Italian pork sausage
1 onion, chopped
1 teaspoon dried basil
1 (4 ounce) can chopped green chilies
2 tablespoons seasoned breadcrumbs
1½ cups shredded mozzarella cheese, divided
1 egg
1 (16 ounce) jar spaghetti sauce

1. Preheat oven to 375°.
2. Cut off top of each pepper and cut pepper in half lengthwise. Discard seeds and white membranes. Place pepper shells in sprayed, 9 x 13-inch baking dish and set aside.
3. Cook sausage and onion in large skillet on medium heat for 5 minutes, stirring to break up sausage; drain.
4. Stir in basil, green chilies, breadcrumbs, 1 cup cheese, and egg. Mix well.
5. Spoon sausage mixture into each green pepper shell.
6. Pour spaghetti sauce over peppers.
7. Cover and bake for 45 minutes. Sprinkle remaining cheese over peppers.

SERVES 6–8.

 ## Who Knew? Light Switch

To make this recipe lower in fat, substitute 1¾ cups of our Homemade Spaghetti Sauce (Light Switch #10) for the jar of spaghetti sauce.

 ## Who Knew?

A great way to save money on peppers is to grow your own! Peppers are perennials and can be grown year-round in 2- to 5-gallon containers of potting soil. Just bring the plants in when the nights drop below 50°, and let them live indoors until the nights are consistently above 50°.

107 Sausage-Apple Ring

Your kids have never seen scrambled eggs and sausage like this! This breakfast-for-dinner dish is sure to impress, even though it doesn't take a lot of work.

2	pounds bulk sausage
1½	cups crushed cracker crumbs
2	eggs, slightly beaten
½	cup milk
¼	cup minced onion
1	cup very finely chopped apple
12	eggs

1. Preheat oven to 350°.
2. Combine sausage, cracker crumbs, beaten eggs, milk, onion, and apple in large bowl. Mix well until ingredients are worked into sausage.
3. Press firmly into 9-inch ring mold. Make sure to press well. Not getting the sausage mixture firmly into the mold will cause holes in the sausage at the bottom.
4. Using a knife, ease around top of edge and center edge of ring mold. Turn onto shallow baking pan or sheet cake pan with edges.
5. Bake for 45 minutes, then drain by letting cool slightly, then spooning off fat in center of ring, then placing several paper towels around ring to absorb fat around edges.
6. Lay plate upside down on top of ring. Cover and refrigerate.
7. When ready to eat, reheat in microwave or in oven at 350° for 15 minutes.
8. While ring is reheating, scramble eggs by beating well and heating over medium heat, stirring constantly. Fill center of ring with scrambled eggs.

SERVES 4–6.

 Who Knew?

Add a pinch of baking soda to a carton of milk right after you open it, and it will last up to a week longer!

108 Select Seafood Manicotti

1 (8 ounce) package manicotti, cooked
1 (15 ounce) container ricotta cheese, softened
3 scallions, finely chopped
1 rib celery, thinly sliced
1 (8 ounce) package frozen salad shrimp, thawed, drained
1 (6 ounce) can crabmeat, drained, flaked
2 cups meatless tomato pasta sauce, divided
¾ cup shredded mozzarella cheese

1. Preheat oven to 350°.
2. Cook manicotti according to package directions. Drain, rinse with cold water, and allow to cool on piece of wax paper.
3. Place ricotta cheese in bowl and stir until fairly smooth. Gently stir in onions, celery, shrimp, and crabmeat.
4. Spread ½ cup pasta sauce in sprayed, 7 x 11-inch glass baking dish.
5. Fill each manicotti shell with seafood mixture and place in sauce. Spoon remaining sauce over manicotti.
6. Cover and bake for 25–30 minutes. Sprinkle with mozzarella cheese and bake uncovered for 5 minutes. Let stand for 5–10 minutes before serving.

SERVES 4–6.

109 Dazzling Shrimp Strata

10–12 thick slices French bread
1 (8 ounce) package shredded Cheddar cheese, divided
1 (16 ounce) package frozen salad shrimp, thawed
1 (10 ounce) package frozen cut spinach, thawed, well drained
1 (4 ounce) can chopped green chilies
¼ cup chopped fresh cilantro
1 (16 ounce) package frozen bell peppers and onions stir-fry, thawed
1½ teaspoons seasoned salt
½ teaspoon dried basil
9 eggs
2 cups milk

1. Arrange bread slices in sprayed, 9 x 13-inch baking dish, cutting cubes from bread to fill in empty spaces.
2. Squeeze spinach between paper towels to completely remove excess moisture.
3. Sprinkle bread with half cheese, then layer shrimp and spinach over cheese.
4. Combine green chilies, cilantro, bell pepper–onion stir-fry, seasoned salt, and dried basil in bowl. Spread over shrimp-spinach layers. Top with remaining cheese.
5. Beat eggs in large bowl and stir in milk. Pour over mixture in baking dish, cover, and refrigerate for at least 8 hours or overnight.
6. When ready to bake, preheat oven to 350°.
7. Bake until knife inserted in center comes out clean, about 45 minutes. Let stand for 10 minutes before slicing to serve.

SERVES 6–8.

 Who Knew? Light Switch

To make this recipe lower in fat, substitute 2 cups of our Low-Fat Four-Cheese Blend (Light Switch #5) for the package of Cheddar cheese.

110 Crab and Broccoli Quiche

1 (15 ounce) package refrigerated piecrust
1 (12 ounce) can white crabmeat, drained
1 (10 ounce) package frozen cut broccoli, thawed, drained
¼ cup finely chopped green bell pepper
1¼ cups shredded provolone cheese
½ cup roasted red bell peppers, drained, chopped
4 large eggs, beaten
1 cup milk
⅛ teaspoon cayenne pepper
¼ teaspoon salt

1. Preheat oven to 400°.
2. Place 1 piecrust on 9-inch glass pie pan and bake until light golden brown, about 10 minutes. (Save second piecrust for another use.)
3. Remove piecrust from oven; reduce heat to 325°. Layer crabmeat, broccoli, bell pepper, cheese, and roasted peppers in piecrust.
4. Combine eggs, milk, cayenne pepper, and salt in bowl. Pour over mixture in piecrust.
5. Bake until knife inserted in center comes out clean, about 55–60 minutes. Let stand for 10 minutes before slicing to serve.

SERVES 6.

 Who Knew?

To keep the edges of the crust from burning, cover them with strips of aluminum foil.

111 Eggplant Frittata

If you have picky eaters in your family, don't tell them this dish is called "Eggplant Frittata," then see what they say after they've cleared their plates! Our boys didn't even know what the eggplant was.

3 cups peeled, finely chopped eggplant
½ cup chopped green bell pepper
3 tablespoons olive oil
1 (8 ounce) jar roasted red peppers, drained, chopped
10 eggs
½ cup half and half
1 teaspoon salt
1 teaspoon Italian seasoning
¼ teaspoon black pepper
⅓ cup grated Parmesan cheese

1. Preheat oven to 325°.
2. Cook eggplant and bell pepper with oil in skillet until tender, about 2–3 minutes. Stir in roasted red peppers.
3. Combine eggs, half and half, salt, Italian seasoning, and pepper in bowl. Beat until well blended.
4. Add eggplant-pepper mixture to egg mixture. Pour into sprayed, 10-inch pie pan.
5. Cover and bake until center sets, about 15 minutes.
6. Sprinkle Parmesan cheese over top. Bake uncovered just until cheese melts slightly, about 5 minutes.
7. Cut into wedges to serve.

SERVES 6–8.

112 Spinach Enchiladas

This recipe will give you enough yummy enchiladas for two meals!

2 (10 ounce) packages frozen chopped spinach, thawed, drained
1 (1 ounce) packet onion soup mix
3 cups shredded Cheddar cheese, divided
3 cups shredded Monterey Jack cheese or mozzarella cheese, divided
12 flour tortillas
1 (1 pint) carton whipping cream

1. Preheat oven to 350°.
2. Squeeze spinach between paper towels to completely remove excess moisture. Combine spinach and onion soup mix in medium bowl.
3. Blend in half of Cheddar cheese and half of Jack cheese.
4. Spread out 12 tortillas. Place about 3 heaping tablespoons spinach mixture down middle of each tortilla. Roll into enchiladas.
5. Place each filled tortilla, seam-side down, into sprayed, 10 x 15-inch baking dish.
6. Pour whipping cream over enchiladas and sprinkle with remaining cheeses. (If freezing for later, place in freezer without whipping cream and remaining cheeses and add just before baking.)
7. Cover and bake for 20 minutes. Uncover and bake for additional 10 minutes.

SERVES 10–12.

 Who Knew? Light Switch

To make this recipe lower in fat, use our Low-Fat Four-Cheese Blend (Light Switch #5) instead of the Cheddar and Monterey Jack cheeses, and use half-and-half rather than whipping cream.

113 Spicy Vegetable Couscous

1 (6 ounce) package herbed-chicken couscous
3 tablespoons butter
3 tablespoons vegetable or canola oil
1 small yellow squash, diced
1 small zucchini, diced
½ red onion, diced
1 red bell pepper, diced
1 (10 ounce) package frozen green peas, thawed
½ teaspoon garlic powder
½ teaspoon ground cumin
½ teaspoon curry powder
¼ teaspoon cayenne pepper
½ teaspoon salt
3–4 tablespoons water, as needed (optional)
1½ cups shredded mozzarella cheese

1. Preheat oven to 350°.
2. Cook couscous according to package directions, but add 3 tablespoons butter instead of amount specified.
3. Heat oil in skillet and sauté squash, zucchini, onion, and bell pepper for 10 minutes. Do not brown.
4. Add peas, garlic powder, cumin, curry powder, cayenne pepper, and salt. Toss.
5. Combine vegetables and couscous. If it seems a little dry, add water.
6. Pour into sprayed, 2½-quart baking dish and sprinkle with mozzarella cheese.
7. Cover and bake for 25 minutes.

SERVES 6–8.

 Who Knew?

If you prefer a milder spice, use only ¹/₈ teaspoon cayenne pepper.

114 Spinach-Cheese Manicotti

It takes a little extra time to fill the manicotti shells, but this is really a special dish and well worth the time!

1 onion, minced
2 teaspoons minced garlic
1 tablespoon vegetable or canola oil
1 (15 ounce) container ricotta cheese
1 (3 ounce) package cream cheese, softened
1 (8 ounce) package shredded mozzarella cheese, divided
1 (3 ounce) package grated Parmesan cheese, divided
2 teaspoons Italian seasoning
½ teaspoon salt
½ teaspoon black pepper
1 (10 ounce) box frozen chopped spinach, thawed, drained
9 manicotti shells, cooked
1 (28 ounce) jar spaghetti sauce

1. Preheat oven to 350°.
2. Sauté onion and garlic with oil in skillet and set aside.
3. Combine ricotta, cream cheese, half of mozzarella, half of Parmesan, Italian seasoning, salt, and pepper in bowl. Beat until they are mixed well.
4. Squeeze spinach between paper towels to completely remove excess moisture.
5. Add spinach and onion-garlic mixture to cheese mixture, and mix well.
6. Spoon mixture into manicotti shells, 1 teaspoon at a time. (Be careful not to tear shells.)
7. Pour half of spaghetti sauce into sprayed, 9 x 13-inch baking dish. Arrange shells over sauce and top with remaining sauce.
8. Cover and bake for 30 minutes. Sprinkle remaining cheeses over top. Bake uncovered until cheese melts.

SERVES 8–10.

115 Pasta Frittata

1 onion, chopped
1 green bell pepper, seeded, chopped
1 red bell pepper, seeded, chopped
2 tablespoons butter
1 (7 ounce) box thin spaghetti, slightly broken, cooked
1 (8 ounce) package shredded mozzarella cheese
5 eggs
1 cup milk
⅓ cup shredded Parmesan cheese
1 tablespoon dried basil
1 teaspoon oregano
½ teaspoon salt
½ teaspoon black pepper

1. Preheat oven to 375°.
2. Sauté onion and bell peppers with butter in skillet over medium heat for 5 minutes. Do not brown.
3. Combine onion-pepper mixture and spaghetti in large bowl and toss. Add mozzarella cheese and toss.
4. In separate bowl, beat eggs, milk, Parmesan cheese, basil, oregano, salt, and pepper. Add spaghetti mixture and pour into sprayed, 9 x 13-inch baking dish.
5. Cover and bake for 15–20 minutes. Uncover and make sure eggs are set. If not, bake for additional 2–3 minutes. Cut into squares to serve.

SERVES 8–10.

Two-Meal Soups And Stews

Who doesn't love the taste of a hearty soup in the fall or winter? This chapter gives you plenty of soups, stews, and chilies to warm your soul and your stomach. Put your plastic containers to good use and save soups without any dairy in your freezer for up to six months. Serve these hearty soups with a couple of healthy wedges of bread and a side salad and they'll not only be enough for an inexpensive dinner—they'll last you two meals! They're also great for a quick microwaved lunch.

116 Chicken-Broccoli Chowder

Even kids love broccoli in this rich, thick soup.

2 (14 ounce) cans chicken broth
1 bunch fresh scallions, finely chopped, divided
1 (10 ounce) package frozen chopped broccoli
1½ cups dry mashed potato flakes
2½ cups chopped rotisserie chicken
1 (8 ounce) package shredded mozzarella cheese
1 (8 ounce) carton heavy cream
1 cup milk
1 cup water
¼ teaspoon salt
⅛ teaspoon black pepper

1. Combine broth, half scallions, and broccoli in large saucepan. Boil, reduce heat, cover, and simmer for 5 minutes.
2. Stir in dry potato flakes and mix until they blend well.
3. Add chicken, cream, milk, water, salt, and pepper. Heat over medium heat, stirring occasionally, until hot, about 5 minutes. Add cheese and stir until melted. (If freezing, freeze and thaw before adding cheese.)
4. Ladle into individual soup bowls and garnish with remaining chopped scallions.

SERVES 8.

117 Chicken-Sausage Stew

1 (16 ounce) package frozen stew vegetables
2 pounds rotisserie or deli chicken, cubed
½ pound Italian sausage, sliced
2 (15 ounce) cans Italian stewed tomatoes
1 (14 ounce) can chicken broth
¼ teaspoon cayenne pepper
¼ teaspoon salt
1 cup cooked rice

1. Combine vegetables, chicken, sausage, tomatoes, broth, cayenne pepper, and salt in large heavy soup pot.
2. Bring to a boil, then reduce heat and simmer for 20 minutes.
3. Stir in cooked rice and simmer for additional 5 minutes.

SERVES 8.

 Who Knew? Light Switch

To make this recipe lower in fat, substitute 1¾ cups of our Healthy Chicken Broth (Light Switch #1) for the can of chicken broth.

118 Northern Chili

2 onions, coarsely chopped
1 tablespoon olive oil
3 (15 ounce) cans great Northern beans, drained
2 (14 ounce) cans chicken broth
2 tablespoons minced garlic
1 (7 ounce) can chopped green chilies
1 tablespoon ground cumin
3 cups cooked, finely chopped rotisserie chicken
1 (8 ounce) package shredded Monterey Jack cheese

1. Cook onions with oil in large saucepan or pot until tender, but not brown, about 5 minutes.
2. Place 1 can of beans in shallow bowl and mash with fork.
3. Combine mashed beans, 2 remaining cans of beans, chicken broth, garlic, green chilies, and cumin in saucepan. Bring to a boil, then reduce heat, cover, and simmer for 30 minutes.
4. Add chopped chicken, stir to blend well, and heat until chili is heated through.
5. When serving, top each bowl with 3 tablespoons cheese.

SERVES 6.

 Who Knew? Light Switch

To make this recipe lower in fat, substitute 2 cups of our Low-Fat Four-Cheese Blend (Light Switch #5) for the package of Monterey Jack cheese.

119 Chicken Chili

This chili is delicious served with hot, buttered flour tortillas for dipping.

2 pounds boneless, skinless chicken breast halves, cubed
1 (16 ounce) package frozen, chopped onions and bell peppers
1 tablespoon olive oil
2 tablespoons minced garlic
2 tablespoons chili powder
1 tablespoon ground cumin
2 (14 ounce) cans chicken broth
¼ teaspoon salt
3 (15 ounce) cans pinto beans with jalapenos, divided

1. Cook chicken with oil in large soup pot over medium heat, stirring occasionally, for 5 minutes. Add onions and bell peppers and continue to cook until chicken is cooked through, about 5 minutes.
2. Add garlic, chili powder, cumin, broth, and salt. Stir to mix well. Bring to a boil over high heat, then reduce heat to low, cover, and simmer for 15 minutes.
3. Place 1 can beans in shallow bowl and mash with fork.
4. Add mashed beans and remaining 2 cans beans to pot. Bring to a boil, then reduce heat and simmer for 10 minutes.

SERVES 8.

120 Brunswick Stew

For this signature Southern dish, cook the meat one day and put your stew together the next. This one-dish meal may take longer than most dishes, but it's really worth it.

3   pounds boneless, skinless chicken pieces
1   (2 pound) boneless pork loin
4   medium potatoes, quartered
3   (28 ounce) cans stewed, diced tomatoes
2   teaspoons sugar
¼   teaspoon salt
⅛   teaspoon black pepper
1   medium onion, chopped
2   (16 ounce) packages frozen butterbeans, thawed
2   (16 ounce) packages frozen corn, thawed

1. Cut pork and chicken into bite-size pieces, trimming off any fat. Cover with water and cook in stew pot until heated through, about 1 hour. Skim off excess fat.
2. Return meat to broth, add potatoes, and cook over medium heat. When potatoes are tender, mash to thicken broth.
3. Add tomatoes, sugar, salt, and pepper and cook until soupy.
4. Add onion and butterbeans. Cook for 10 minutes on low, stirring frequently.
5. Add corn and cook for 5 minutes. Keep scraping bottom of pan to prevent sticking.

SERVES 8–10.

121 Favorite Chicken-Tomato Stew

1   pound boneless, skinless chicken breast halves, cut into strips
1   tablespoon olive oil
1   medium onion, chopped
1   green bell pepper, seeded, chopped
2   (14 ounce) cans chicken broth
2   (15 ounce) cans Mexican stewed tomatoes
2   (15 ounce) cans navy beans with liquid
1   cup salsa
2   teaspoons ground cumin
¼   teaspoon salt
⅛   teaspoon black pepper
1½ cups crushed tortilla chips

1. Cook chicken with oil in soup pot on medium heat for 10 minutes, stirring occasionally.
2. Add onion, bell pepper, broth, tomatoes, navy beans, salsa, cumin, salt, and pepper.
3. Bring to a boil over high heat, then reduce heat to medium and simmer for 25 minutes, stirring often.
4. Ladle into individual soup bowls and sprinkle crushed tortilla chips on top of stew. Serve immediately.

SERVES 8.

122 Zesty Chicken Stew

8 chicken thighs
¼ cup flour
3 tablespoons olive oil
¾ teaspoon dried oregano
¾ teaspoon dried basil
1 teaspoon salt
1 teaspoon black pepper
1 large onion, chopped
1 cup white cooking wine
1 (14 ounce) can chicken broth
3 medium new (red) potatoes, peeled, diced
1 (15 ounce) can diced tomatoes, drained
1 (8 ounce) can sliced carrots, drained
3 tablespoons chopped fresh cilantro

1. Lightly dredge chicken in flour and shake to remove excess.
2. Cook chicken with oil in skillet over medium-high heat until brown on all sides, about 4 minutes per side; set aside.
3. Combine oregano, basil, salt, and pepper in bowl and sprinkle mixture evenly over chicken.
4. Sauté onion in remaining oil in soup pot over medium-high heat until tender, about 4 minutes. Stir in wine and cook for 2 more minutes.
5. Return chicken to pan and add broth, potatoes, tomatoes, and carrots.
6. Reduce heat and simmer, stirring occasionally, for 45 minutes.
7. Remove chicken and de-bone, then add back to soup. Stir in cilantro and serve over brown or white rice.

SERVES 8.

123 Hearty 15-Minute Turkey Soup

Serve this tasty, spiced soup with some cornbread! Use leftover turkey, or ask for a slab of turkey at the deli counter.

1 (14 ounce) can chicken broth
3 (15 ounce) cans navy beans with liquid
1 (28 ounce) can stewed tomatoes with liquid
3 cups cooked, chopped white meat turkey (about 1 pound)
2 teaspoons minced garlic
¼ teaspoon cayenne pepper
¼ teaspoon salt
⅛ black pepper
1 (6 ounce) package baby spinach, stems removed

1. Combine broth, beans, stewed tomatoes, turkey, garlic, cayenne pepper, salt, and black pepper in soup pot.
2. Bring to a boil, then reduce heat to medium and simmer for 10 minutes.
3. Stir in baby spinach. Cook, stirring, for 8 minutes.

SERVES 8.

124 Hot Gobble-Gobble Soup

This turkey soup has a spicy kick to it—not too much, but just right! Use leftover turkey or ask at the deli counter for a large slab that isn't cut into slices.

6–8 **cups cooked, chopped turkey**	1. Combine all ingredients in large soup pot.
1 **(48 ounce) carton + 1 (14 ounce) can chicken broth**	2. Bring to a boil, then reduce heat and simmer, stirring occasionally, for 2 hours.
4 **(10 ounce) cans diced tomatoes with green chilies**	
2 **(15 ounce) cans whole corn, drained**	
2 **large onions, chopped**	
2 **(10 ounce) cans tomato soup**	
1½ **teaspoon garlic powder**	
1½ **teaspoon dried oregano**	
¼ **cup water**	

SERVES 12.

 Who Knew? Light Switch

To make this recipe even healthier, substitute 2 quarts of our Healthy Chicken Broth (Light Switch #1) for the carton and can of chicken broth.

---

125 Beefy Bean Chili

3 **pounds ground beef**	1. Cook ground beef in large soup pot over medium heat, stirring occasionally, until meat crumbles and is brown, about 12 minutes.
6 **ribs celery, chopped**	
2 **medium onions, chopped**	2. Add celery, onion, bell pepper, and minced garlic. Cook until vegetables are tender but not brown, about 8 minutes.
2 **bell peppers, seeded, chopped**	
1 **tablespoon minced garlic**	
2 **(15 ounce) cans tomato sauce**	3. Stir in tomato sauce, chili powder, water, salt, and pepper and mix well. Bring mixture to a boil, then reduce heat to low and simmer for 20 minutes.
3 **tablespoons chili powder**	
4 **cups water**	
½ **teaspoon black pepper**	4. Add beans and simmer for additional 15 minutes.
1 **teaspoon salt**	
2 **(15 ounce) cans pinto beans with liquid**	5. Ladle into individual serving bowls and top each serving with several tablespoons crushed tortilla chips.
2 **(15 ounce) cans black beans with liquid**	
2–4 **cups crushed tortilla chips**	

SERVES 12.

126 Big-Time Chili

This chili is not for lightweights! Cayenne pepper and chili powder give it a super-spicy kick that's so powerful it may have your nose running!

¼ cup olive oil
3 medium to large onions, chopped
4 pounds ground beef
1 (15 ounce) can black beans
1 (15 ounce) can kidney beans
2 (15 ounce) cans diced tomatoes
1 (6 ounce) can tomato paste
1 teaspoon cayenne pepper
2 tablespoons garlic powder
3 tablespoons chili powder
1 tablespoon ground cumin
1½ tablespoons paprika
1 tablespoon salt
Water, as necessary

1. Heat olive oil in large saucepan over medium heat. When hot, add onions and ground beef. Cook, stirring and breaking up beef, until onion is tender and beef is browned. Drain.
2. Add all remaining ingredients and increase heat to medium-high. When mixture begins to bubble, stir and reduce heat to low. Simmer, covered, for 3 hours.
3. Stir several times throughout cooking time and add water if liquid level gets too low.

SERVES 12.

127 Down-Home Beefy Soup

1½ tablespoons olive oil
3 pounds lean ground beef
1 tablespoon minced garlic
2 (16 ounce) packages frozen onions and peppers
1 (48 ounce) carton beef broth
5 cups water
4 (15 ounce) cans Italian stewed tomatoes
2 tablespoons Italian seasoning
3 cups uncooked macaroni noodles

1. Add olive oil to soup pot and cook over medium heat. When hot, add beef and garlic. Cook, stirring and breaking up beef, until starting to brown, about 10–15 minutes. Add onion and pepper mix and continue to cook, stirring, until vegetables are heated through and beef is browned. Drain.
2. Add beef broth, water, stewed tomatoes, and Italian seasoning and cook over high heat. Bring to boiling and boil for 2 minutes.
3. When ready to eat, cook macaroni according to package directions. Add to warm soup.

SERVES 12–16.

 Who Knew? Light Switch

To make this recipe lower in fat, substitute 6¼ cups of our Healthy Beef Broth (Light Switch #2) for the carton of beef broth.

128 Beef-Veggie Soup

1 pound lean ground beef
1 (1 ounce) packet onion soup mix
2 (14 ounce) cans beef broth
2 (15 ounce) cans stewed tomatoes
2 (16 ounce) packages frozen
   mixed vegetables
1 cup water
1 cup shell macaroni

1. Place beef in soup pot and cook, stirring, over medium-high heat until meat is no longer pink, about 8–12 minutes. Drain.
2. Add soup mix, broth, tomatoes, mixed vegetables, and water. Bring to boil. Add macaroni and reduce heat to medium. Cook until macaroni is tender, stirring occasionally, about 15 minutes.

SERVES 8.

 Who Knew?

Add a few tablespoons of black coffee to this (and other beef soups and stews) to give them a nice dark color and a rich taste that may become your secret ingredient! This also works well for gravies.

129 Albondigas Soup

This tasty dish is a traditional meatball-potato soup from Mexico.

4 pounds lean ground beef
2 cups breadcrumbs
2 medium onions, chopped
4 eggs
1 tablespoon ground cumin
4 cloves garlic, minced
1 tablespoon salt, divided
¾ teaspoon black pepper
1 tablespoon olive oil
½ cup (1 stick) butter
¼ cup flour
2 quarts hot water
¼ cup snipped cilantro
4 large potatoes, peeled, cubed

1. Combine beef, breadcrumbs, onions, eggs, cumin, garlic, 2 teaspoons salt, and pepper in bowl. Mix well and form into meatballs about 1¼ inches in diameter.
2. Heat oil in large skillet over medium-high heat. When hot, add meatballs and cook, turning and flipping occasionally, until meatballs are cooked through. Transfer to bowl and set aside.
3. Heat butter in same skillet. When butter is melted, sprinkle flour on top. Stir constantly until flour begins to turn brown; do not burn.
4. Immediately add water, cilantro, and remaining salt and continue to stir until liquid boils.
5. Add potatoes, then reduce heat to low and simmer, covered, until potatoes are cooked through, about 45 minutes–1 hour. Add meatballs and cook until heated through.

SERVES 12.

130 Southwestern Soup

1½ pounds lean ground beef
1 large onion, chopped
2 (15 ounce) cans pinto beans with liquid
1 (15 ounce) can ranch-style beans, drained
2 (15 ounce) cans whole kernel corn with liquid
2 (15 ounce) cans Mexican stewed tomatoes
1½ cups water
2 (1 ounce) packets taco seasoning

1. Brown beef and onion in large soup pot, stirring until beef crumbles; drain. Add beans, corn, tomatoes, and water.
2. Bring to a boil, then reduce heat and stir in taco seasoning. Simmer for 25 minutes.

SERVES 8.

131 Spaghetti Soup

If your family loves spaghetti, they'll love this soup version! To ensure that the noodles don't get too soft, freeze this soup as soon as it cools until you're ready to eat it.

2 quarts water
¼ teaspoon salt
1 (7 ounce) package spaghetti pasta
1 (18 ounce) package frozen, cooked meatballs, thawed
1 (28 ounce) jar spaghetti sauce
1 (15 ounce) can stewed tomatoes
1 cup grated Parmesan cheese

1. In large soup pot, boil water over high heat. Add salt and spaghetti. Reduce heat to medium and cook spaghetti for 6 minutes. Do not drain.
2. When spaghetti is done, add meatballs, spaghetti sauce, and stewed tomatoes and cook until mixture heats through.
3. Add grated Parmesan cheese to individual bowls for garnish.

SERVES 8.

 Who Knew? Light Switch

To make this recipe lower in fat, substitute our Low-Fat Meatballs (Light Switch #12) for the package of frozen meatballs.

132 Easy Meaty Minestrone

Adding meatballs and more beans to a traditional can of minestrone soup is a great way to turn it from a lunch into a dinner.

4 (26 ounce) cans minestrone soup
2 (15 ounce) cans pinto beans with liquid
2 (18 ounce) packages frozen, cooked meatballs, thawed
1 cup water
¾ cup grated Parmesan cheese

1. Combine soup, beans, meatballs, and water in large saucepan. Boil, reduce heat, and simmer for 15 minutes.
2. Ladle into individual soup bowls and sprinkle with about 1 tablespoon grated Parmesan cheese.

SERVES 12,

 Who Knew? Light Switch

To make this recipe lower in fat, substitute our Low-Fat Meatballs (Light Switch #12) for the package of frozen meatballs.

133 Meat and Potatoes Stew

½ cup flour
1 teaspoon salt
¼ teaspoon black pepper
2 pounds stew beef, cubed
1 tablespoon olive oil
4 cups water
4 beef bullion cubes
1 bay leaf
2 cloves garlic, smashed
3 medium onions
6 carrots, peeled, sliced
2½ pounds russet potatoes, peeled, cubed
1 (10 ounce) package frozen peas

1. Mix flour, salt, and pepper in bowl. Add beef cubes and toss to coat.
2. Heat olive oil in a soup pot or Dutch oven over medium-high heat. When hot, add beef and cook, stirring, until browned on all sides. Drain.
3. Boil water and add bullion cubes; stir to dissolve. Add to pot along with bay leaf and garlic. Bring to a boil over high heat, then reduce heat to low. Simmer until meat is cooked through, about 10–20 minutes.
4. Add onions, carrots, and potatoes. Cook for 10 minutes, then add peas and cook until all vegetables are tender, about 20 minutes. Add water if needed during cooking time.

SERVES 10.

 Who Knew?

The tannic acid in strong black tea can tenderize meat in a stew, as well as reduce the cooking time. Just add ½ cup strong tea to the stew when you add the broth.

134 Baked Pinto Bean Stew

Here's another take on pinto beans, this time in a hearty stew with a hint of cinnamon.

2 cups dried pinto beans
10 cups water
2 pounds beef stew meat
2 onions, chopped
2 (6 ounce) cans tomato paste
½ cup packed brown sugar
1 teaspoon dry mustard
½ teaspoon ground cinnamon
½ teaspoon salt
¼ teaspoon black pepper

1. Preheat oven to 325°.
2. Place beans in oven-safe pot. Bringing to boiling over high heat. Boil for 2 minutes.
3. Add remaining ingredients, cover, and bake for 2 hours.
4. Remove from oven and stir mixture well. Return to oven, cover, and bake until beans and beef are heated through, about 3 hours.

SERVES 12.

135 Steakhouse Stew

2 tablespoons olive oil
2 pounds boneless beef sirloin steak, cubed
2 cups water
2 (15 ounce) cans stewed tomatoes
2 (10 ounce) cans French onion soup
2 (10 ounce) cans tomato soup
2 (16 ounce) packages frozen stew vegetables, thawed

1. Add oil to large skillet or soup pot and cook over medium-high heat. When hot, add cubed steak and cook, stirring, until steak is browned on all sides, about 10 minutes.
2. Add remaining ingredients and increase heat to high. When boiling, reduce heat to low and simmer for 35 minutes.

SERVES 12.

 ## Who Knew?

If you or someone in your family has trouble with the acidity of the tomatoes in this recipe (or others), add some chopped carrots in step 2. They will naturally decrease the acid in the dish!

136 Chile Verde Con Carne

Chile con carne translates to "chili with meat," and *verde* refers to the fresh green chilies in this tasty dish.

¼ cup (1/2 stick) butter
2 tablespoons olive oil
4–6 pounds sirloin or tenderloin, cubed
2 large onions, chopped
1 head garlic, peeled and minced
16–20 fresh New Mexico green chilies, peeled, seeded, chopped
1½ tablespoons ground cumin
1 tablespoon oregano
2 cups water
1½ teaspoon salt
1½ teaspoon black pepper

1. Heat butter and olive oil in large skillet over medium-high heat. When butter has melted, add cubed sirloin and cook, stirring, until meat is brown on all sides, about 10 minutes.
2. Reduce heat to low and add all remaining ingredients. Cover and simmer for 2–3 hours, stirring occasionally. Add 1–2 cups additional water if liquid level gets low.
3. When finished, uncover, taste for flavor, and add salt, pepper, and oregano, if needed.

SERVES 12.

 Who Knew?

To save time, 2 (7 ounce) cans of green chilies may be used instead of roasting fresh green chilies, but the flavor of fresh chilies is the secret to the best chili.

137 Green Chile Stew Pot (Caldillo)

This traditional Mexican dish is called *Caldillo* in Spanish, and is often served on special occasions.

4 pounds round steak, cubed
3 tablespoons salt, divided
2 tablespoons vegetable or canola oil
4 medium onions, chopped
4 potatoes, peeled, diced
4 cloves garlic, minced
12–16 fresh green chilies, roasted, peeled, seeded, diced
1 teaspoon black pepper
Water

1. Sprinkle round steak with 2 tablespoons salt.
2. Heat oil in large skillet over medium-high heat and add meat when hot. Cook, stirring, until meat is brown on all sides, about 12–15 minutes. Add onions, potatoes, and garlic and cook until onions are translucent, about 5–8 minutes.
3. Pour all ingredients from skillet into large stew pot. Add chilies, remaining salt, pepper, and enough water to cover all ingredients.
4. Bring to a boil over high heat, then reduce heat to low and simmer until meat and potatoes are cooked through, about 1–2 hours.

SERVES 12.

138 Chunky Beefy Noodle Soup

2 pounds beef round steak, cubed
2 medium onions, chopped
4 ribs celery, chopped
2 tablespoons oil
5 cups water
1½ teaspoon salt
1½ tablespoons chili powder
¾ teaspoon dried oregano
2 (15 ounce) cans stewed tomatoes
1 (48 ounce) carton beef broth
1 (8 ounce) package egg noodles
2 green bell peppers, seeded, chopped

1. Cook and stir cubed steak, onions, and celery in soup pot with oil until beef browns on all sides, about 15 minutes.
2. Stir in water, salt, chili powder, oregano, stewed tomatoes, and beef broth. Bring to a boil, then reduce heat and simmer until beef is cooked through, about 1 hour 30 minutes–2 hours.
3. Stir in noodles and bell peppers and heat to boiling. Reduce heat and simmer until noodles are tender, about 10–15 minutes.

SERVES 12.

 Who Knew? Light Switch

To make this recipe lower in fat, substitute 6¼ cups of our Healthy Beef Broth (Light Switch #2) for the carton of beef broth, and No Yolks egg noodle substitute for the egg noodles.

139 Border-Crossing Stew

2 tablespoons vegetable or olive oil
3 pounds round steak, trimmed and cut into cubes
4 small to medium onions, chopped
2 (14 ounce) cans beef broth
2 (15 ounce) cans Mexican stewed tomatoes
2 (7 ounce) cans chopped green chilies
6 baking potatoes, peeled, cubed
3 teaspoons minced garlic
3 teaspoons ground cumin
2 cups water
½ teaspoon salt
¼ teaspoon black pepper

1. Cook oil in large skillet over medium-high heat. When hot, add cubed steak and onions. Cook, stirring often, until onions are tender and steak is browned on all sides, about 10 minutes.
2. Add beef broth, tomatoes, green chilies, potatoes, garlic, cumin, water, salt, and pepper. Mix well to combine.
3. Bring to a boil, then reduce heat to medium-low and cook, covered, until potatoes are tender, about 35 minutes.

SERVES 12.

140 Easy Chunky Chili

This recipe works great with beef, pork, and even chicken, so buy whatever is on sale!

4 pounds cubed stew meat
2 tablespoons olive oil
2 (10 ounce) cans beef broth
2 medium onions, chopped
4 (15 ounce) cans diced tomatoes
2 (10 ounce) cans tomatoes with green chilies
2 (15 ounce) cans pinto beans with liquid
2 (15 ounce) cans kidney beans with liquid
2 tablespoons chili powder
1 tablespoon ground cumin
2 teaspoons oregano

1. If stew meat is in large chunks, cut each chunk in half.
2. Add oil to large skillet. When hot, add meat and cook, stirring, over medium-high heat until meat is browned on all sides, about 8–10 minutes.
3. Add all remaining ingredients. Bring to a boil, then reduce heat and cook on low heat for 1 hour.

SERVES 12.

141 Stroganoff Stew

2 (1 ounce) packets onion soup mix
4 (10 ounce) cans golden mushroom soup
4 (10 ounce) soup canfuls water
4 pounds stew meat
2 (8 ounce) cartons sour cream
6 cups egg noodles, cooked, drained

1. Preheat oven to 275°.
2. Combine soup mix, mushroom soup, and water and pour over stew meat in roasting pan.
3. Cover tightly and bake for 6 hours.
4. When ready to serve, stir in sour cream, return mixture to oven until it heats through, and serve over noodles.

SERVES 12.

 Who Knew? Light Switch

To make this recipe lower in fat, substitute 2 cups of our Low-Fat Sour Cream Substitute (Light Switch #8) for the cartons of sour cream, and the egg noodles for No Yolks egg noodle substitute.

142 Oven-Baked Beef Stew

2 tablespoons flour
½ teaspoon salt
¼ teaspoon black pepper
1½ pounds beef chuck, cubed
1½ cups chopped onion
½ teaspoon basil
4 potatoes, peeled, cubed
4 carrots, peeled, sliced
½ cup dry red wine
2 (10 ounce) cans tomato soup
2½ cups water

1. Preheat oven to 325°.
2. Combine flour with salt and pepper and pat onto both sides of meat. In large, oven-safe skillet, cook meat on medium-high heat until browned on all sides, about 8–12 minutes. Drain.
3. Add all remaining ingredients; cover and bake for 1 hour.

SERVES 8–12.

143 Quick-Step Posole

Pork shoulder is not only one of the most delicious cuts of pork, it's also one of the cheapest! The only secret is that you have to cook it for a long time, like in this recipe.

3–4 pounds pork shoulder, cubed
1½ teaspoons salt
¾ teaspoon black pepper
½ cup flour
¼ cup olive oil
2 large onions, chopped
2 cloves garlic, minced
4 ribs celery, chopped
2 (8 ounce) cans hominy, drained
1 (10 ounce) bottle red chili sauce
1 (32 ounce) carton pork or
    beef broth

1. Sprinkle pork with salt and pepper and dredge in flour on all sides.
2. Heat oil in large saucepan over medium-high heat. Add pork cubes and cook, stirring, until brown on all sides, about 8 minutes.
3. Add onions, garlic, and celery; cook until onions are translucent, about 5 minutes.
4. Add hominy and red chili sauce to saucepan. Cover and cook on low heat, stirring occasionally, for 10 minutes.
5. Add broth and simmer on low heat for 1 hour, stirring occasionally.

SERVES 12.

 Who Knew?

If you don't have a garlic press, try using a lemon zester to mince garlic. It's faster and easier than using a knife!

144 Pinto Bean Soup

This amazingly simple recipe is great for "cooking Sundays." Start it at the beginning of your cooking session, then leave it on the stove until you're almost done.

4 pounds dry pinto beans
2 smoked ham hocks or 4 cups cooked, chopped ham
1 dried bay leaf
½ teaspoon salt
1 (14 ounce) can beef broth

1. Rinse beans, then cover with cold water in soup pot and soak overnight.
2. Drain beans, cover with water, and bring to a boil over high heat.
3. Add ham, bay leaf, and salt to pot, reduce heat to very low, and simmer slowly for 3–4 hours. (You may need to add more water during cooking time.)
4. When beans are tender, drain half of liquid. Remove 4–6 cups beans and smash with potato masher. Return smashed beans to pot and add beef broth.
5. Cook over medium heat for 10 minutes.

SERVES 12.

 Who Knew?

How do you tell if a bean is fully cooked? Squeeze it! There should be no hard core at the center.

145 Ham Bone Soup

If you don't see them in the case, ask for ham hocks at the deli counter. They may need to fetch them from the back, but they're very inexpensive, and will add an amazing depth of flavor to this simple soup.

4 cups dried navy beans
3 quarts water
1 pound ham hocks
   Salt and pepper to taste

1. Cover beans with water and soak overnight.
2. Drain, then place beans in large soup pot with water and ham hocks. Bring to a boil over high heat, then reduce heat to low and simmer until beans are tender, about 2–3 hours.
3. Season with salt and pepper to taste.

SERVES 8.

 Who Knew?

You can make dry beans less gassy by adding fennel seeds to the water while you're soaking them overnight. Use a teaspoon of fennel for every 2 cups of beans.

146 Split Pea Soup

This is a wonderful way to use up leftover ham. If you happen to have a meaty ham bone, you can use that along with, or instead of, the chopped ham.

2 (16 ounce) packages dried green split peas
Water
2 onions, chopped
2 large potatoes, peeled, diced
4 ribs celery, chopped
2 cups cooked, shredded or chopped ham
2 cups shredded carrots
2 teaspoons minced garlic
½ teaspoon salt
¼ teaspoon black pepper
1 (5½ ounce) package seasoned croutons

1. Rinse peas and place in large, heavy soup pot. Fill with water until water is covering the peas by 2 inches. Soak overnight.
2. Drain, then add onions, potatoes, celery, ham, carrots, garlic, salt, and pepper. Fill pot with water until covering all ingredients.
3. Bring to a boil over high heat, then reduce heat to low, cover, and simmer for 2 hours 30 minutes–3 hours, stirring occasionally.
4. Let cool slightly, then blend mixture in food processor or blender in batches.
5. When smooth, return mixture to soup pot, then cover and simmer until heated through, about 5 minutes. Garnish with croutons.

SERVES 12.

147 Turnip Greens Stew

4 cups chopped ham
1 (48 ounce) carton chicken broth
4 (16 ounce) packages frozen, chopped turnip greens
2 (16 ounce) packages frozen, chopped onions and bell peppers
1 (10 ounce) package frozen corn
2 teaspoons sugar
1½ teaspoons pepper

1. Combine all ingredients in large stew pot. Bring to a boil over high heat, then cover, reduce heat to low, and simmer, stirring occasionally, for 30 minutes.

SERVES 12–16.

 Who Knew? Light Switch

To make this recipe even healthier, substitute 6¼ cups of our Healthy Chicken Broth (Light Switch #1) for the carton of chicken broth.

148 Ham and Lentil Stew

2 (1 ounce) packets onion-mushroom
  soup mix
2 (14 ounce) cans chicken broth
2 cups lentils, rinsed, drained
2 cups brown rice
4 cups chopped onion
4 cups chopped celery
2 (16 ounce) packages baby
  carrots, sliced
2 cups water
4 (15 ounce) cans diced tomatoes
  with liquid
4 cups cubed ham
2 tablespoons apple-cider vinegar

1. Combine soup mix, chicken broth, lentils, rice, onion, celery, carrots, and water in stew pot. Bring to a boil, then reduce heat and simmer for 45 minutes.
2. Stir in tomatoes, ham, and vinegar and cook on medium heat until mixture is heated through.

SERVES 12.

 Who Knew?

For an added treat, add a 3-inch square rind of Parmesan cheese (or another hard cheese) to this soup while you're simmering it. When you're serving the soup, break up the delicious, melty rind and include it in each bowl. It's completely edible.

149 Soul Food Soup

Stock up on navy beans. It's time for Soul Food Soup!

6 (15 ounce) cans navy beans
  with liquid
3 large onions, chopped
1½ tablespoons minced garlic
6 medium yukon gold potatoes,
  peeled, cubed
4 cups diced ham
2 (32 ounce) cartons chicken broth
2 (10 ounce) packages frozen
  chopped turnip greens
½ teaspoon salt
¼ teaspoon black pepper

1. Place 2 cans of beans in shallow bowl and mash with potato masher or fork.
2. Spray large soup pot and add mashed beans, remaining cans of beans, onions, garlic, potatoes, ham, broth, turnip greens, salt, and pepper. Mix well.
3. Bring to a boil over high heat and boil for 5 minutes. Reduce heat to low and simmer until potatoes and greens are tender, about 45 minutes.

SERVES 12.

150 Good Ol' Bean Soup

Here's another one of our favorite bean soup recipes, this time with chicken broth as a base.

¼ cup olive oil
2 cups peeled, shredded carrots
2 (16 ounce) packages frozen, chopped onions and peppers
1 (48 ounce) carton chicken broth
3 (15 ounce) cans pinto beans with jalapenos with liquid
2 cups cooked, diced ham
1 cup water

1. Combine oil, carrots, and onions and peppers in soup pot and cook over medium heat, stirring occasionally, until vegetables are tender and heated through, about 10 minutes. Drain if necessary.
2. Add broth, pinto beans, ham, and water.
3. Bring to a boil over high heat, then reduce heat to low and simmer for 15 minutes.

SERVES 12.

 Who Knew?

To easily shred carrots, simply run them through the largest holes on your cheese grater.

---

151 Ham and Sausage Stew

3 cups cooked, diced ham
1 pound Polish sausage, sliced
3 (14 ounce) cans chicken broth
2 (15 ounce) cans Mexican stewed tomatoes
1 tablespoon ground cumin
¼ teaspoon salt
1 tablespoon olive oil
2 (15 ounce) cans navy beans with liquid
2 (15 ounce) cans whole kernel corn, drained
8 flour tortillas

1. Combine ham, sausage, chicken broth, tomatoes, cumin, and salt in large roasting pan.
2. Add oil and cook on high heat for 5 minutes.
3. Add navy beans and corn, then reduce heat and simmer for 35 minutes.
4. Serve with warmed, buttered flour tortillas.

SERVES 8.

152 Frogmore Stew

According to legend, Frogmore Stew was invented many years ago by a South Carolina fisherman, who used whatever he could find—including sausage, seafood, and corn—in a stew. Here's an easy version of the famous dish.

2 gallons water
3 tablespoons seafood seasoning
3 pounds smoked link sausage, sliced
3 onions, peeled, chopped
1 lemon, sliced, seeded
½ teaspoon salt
½ cup (1 stick) butter
6 ears corn, halved or 2 (10 ounce) packages frozen corn
3 pounds large shrimp, peeled

1. Combine water, seasoning, sausage, onions, lemon, and salt in very large stew pot and boil. Simmer for 45 minutes.
2. Add butter and corn and cook for 10 minutes.
3. Add shrimp, cook for additional 5 minutes, and drain water. Serve immediately.

SERVES 8.

 Who Knew?

No matter what kind of cutting board you prefer, here are some safety and cleaning tips for them. Reserve one cutting board only for raw meats, poultry, and fish; use other cutting boards for prepping vegetables, cheeses, and cooked meats.

153 Sausage Chowder

1 tablespoon olive oil
2 pounds pork sausage, sliced and chopped into bite-sized pieces
4 (15 ounce) cans kidney beans, rinsed, drained
2 (15 ounce) cans diced tomatoes
2 medium potatoes, peeled, cubed
2 green bell peppers, seeded, chopped
2 medium onions, chopped
1 tablespoon minced garlic
½ teaspoon thyme
½ teaspoon salt
¼ teaspoon black pepper

1. Add oil to large soup pot and heat over medium heat. When hot, add sausage and cook, stirring, until sausage is cooked through, about 12 minutes. Drain.
2. Add beans, tomatoes, potatoes, bell peppers, onions, garlic, thyme, salt, and pepper. Bring to a boil over high heat, then reduce heat to low and simmer for 1 hour.

SERVES 12.

154 Creamed Broccoli Soup

8 slices bacon
6 potatoes, peeled
2 small onions, minced
4 cups water
1½ teaspoon salt
2 (10 ounce) packages frozen, chopped broccoli
½ cup (1 stick) butter
6 tablespoons flour
2 (1 pint) cartons cream

1. Fry bacon in deep skillet, drain, and set aside.
2. Shred potatoes with cheese grater. With bacon drippings still in skillet, add potatoes, onion, water, and salt. Cover and cook for 10 minutes. Add broccoli and cook for additional 5 minutes.
3. In separate large saucepan, melt butter and add flour. Stir and cook until mixture bubbles.
4. Gradually add cream. Cook, stirring constantly, until it thickens.
5. Stir in potato-broccoli mixture and heat just until heated through.
6. Crumble bacon and sprinkle on top of each serving.

SERVES 8.

 Who Knew?

To easily store unused bacon in the freezer, roll each into a ball and keep in a resealable plastic bag. When you cook the bacon, simply heat it in a microwave for a few seconds, unroll it, and fry away!

155 Rich Corn Chowder

16 ears fresh corn
12 slices bacon
2 small onions, chopped
1 red bell pepper, seeded, chopped
2 small baking potatoes, peeled, cubed
2 cups water
½ teaspoon salt
¼ teaspoon black pepper
2 (1 pint) cartons cream, divided
1 tablespoon sugar
¾ teaspoon dried thyme
1½ tablespoons cornstarch

1. Cut corn from cobs into large bowl and scrape well to remove all milk.
2. Fry bacon in large soup pot over medium heat. Remove bacon and save drippings in pan. Crumble bacon and set aside.
3. Cook onion and bell pepper in bacon drippings over medium heat until tender, about 8–10 minutes. Drain.
4. Stir in corn, potatoes, water, salt, and pepper. Bring to a boil over high heat, then cover, reduce heat to low, and simmer for 15 minutes, stirring occasionally.
5. Stir in 3 cups cream, sugar, and thyme.
6. Combine cornstarch and remaining cream and stir until smooth. Gradually add to corn mixture, stirring constantly.
7. Cook on medium-low heat until soup thickens, stirring constantly, about 15 minutes.

SERVES 12.

156 Rich Cheese Soup

8 slices bacon
1 large onion, finely chopped
4 ribs celery, finely sliced
2 medium leeks, halved lengthwise, sliced
1 (32 ounce) carton plus 1 (14 ounce) can chicken broth
1¹⁄₃ cups quick-cooking oats
1½ cups shredded Swiss cheese
2 (8 ounce) cartons whipping cream

1. Cook bacon in large saucepan over medium-high heat until crisp, about 2–3 minutes per side; drain, cool, and crumble. Save drippings in saucepan.
2. Cook onions, celery, and leeks in pan drippings over medium heat, stirring often, for 10 minutes.
3. Add broth and oats. Bring to a boil, then reduce heat and simmer for 15 minutes. Cool slightly.
4. Place half of mixture in blender and process until smooth. Repeat with remaining mixture.
5. Return all of mixture to saucepan and stir in cheese and cream. Heat until cheese melts; do not boil. Ladle into individual soup bowls and sprinkle with crumbled bacon.

SERVES 8.

 ## Who Knew?

If you're making soup or stew and it comes out too salty, use one of these methods to make it less so: Add a can of peeled tomatoes or a small amount of brown sugar; or stir in a slice or two of raw apple or potato, let simmer a few minutes, then discard the apple or potato.

---

157 Quickie Corny Soup

6 strips bacon
2 bunches scallions, minced
2 (15 ounce) cans cream-style corn
2 (10 ounce) cans cream of celery soup
2 soup canfuls milk
³⁄₈ teaspoon salt
³⁄₁₆ teaspoon black pepper

1. Cook bacon in large skillet over medium heat. Set aside on paper towels and crumble when cool.
2. Add scallions to bacon drippings in skillet and cook, stirring, until translucent. Drain.
3. Add cream-style corn, soup, milk, bacon, salt, and pepper. Heat on medium heat until heated through, about 10 minutes. Do not boil.

SERVES 12.

 ## Who Knew?

Did you know you could freeze corn on the cob? After shucking the corn, boil it for 5 minutes, then plunge into ice water and pat dry. Pack in a freezer bag before freezing. To cook, place the frozen corn in boiling water for 10–15 minutes.

158 Cod and Corn Chowder

5 cups water
2 pounds cod, cut into bite-size pieces
4 large baking potatoes, thinly sliced
6 ribs celery, sliced
2 medium onions, chopped
2 (15 ounce) cans whole kernel corn
½ teaspoon salt
¼ teaspoon black pepper
2 (8 ounce) cartons whipping cream
12 slices bacon, cooked, crumbled

1. In large soup pot, combine water, cod, potatoes, celery, onion, corn, salt, and pepper. Stir to mix well.
2. Bring to a boil over high heat. Reduce heat to low, cover, and simmer until fish and potatoes are done, about 20 minutes.
3. Stir in cream and heat just until heated through.
4. When ready to serve, sprinkle crumbled bacon over each serving.

SERVES 12.

159 Anniversary Seafood Bisque

Jeanne debuted this recipe on our twelfth wedding anniversary! It was a big hit.

2 pounds new (red) potatoes, washed and chopped into bite-sized pieces
½ cup (1 stick) butter
2 (8 ounce) packages frozen salad shrimp, thawed
2 (6 ounce) cans crab, drained, flaked
2 teaspoons minced garlic
1 cup flour
4 (14 ounce) cans chicken broth, divided
2 cups milk, cream, or half-and-half
½ teaspoon salt
¼ teaspoon black pepper

1. Cook potatoes in boiling water until cooked through, about 10 minutes. Drain.
2. Melt butter in large saucepan over medium heat. Add potatoes, shrimp, crab, and garlic and cook for 10 minutes.
3. Stir in flour and cook, stirring constantly, for 3 minutes.
4. Gradually add chicken broth. Cook and stir until mixture thickens.
5. Stir in cream, salt, and pepper, stirring constantly, and cook just until mixture is heated through; do not boil.

SERVES 12.

160 Cauliflower-Crab Chowder

1 (16 ounce) package frozen
cauliflower
¾ cup water
¼ cup (½ stick) butter
¼ cup flour
1 (14 ounce) can chicken broth
1½ cups milk
1 (3 ounce) package cream
cheese, cubed
1 (2 ounce) jar chopped
pimento, drained
1 teaspoon dried parsley
¼ teaspoon salt
⅛ teaspoon black pepper
1 (8 ounce) package refrigerated
imitation crabmeat, drained

1. Cook cauliflower in water in large saucepan until tender-crisp.
2. In separate saucepan, melt butter, stir in flour, and mix well.
3. Add broth, milk, and cream cheese and cook, stirring constantly, until thick and bubbly.
4. Add mixture to saucepan with cauliflower and stir in pimento, parsley, salt, and pepper.
5. Stir in crab and heat just until heated through.

SERVES 8.

 Who Knew? Light Switch

To save money and make this recipe even healthier, use 1¾ cups of our Healthy Chicken Broth (Light Switch #1) instead of the can of chicken broth.

161 Spiked Crab Soup

This wine-infused soup isn't child friendly, but serve it as the first course at a dinner party and you're sure to receive raves.

2 (1 ounce) packets dry onion soup mix
4 cups water
2 (6 ounce) cans crabmeat with
liquid, flaked
2 (8 ounce) cartons whipping cream
½ teaspoon salt
⅛ teaspoon black pepper
1 cup white wine

1. Dissolve soup mix with water in saucepan.
2. Add crabmeat, crab liquid, and whipping cream. Sprinkle with salt and pepper.
3. Heat, but do not boil, and simmer for 20 minutes.
4. Stir in wine, heat, and serve warm.

SERVES 12.

162 Super Easy Gumbo

It doesn't get any easier than this! Add some seafood to cans of gumbo for a simple (yet delicious) supper.

2 (10 ounce) cans pepper-pot soup
2 (10 ounce) cans chicken gumbo soup
2 (6 ounce) cans white crabmeat, flaked
2 (6 ounce) cans tiny shrimp, thawed or ½ of 1 (32 ounce) package salad frozen shrimp, shelled
3 soup canfuls water

1. Combine all ingredients in saucepan.
2. Bring to a boil over high heat, then reduce heat to low and simmer, covered, for 15 minutes.

SERVES 8.

 Who Knew?

To help a semisolid or condensed soup slide right out of the can, shake the can first, then open it from the bottom.

163 Oyster and Vegetable Chowder

½ cup (1 stick) butter
6 (8 ounce) cans whole oysters with liquor
2 (16 ounce) packages frozen broccoli florets
2 (10 ounce) packages frozen corn
2 (1 pint) cartons cream
2 cups milk
2¼ teaspoons salt
¾ teaspoon pepper

1. Melt butter in large saucepan and stir in oysters, broccoli, and corn.
2. Cook over medium heat, stirring often, until vegetables are tender, about12 minutes.
3. Stir in cream, milk, salt, and pepper.
4. Cook over low heat, stirring often, until mixture is heated through.

SERVES 12.

 Who Knew? Light Switch

To make this recipe lower in fat, substitute an equal amount of butter for the cream, and use half the amount of butter. Add a bit of olive oil if broccoli and corn get stuck to the bottom of the saucepan.

164 Easy Oyster Stew

If you want a little snap to this stew, add a pinch or two of cayenne pepper.

4 tablespoons butter
6 fresh scallions, finely chopped
2 (12 ounce) cans oysters with liquor
2 (1 pint) cartons whipping cream
4 cups milk
½ teaspoon salt
¼ teaspoon black pepper

1. Melt butter in soup pot over medium heat. Add scallions and cook, stirring, until tender, about 3 minutes. Add oysters, cream, milk, salt, and pepper.
2. Reduce heat to low and cook until oyster edges begin to curl and mixture is hot, but not boiling.

SERVES 12.

 ## Who Knew?

Always buy milk in cardboard cartons instead of see-though plastic. Translucent containers allow light to seep in, which causes the milk to spoil sooner, and it also destroys up to 40% of the milk's vitamin D. Also, don't store milk on the door of your refrigerator. Items stored there are susceptible to warm air that enters the fridge each time you open it.

---

165 New England Clam Chowder

This traditional New England clam chowder is not only easy to make, it's very low in fat!

1 tablespoon butter
2 large onions, chopped
2 (20 ounce) cans minced clams with liquid
¼ teaspoon black pepper
2 pounds new potatoes, cleaned, diced
2 quarts water
1 teaspoon salt
1½ tablespoon cornstarch
1 (13 ounce) can evaporated milk

1. Melt butter in saucepan over medium-high heat. Add onions and cook, stirring, until onions begin to turn translucent, about 10–15 minutes.
2. Add liquid from clams, water, cornstarch, salt, and pepper and mix well. Add potatoes.
3. Bring to a boil, then lower heat to low and simmer, covered, until potatoes are tender, about 10 minutes.
4. Add evaporated milk and clam meat. Cook, stirring, until heated through; do not boil.

SERVES 10.

166 One-Pot Chowder

4 (10 ounce) cans New England
  clam chowder
2 (10 ounce) cans cream of
  celery soup
2 (10 ounce) cans cream of
  potato soup
2 (10 ounce) cans French onion soup
2 (15 ounce) cans cream-style corn
2 cups milk

1. Combine all ingredients in saucepan.
2. Heat over medium heat, stirring occasionally,
for 20 minutes.

SERVES 12–16.

 Who Knew?

When serving creamed soups from the can, beat or whisk for a 10–15 seconds before
heating and your soup will be silky smooth.

167 Italian Minestrone

To make this easy minestrone recipe completely vegetarian, substitute vegetable broth for the beef broth.

¼ cup (½ stick) butter
1 (16 ounce) package frozen onions
  and bell peppers
3 ribs celery, chopped
2 teaspoons minced garlic
2 (15 ounce) cans diced tomatoes
1 teaspoon dried oregano
1 teaspoon dried basil
¼ teaspoon salt
⅛ teaspoon black pepper
2 (14 ounce) cans beef broth
2 (15 ounce) cans kidney
  beans, drained
2 medium zucchini, cut in half
  lengthwise, sliced
1 cup elbow macaroni

1. Melt butter in soup pot over medium-high heat.
Add onions and bell peppers, celery, and garlic and
cook, stirring occasionally, for 2 minutes.
2. Add tomatoes, oregano, basil, salt, and pepper. Bring
to a boil, then reduce heat and simmer for 15 minutes,
stirring occasionally.
3. Stir in beef broth, beans, zucchini, and macaroni and
bring to a boil. Reduce heat and simmer until macaroni
is tender, about 15 minutes.

SERVES 8.

168 Broccoli–Wild Rice Soup

This is a hearty and delicious soup that's full of flavor. Your family will never guess the secret ingredient is cream cheese!

2 (6 ounce) packages chicken-flavored wild rice mix
12 cups water
2 (10 ounce) packages frozen chopped broccoli
4 teaspoons dried minced onion
2 (10 ounce) cans cream of chicken soup
2 (8 ounce) packages cream cheese, cubed

1. Combine rice, rice seasoning packet, and water in large saucepan. Bring to a boil, then reduce heat, cover, and simmer for 10 minutes, stirring once.
2. Stir in broccoli and onion and simmer for 5 minutes.
3. Stir in soup and cream cheese. Cook and stir on low heat until cheese melts.

SERVES 12.

 Who Knew? Light Switch

To make this recipe lower in fat, substitute 2½ cups of our Low-Fat Cream of Chicken Soup Base (Light Switch #3) for the cans of cream of chicken soup.

---

169 Creamy Parsley Soup

3 pounds zucchini, chopped
4 (14 ounce) cans chicken broth
4 cups loosely packed parsley
2 (8 ounce) cartons whipping cream
Salt and pepper to taste

1. Combine zucchini and chicken broth in soup pot and cook on medium high until zucchini is tender and broth is warm, about 10 minutes.
2. Add parsley and cook for additional 5 minutes.
3. Remove from heat and pour into blender or food processor. Blend until smooth.
4. Return mixture to soup pot and cook over low heat. Slowly stir in cream and cook until heated through. Season with salt and pepper to taste.

SERVES 8.

170 Beans 'n' Rice Soup

This quick soup is great for freezing and reheating for lunches and last-minute dinners.

2 tablespoons olive oil
2 medium onions, chopped
1 red bell pepper, seeded, chopped
2 tablespoons minced garlic
2 (28 ounce) cans diced tomatoes
2 (15 ounce) cans black beans, rinsed, drained
2 (10 ounce) packages frozen corn
1 cup rice, cooked (½ cup uncooked)
2 cups water
1½ teaspoons ground cumin

1. Cook olive oil in large soup pan over medium-high heat. When hot, add onion, bell pepper, and garlic. Cook, stirring, until peppers are crisp-tender, about 6–8 minutes. Stir in tomatoes, beans, corn, rice, water, and cumin.
2. Cover pot and bring to a boil. Reduce heat and simmer for 15 minutes.

SERVES 8.

171 Mexican Bean Soup

2 (15 ounce) cans refried beans
2 (15 ounce) cans pinto beans with jalapenos
2 (8 ounce) cans tomato sauce
1 cup hot salsa
2 onions, chopped
2 bell peppers, seeded, chopped
4 (14 ounce) cans beef broth
2 cups water

1. Combine all ingredients in large soup pot and mix well.
2. Bring to a boil over high heat, then reduce heat to low and simmer for 30 minutes.

SERVES 12.

 Who Knew? Light Switch

To save money and make this recipe even tastier, substitute our Super Healthy Salsa (Light Switch #7) for the jarred salsa.

172 Ranchero Black Bean Soup

      2 cups dried black beans
      2 quarts water
      2 (48 ounce) cartons beef broth
      2 large bunches scallions, chopped
    10 ribs celery, chopped
      6 cloves garlic, minced
      1 cup (2 sticks) butter
      2 bay leaves
    10 peppercorns
    1½ teaspoon salt
      ¾ teaspoon cayenne pepper
      1 cup rice, uncooked

1. Rinse and soak beans in water overnight. Drain, then transfer beans to large saucepan. Add beef broth and cook on high heat until boiling. Reduce heat to low and simmer, covered, for 2 hours.
2. Add butter to separate skillet and cook over medium-high heat. When melted, add scallions, celery, and garlic and cook, stirring, until celery is tender, about 8 minutes.
3. Transfer celery mixture to saucepan with beans. Add bay leaves, peppercorns, salt, and cayenne pepper.
4. Simmer covered over low heat for 1 hour. Add rice and continue to cook, stirring occasionally, until beans are tender, about 1 more hour. Add water if liquid level becomes low.
5. Remove bay leaves and peppercorns before serving.

SERVES 12.

 Who Knew? Light Switch

You'll love the taste of our Healthy Beef Broth (Light Switch #2) in this recipe! Just substitute 11 cups for the 2 cartons of beef broth.

---

173 El Paso Tomato Soup

    4 (10 ounce) cans tomato soup
    2 (14 ounce) cans chopped Mexican stewed tomatoes with onions
    2 (10 ounce) cans chopped tomatoes and green chilies
    2 (14 ounce) cans chicken broth
    2 (14 ounce) canful water

1. Mix all ingredients in large saucepan. Heat over high heat until boiling, then reduce heat to low and simmer for 8 minutes, stirring occasionally.

SERVES 8.

174 At-Home Broccoli Soup

This soup is perfect after a long day away from home.

½ cup (1 stick) butter
4 medium onions, finely chopped
6 tablespoons flour
6 (14 ounce) cans chicken broth
2 (16 ounce) packages frozen chopped broccoli
2 cups shredded carrots
2 (5 ounce) cans evaporated milk
½ teaspoon salt
¼ teaspoon black pepper

1. Melt butter in soup pot over medium-high heat. Add onions and cook, stirring, until they turn golden, about 5–6 minutes.
2. Add flour and stir constantly until light brown.
3. Stir in broth and bring to a boil over high heat, then reduce heat to low and simmer for 10 minutes, stirring constantly.
4. Add broccoli and carrots and cook, covered, on medium heat for 10 minutes, stirring occasionally. Stir in evaporated milk, salt, and pepper. Heat just until soup is heated through.

SERVES 12.

175 Cream of Carrot Soup

¼ cup (½ stick) butter
2 small onions, chopped
12 carrots, chopped
¼ cup dry white wine
1 (48 ounce) carton chicken broth
2 cups water
¼ teaspoon ground nutmeg
½ teaspoon salt
¾ teaspoon black pepper
2 (8 ounce) cartons whipping cream, whipped

1. Melt butter in large saucepan over medium-high heat. Add onions and cook, stirring, until onions are tender, about 5 minutes.
2. Add carrots, wine, chicken broth, water, nutmeg, salt, and pepper. Bring to a boil, then reduce heat to low and simmer until carrots are tender, about 30 minutes.
3. Pour half of mixture into blender; cover and blend on medium speed until mixture is smooth. Return to saucepan. Repeat with remaining mixture.
4. Heat just until heated through. Stir in cream.

SERVES 12.

 Who Knew? Light Switch

To make this recipe lower in fat, substitute 6¼ cups of our Healthy Chicken Broth (Light Switch #1) for the carton of chicken broth, and use only half the amount of whipping cream.

176 Creamy Corn Soup

¼ cup (½ stick) butter
1 (16 ounce) package frozen onions and bell peppers
1 (16 ounce) package frozen whole kernel corn
1 (15 ounce) can cream-style corn
1 (10 ounce) can diced tomatoes and green chilies
2 (14 ounce) cans chicken broth
¼ cup water
¼ cup flour
1 (1 pint) carton half and half

1. Melt butter and sauté onions and bell peppers in soup pot on medium heat for 5 minutes.
2. Stir in whole kernel corn, cream-style corn, tomatoes and green chilies, and chicken broth. Bring to a boil, then reduce heat and simmer for 20 minutes.
3. Mix water with flour in bowl until they blend well. Stir into soup and heat, stirring constantly, until soup thickens.
4. Stir in cream and heat soup, stirring constantly, until heated through. (Do not boil.)

SERVES 8.

 ## Who Knew?

If you have trouble keeping this soup from getting lumpy, omit the flour and water and use ¼ cup of instant mashed potatoes to thicken it instead.

177 Merry Split Pea Soup

Here's another version of split pea soup that's completely vegetarian. If you prefer a meatier taste, try using chicken broth rather than vegetable broth.

2 (1 pound) packages split peas
4 quarts water
2 teaspoons dried parsley
1 teaspoon garlic salt
1 (48 ounce) carton vegetable broth
3 cups chopped onion
2½ cups chopped celery
1½ teaspoons black pepper
1½ cups chopped carrots

1. Soak peas overnight in water. Drain, rinse, and place peas in large soup pot. Pour water over peas.
2. Add parsley, garlic salt, chicken broth, onions, celery, and pepper.
3. Cover and simmer for 1 hour 30 minutes–2 hours. Add carrots. Cover and simmer for additional 45 minutes.

SERVES 12.

178 Creamy Mushroom Soup

½ cup (1 stick) butter
6 (8 ounce) packages fresh
   mushrooms, chopped
2 small onions, finely chopped
1 cup flour
1 (48 ounce) carton chicken broth
2 (1 pint) cartons half-and-half
½ cup dry white wine
1½ teaspoons dried tarragon
¼ cup white wine Worcestershire
   marinade for chicken
1 teaspoon salt

1. Melt butter over medium heat in large soup pot. Add mushrooms and onions and cook, stirring, until tender, about 8–12 minutes. Add flour and stir or whisk until smooth.
2. Add broth, half-and-half, wine, tarragon, Worcestershire marinade, and salt; stir constantly over medium-high heat.
3. Heat until mixture begins to bubble, then reduce heat to medium-low and cook until mixture thickens, stirring often, about 20 minutes.

SERVES 12.

179 Mashed Potato Soup with Cauliflower

The hearty flavor of this soup comes not only from the cauliflower and mashed potatoes, but from caraway seeds, an ingredient commonly found in rye bread.

1½ cups water
1 cup instant mashed potato flakes
½ cup finely chopped scallions,
   whites only
½ teaspoon caraway seeds
1½ teaspoons salt
1 teaspoon pepper
2 (14 ounce) cans chicken broth
1 (16 ounce) package frozen
   cauliflower florets
1 (8 ounce) package shredded
   Cheddar cheese, divided

1. Boil water over high heat in soup pot. Reduce heat to medium to add mashed potato flakes, scallions, caraway seeds, salt, pepper and chicken broth. Simmer for 10 minutes.
2. Stir in cauliflower florets and cook until cauliflower is tender, about 10 minutes. Add half Cheddar cheese and stir until melted.
3. Sprinkle individual soup bowls with remaining cheese.

SERVES 8.

 Who Knew? Light Switch

To make this recipe lower in fat, substitute 2 cups of our Low-Fat Four-Cheese Blend (Light Switch #5) for the package of Cheddar cheese.

180 Potato-Pepper Soup

2 (18 ounce) packages frozen
   hash-brown potatoes with
   onions and peppers
2 red bell peppers, seeded, chopped
4 (14 ounce) cans chicken broth
2 cups water
2 (10 ounce) cans cream of
   celery soup
2 (10 ounce) cans cream of
   chicken soup
2 (8 ounce) cartons whipping cream
8 fresh scallions, chopped

1. Combine potatoes, bell peppers, chicken broth, and water in large saucepan. Bring to a boil over high heat. Cover, reduce heat to low, and simmer for 25 minutes.
2. Stir in both soups and whipping cream, stirring well. Garnish with scallions, shredded Cheddar cheese, or diced, cooked ham.

SERVES 12.

181 Baked Potato Soup

10 large baking potatoes
1½ cups (3 sticks) butter
1⅓ cup flour
12 cups milk
2 (8 ounce) packages shredded
   Cheddar cheese, divided
2 (3 ounce) packages real bacon bits
2 bunches fresh scallions,
   chopped, divided
½ teaspoon salt
¼ teaspoon black pepper
2 (8 ounce) cartons sour cream

1. Preheat oven to 400°. Place potatoes directly on rack and bake for 1 hour, turning halfway through. Remove potatoes and let cool. Cut potatoes in half lengthwise, scoop out flesh, and set aside. Discard potato shells.
2. Melt butter in large soup pot over low heat. Add flour and stir until smooth.
3. Gradually add milk and cook over medium heat, stirring constantly, until mixture thickens.
4. Stir in potatoes, half of cheese, bacon bits, 2 tablespoons scallions, salt, and pepper. Cook until hot, but do not boil.
5. Stir in sour cream and cook just until hot.
6. Spoon into individual soup bowls and sprinkle remaining cheese and scallions over each serving.

SERVES 12.

 ### Who Knew? Light Switch

To make this recipe lower in fat, substitute 4 cups of our Low-Fat Four-Cheese Blend (Light Switch #5) for the packages of Cheddar cheese, and 2 cups of our Low-Fat Sour Cream Substitute (Light Switch #8) for the cartons of sour cream.

182 Potato-Leek Soup

4 pounds baking potatoes, peeled, cubed
4 (14 ounce) cans chicken broth
½ cup (1 stick) butter
6 ribs celery, thinly sliced
1½ cups thinly sliced leeks, white only
2 (1 pint) cartons cream
½ teaspoon ground nutmeg
½ teaspoon salt
¼ teaspoon black pepper

1. Combine potatoes and chicken broth in large soup pot. Bring to a boil over high heat, then reduce heat and simmer over medium-low heat until potatoes are tender, about 10–15 minutes. Do not drain.
2. Transfer half potato mixture to blender and blend until smooth. Repeat with remaining potato mixture and return to soup pot.
3. Melt butter in saucepan and cook celery and leeks until tender, about 5 minutes.
4. Spoon into soup pot and add cream, nutmeg, salt, and pepper. Heat, stirring constantly, until mixture is heated through.

SERVES 12.

 Who Knew?

Don't have any nutmeg on hand? Simply use a dash of allspice or cloves.

183 Pumpkin Soup

This decadent soup is perfect for Thanksgiving or another fall feast. If you have sour cream or plain yogurt on hand, scoop a dollop on top of each soup serving for a great garnish.

6 tablespoons butter
2 (8 ounce) packages fresh mushrooms, sliced
½ cup flour
2 (32 ounce) cartons vegetable broth
2 (15 ounce) cans cooked pumpkin
2 (1 pint) cartons cream
½ cup honey
2 tablespoons sugar
¾ teaspoon curry powder
½ teaspoon ground nutmeg

1. Melt butter over medium heat in large saucepan. Add mushrooms and cook, stirring occasionally, until mushrooms are tender, about 10–12 minutes.
2. Add flour, stir well until there are no lumps, and gradually add broth. Heat over high heat until mixture starts to bubble, then reduce heat to medium-low and cook until mixture thickens, about 2 minutes.
3. Stir in pumpkin, cream, honey, sugar, curry powder, and nutmeg. Stir constantly until soup is heated through.

SERVES 12.

184 Easy Veggie Soup

4 (14 ounce) cans beef broth
1 cup diced celery
2 (16 ounce) cans mixed vegetables
2 bay leaves
3 cups water
1½ teaspoon salt
1½ teaspoon black pepper

1. Combine beef broth, celery, mixed vegetables, and bay leaves in large soup pot.
2. Add water, salt, and pepper and simmer on medium-low heat for 45 minutes.
3. Add more salt and black pepper if desired, remove bay leaves, and serve.

SERVES 8–12.

 Who Knew?

If you don't have any bay leaves, add a few teaspoons of thyme instead.

185 Spinach-Rice Soup

1 (48 ounce) carton plus 1 (32 ounce carton) chicken broth
4 (12 ounce) packages frozen creamed spinach, thawed
2 (10 ounce) cans cream of onion soup
2 (4 ounce) cans chopped pimentos
1 cup uncooked rice
½ teaspoon salt
¼ teaspoon black pepper

1. Combine broth, spinach, soup, pimentos, rice, salt, and pepper in soup pot.
2. Bring to a boil over high heat, then reduce heat to low and simmer until rice is tender, about 15–20 minutes.

SERVES 12.

186 Zesty Squash Soup

¼ cup (½ stick) butter
2 medium onions, finely chopped
¼ cup flour
4 (16 ounce) packages frozen yellow squash, thawed
2 (32 ounce) cartons chicken broth
1 cup water
2 (7 ounce) cans chopped green chilies
½ teaspoon salt
¼ teaspoon black pepper
1½ cups whipping cream

1. Melt butter in large soup pot and sauté onion for 3 minutes, stirring constantly. Stir in flour and cook for 1 minute. stirring until flour is absorbed and not lumpy.
2. Add squash, broth, water, green chilies, salt, and pepper. Bring to a boil over high heat, then reduce heat to low and simmer for 25 minutes.
3. Puree soup in batches in blender until mixture is smooth.
4. Return pureed soup to pot, add whipping cream, and heat just until soup is heated through.

SERVES 12–16.

187 Johnny Appleseed's Squash Soup

This soup, which is also delicious cold, uses a unique ingredient to help thicken the soup: white bread! You won't believe it until you've tried it.

1 large butternut squash
6 tart green apples, peeled, cored, chopped
2 medium onions, chopped
½ teaspoon dried rosemary
½ teaspoon dried marjoram
6 (14 ounce) cans chicken broth
4 slices white bread
½ cup whipping cream

1. Cut butternut squash in half and scoop out seeds.
2. Combine squash, apples, onions, rosemary, marjoram, broth, and bread in large saucepan. Bring to a boil over high heat, then reduce heat to low and simmer for 45 minutes.
3. Remove squash, scoop out flesh from peel, and discard peel. Add flesh back to mixture.
4. Puree mixture in blender until smooth. Return to saucepan and cook over medium heat for 10 minutes.
5. Just before serving, mix in cream.

SERVES 12.

188 French Onion Soup

¼ cup (½ stick) butter
8 yellow onions, thinly sliced
2 (32 ounce) cartons beef broth
8 slices French bread, crust trimmed, toasted
8 slices Swiss cheese

1. Melt butter in large soup pot over medium-low heat. Add onions and cook until onions are brown, about 20–30 minutes. Scrape onions from bottom of pot and stir occasionally.
2. Add beef broth and cook on medium heat for 1 hour.
3. Just before time to serve, pour soup into individual ovenproof soup bowls. Top with slices of toasted bread and cover with slices of cheese.
4. Place bowls on baking sheet and place under broiler until cheese melts, about 1–2 minutes. Serve immediately.

SERVES 8.

 Who Knew?

If you don't have oven-proof bowls, simply melt the cheese over the toasted bread on a baking sheet, then place in soup bowls and let sit for 1 minute before serving.

189 Curried Zucchini Soup

This delicious soup will make you happy you bought that curry powder! Buy some large garlic-flavored croutons when you find them on sale and save them as a garnish for this recipe.

½ cup (1 stick) butter
6 cups coarsely chopped zucchini
4 ribs celery, thinly sliced
1 tablespoon Italian seasoning
1 teaspoon curry powder
2 (10 ounce) cans cream of potato soup
2 (10 ounce) cans French onion soup
4 cups milk

1. Melt butter in soup pot over medium-low heat. Add zucchini, celery, Italian seasoning, and curry powder and stir constantly for 5 minutes.
2. Stir in potato soup, onion soup, and milk. Bring to a boil over medium-high heat, then reduce heat to low and simmer for 10 minutes.

SERVES 12.

190 Warm-Your-Soul Soup

2 (48 ounce) cartons chicken broth
2 (10 ounce) cans Italian stewed tomatoes with liquid
1 cup chopped onion
1½ cup chopped celery
1 (12 ounce) package fettuccini pasta
Salt and pepper to taste

1. Combine chicken broth, tomatoes, onion, and celery in large soup pot. Bring to a boil over high heat, then reduce heat to low and simmer until onion and celery are tender.
2. Add pasta and cook until al dente (firm but tender). Season with salt and pepper to taste.

SERVES 8–12.

 Who Knew? Light Switch

To make this recipe even healthier, substitute 3¼ quarts of our Healthy Chicken Broth (Light Switch #1) for the cartons of chicken broth.

191 Creamy Tomato Soup

½ cup (1 stick) butter
2 medium onions, chopped
4 (28 ounce) cans diced tomatoes with liquid
3 (6 ounce) cans tomato paste
¼ cup flour
¼ cup light brown sugar
2 (14 ounce) cans chicken broth
2 (8 ounce) cartons whipping cream
½ teaspoon salt

1. Melt butter in large soup pot over medium-high heat. Add onions and cook for 4 minutes, stirring constantly.
2. Drain diced tomatoes and set aside liquid. Combine tomato paste and flour. Add drained tomatoes, tomato paste mixture, and brown sugar to soup pot. Cook on medium heat, stirring often, for 10 minutes.
3. Gradually stir in broth and reserved tomato liquid; simmer on low heat for 15 minutes.
4. Puree soup in batches in food processor until mixture is smooth. Pour pureed mixture back into soup pot and bring to a boil.
5. Immediately remove from heat. Stir in whipping cream and salt.

SERVES 12.

 Who Knew?

To lessen your clean-up time when using a food processor or blender, protect the lid by first covering the bowl of food with a piece of plastic wrap. The lid will stay clean and you can toss the plastic wrap in the trash when you're finished.

192 Spicy Tomato Soup

¼ cup (½ stick) butter
2 medium onions, chopped
4 ribs celery, sliced
2 bell peppers, seeded, chopped
2 teaspoons minced garlic
4 (15 ounce) cans Italian stewed tomatoes
2 (14 ounce) cans vegetable broth
¾ teaspoon cayenne pepper
½ teaspoon salt
¼ teaspoon black pepper
⅔ cup sour cream

1. Melt butter in large saucepan and cook onions, celery, bell peppers, and garlic over medium heat until vegetables are tender, about 10 minutes; do not brown.
2. Stir in tomatoes, then transfer in batches to food processor. Process until soup is almost smooth.
3. Return soup mixture to saucepan and add broth, cayenne pepper, salt, and black pepper. Heat until soup is heated through, about 5 minutes.
4. Stir in sour cream just before serving.

SERVES 8.

193 Cheesy Vegetable Soup

This money-saving recipe is a great way to fill up without using meat.

4 large potatoes, peeled, diced
2 (16 ounce) packages frozen onions and peppers
1 (48 ounce) carton chicken broth
4 cups water
2 (4 ounce) cans sliced mushrooms, drained
2 (16 ounce) packages frozen mixed vegetables
1½ teaspoons salt
2 (10 ounce) cans cream of celery soup
1 (8 ounce) package Velveeta cheese, cubed

1. Combine potatoes, onions and peppers, chicken broth, and water in large soup pot. Cook over medium heat until potatoes are tender, about 15–20 minutes.
2. Stir in mushrooms, mixed vegetables, and salt and cook for additional 10 minutes.
3. Stir in celery soup and cheese. Heat on medium low, stirring constantly, until cheese melts. Serve immediately and do not freeze.

SERVES 12.

 Who Knew? Light Switch

To make this recipe lower in fat, substitute 2½ cups of our Low-Fat Cream of Celery Soup Base (Light Switch #4) for the cans of cream of celery soup, and 1½ cups of our Melty Cheese Sauce (Light Switch #6) for the 2 packages of Velveeta cheese.

194 Southwest Vegetarian Chili

Sage leaves add a fresh, smoky flavor to this chili that will have your family wondering what your secret ingredient is!

8   scallions, sliced
2   tablespoons minced garlic
1   tablespoon olive oil
4   (15 ounce) cans diced tomatoes with liquid
2   (15 ounce) cans pinto beans, rinsed, drained
1⅛ teaspoons cayenne pepper
3   tablespoons chili powder
2   teaspoons ground cumin
½   teaspoon salt
9   fresh sage leaves, chopped

1. Sauté scallions and garlic with olive oil in large saucepan over medium heat for 3 minutes. Add tomatoes, beans, cayenne pepper, chili powder, cumin, coriander, and salt.
2. Heat chili to boiling over high heat, then reduce heat to low and simmer for 25 minutes, stirring several times throughout cooking time.
3. Add sage, and cook for 3 more minutes.

SERVES 8.

195 Cheese-Topped Broccoli Soup

1   (48 ounce) carton plus 1 (32 ounce) carton chicken broth
2   cups water
4   ribs celery, sliced
2   medium onions, chopped
2   medium baking potatoes, peeled, chopped
2   (16 ounce) packages frozen, chopped broccoli
1   (1 pint) carton cream
1   cup milk
½   teaspoon salt
½   teaspoon black pepper
2½ cups grated Parmesan cheese

1. Combine broth, water, celery, onions, and chopped potatoes in large, heavy soup pot.
2. Bring to a boil over high heat, then reduce heat to low and simmer, covered, until vegetables are tender, about 20 minutes.
3. Stir in broccoli and continue to simmer until broccoli is tender, about 15 minutes.
4. Stir in cream, milk, salt, and pepper.
5. Heat on medium, stirring constantly, until soup is heated through. (Do not boil.) Ladle into individual soup bowls and sprinkle with Parmesan cheese.

SERVES 12.

196 Eight-Can Soup Bowl

It doesn't get much easier than this! Stock up when these items are on sale, because you can keep them almost indefinitely. Throw in some cooked chicken for a heartier soup.

2 (14 ounce) cans chicken broth
2 (10 ounce) cans cream of chicken soup
2 (15 ounce) cans ranch-style beans
2 (10 ounce) cans tomatoes with green chilies
1 large bag tortilla chips, crushed coarsely
1 (12 ounce) package shredded four-cheese blend
1 (8 ounce) carton sour cream

1. Combine broth, chicken soup, beans, and tomatoes with green chilies in saucepan. Simmer for 30 minutes.
2. Serve over tortilla chips and top with cheese and sour cream.

SERVES 12.

 Who Knew? Light Switch

To make this recipe lower in fat, substitute 1¼ cup of our Low-Fat Cream of Chicken Soup Base (Light Switch #3) for the can of cream of chicken soup, 3 cups of our Low-Fat Four-Cheese Blend (Light Switch #5) for the package of four-cheese blend, and 1 cup of our Low-Fat Sour Cream Substitute (Light Switch #8) for the carton of sour cream.

---

197 Creamy Asparagus Soup

4 tablespoons butter
2 onions, finely chopped
2 red bell peppers, seeded, chopped
1 pound asparagus, chopped
4 (10 ounce) cans cream of chicken soup
2 cups milk, cream, or half-and-half
2 teaspoons lemon juice
½ teaspoon dried tarragon
½ teaspoon salt
¼ teaspoon black pepper

1. Melt butter in soup pot over medium-high heat. Add onion and bell pepper and cook, stirring, for 3 minutes. Add asparagus and continue to cook, stirring, until all vegetables are tender. Remove from heat.
2. Pour mixture into food processor or blender and blend until smooth.
3. Return onion-asparagus mixture to soup pot and add chicken soup, milk, lemon juice, tarragon, salt, and pepper.
4. Cook on medium-high heat, stirring constantly, until soup is heated through. Do not boil.

SERVES 12.

Easy Casseroles

In terms of dinner-making, nothing is as satisfying as pulling a big casserole out of the oven and yelling, "Dinner is ready!" to a bunch of hungry kids. Better still is preparing the casserole days (or even weeks) ahead of time! Prepare these casseroles up to the baking step, then leave them in the fridge for up to five days, until you're ready to heat them up. Or, bake the casserole and then freeze for later. Make sure to add any crunchy toppings just before you bake them, and be aware that casseroles with lots of cheese won't reheat as well after you freeze them. A cooked casserole, however, can last in your fridge for several weeks!

198 Quick Chicken Casserole

¼ cup (½ stick) butter
4 boneless, skinless chicken breast halves, chopped
8 ounces fresh mushrooms, sliced
1 (14 ounce) jar artichoke hearts, drained
2 tablespoons flour
1 (14 ounce) can chicken broth

1. Preheat oven to 350º.
2. Melt butter in skillet over medium heat. Add chicken pieces and cook, stirring, for 5 minutes. Add mushrooms and continue to cook, stirring, until chicken is cooked through and mushrooms and tender.
3. Keeping melted butter in skillet, transfer chicken and mushrooms to sprayed, 3 quart baking dish. Top with artichoke hearts.
4. Add flour to remaining butter and juices in skillet. Stir to blend. Add broth and cook over medium-high heat until thickened, about 6–10 minutes. Pour over chicken.
5. Baked, covered, for 45 minutes. Let sit for 5–10 minutes before serving.

SERVES 4.

199 Creamy, Cheesy Chicken

4 cups cooked rice (2 cups uncooked)
6 tablespoons (¾ stick) butter, divided
¼ cup flour
2 cups milk
2 teaspoons chicken bouillon granules
1 teaspoon parsley flakes
½ teaspoon celery salt
½ teaspoon salt
4 cups cooked, cubed chicken
2 (8 ounce) packages Velveeta cheese, cubed
1 (8 ounce) carton sour cream
1½ cups crushed round buttery crackers

1. Preheat oven to 325°.
2. Spread cooked rice into sprayed, 9 x 13-inch baking dish and set aside.
3. Melt 4 tablespoons butter in large saucepan. Stir in flour and mix until smooth. Gradually stir in milk, bouillon, parsley flakes, celery salt, and salt.
4. Cook over medium heat, stirring constantly, until sauce thickens, about 2 minutes.
5. Reduce heat and add chicken, cheese, and sour cream. Stir until cheese melts.
6. Spoon chicken mixture over rice in baking dish.
7. Melt remaining 2 tablespoons butter and toss with cracker crumbs. Sprinkle over casserole.
8. Bake until hot, about 35 minutes.

SERVES 8.

 Who Knew? Light Switch

To make this recipe lower in fat, substitute 3 cups of our Melty Cheese Sauce (Light Switch #6) for the 2 packages of Velveeta cheese, and 1 cup of our Low-Fat Sour Cream Substitute for the carton of sour cream.

200 Award-Winning Casserole

This chicken-chili casserole won us first prize at a church competition many years ago.

2 tablespoons olive oil
3 boneless, skinless chicken breasts, chopped into cubes
1 bell pepper, seeded, chopped
1 medium onion, chopped
½ cup chicken broth or water
1 (4 ounce) can chopped green chilies, drained
1½ teaspoon dried oregano
½ teaspoon garlic powder
½ teaspoon salt
½ teaspoon black pepper
1 (7 ounce) can whole green chilies, drained
1½ cups shredded Monterey Jack cheese
1½ cups shredded sharp Cheddar cheese
3 large eggs
1 tablespoon flour
1 cup cream

1. Preheat oven to 350°.
2. Heat oil over medium heat in skillet. When hot, add chicken, bell pepper, and onion. Cook, stirring, until onion and bell pepper is tender-crisp, about 5 minutes. Add broth, green chilies, oregano, cilantro, garlic powder, salt, and pepper and mix well. Cook, stirring occasionally, until chicken is cooked through, about 10–15 minutes.
3. Seed whole chilies and spread into sprayed, 9 x 13-inch baking dish. Cover with meat mixture and sprinkle with cheeses.
4. Combine eggs and flour in bowl and beat with fork until fluffy. Add cream, mix well, and pour over top of meat in baking dish.
5. Bake until light brown, about 30–35 minutes.

SERVES 8.

201 Chicken 'n' Rice Casserole

1 cup rice (uncooked)
1 (10 ounce) can cream of mushroom soup
½ soup canful water
1 (1 ounce) packet onion soup mix
4 boneless, skinless chicken breasts, chopped

1. Preheat oven to 350°.
2. Place rice into sprayed, 2-quart baking dish. In large bowl, combine soup, water, onion soup mix, and chicken. Pour over rice.
3. Cover and baked until rice is tender, chicken is cooked through, and liquid is absorbed, about 1 hour.

SERVES 4.

202 Across the Road Chicken Casserole

2 cups crushed tortilla chips
4 boneless, skinless chicken breast halves, cooked
1 (15 ounce) can garbanzo beans (chickpeas), drained
1 (15 ounce) can pinto beans, drained
1 (15 ounce) can whole kernel corn, drained
1 (16 ounce) jar hot salsa
1 red onion, chopped
2 teaspoons ground cumin
1 teaspoon dried cilantro leaves
1 green bell pepper, seeded, diced
2 teaspoons minced garlic
1 teaspoon salt
1 (16 ounce) package shredded Mexican four-cheese blend

1. Preheat oven to 350°.
2. Scatter crushed tortilla chips evenly in sprayed, 9 x 13-inch baking dish.
3. Cut chicken breasts in thin slices. Combine chicken, beans, corn, salsa, onion, cumin, cilantro, bell pepper, garlic, and salt in large bowl; mix well.
4. Spoon half of mixture evenly over chips.
5. Combine cheeses in separate bowl and sprinkle half over mixture in baking dish.
6. Cover with remaining chicken-bean mixture and then top with remaining cheese.
7. Bake for 35 minutes. Let stand for 10 minutes before serving.

SERVES 8–10.

 Who Knew? Light Switch

To make this recipe lower in fat, substitute 2 cups of our Super Healthy Salsa (Light Switch #7) for the jar of salsa, and 4 cups of our Low-Fat Four-Cheese Blend (Light Switch #5) for the package of Mexican four-cheese blend.

 Who Knew?

Save those bits of crushed tortilla chips at the bottom of the bag! They not only come in handy in recipes like this, but they're great on top of salad in lieu of croutons.

203 Chicken-Ham Lasagna

This unique, tomato-free lasagna is perfect for getting rid of some leftovers!

¼ cup (½ stick) butter
1 (4 ounce) can chopped mushrooms, drained
1 large onion, chopped
½ cup flour
1 teaspoon salt
¼ teaspoon black pepper
1 (14 ounce) can chicken broth
1 cup milk
1 (3 ounce) package grated Parmesan cheese
1 pound broccoli, chopped
9 lasagna noodles, cooked, drained
1½ cups cooked, finely diced ham, divided
2 cups cooked, shredded chicken breasts
1 (12 ounce) package shredded Monterey Jack cheese, divided

1. Preheat oven to 350°.
2. Melt butter in large skillet over medium-high heat. Add mushrooms and onion and cook, stirring, until onion is tender, about 5 minutes. Stir in flour, salt, and pepper until blended well.
3. Gradually stir in broth and cream. Cook, stirring constantly, until mixture thickens, about 3 minutes. Stir in Parmesan cheese and chopped broccoli.
4. Spread about ½ cup of mixture in sprayed, 10 x 15-inch baking dish.
5. Layer 3 noodles on top, then $1/3$ of remaining broccoli mixture, ½ cup ham, 1 cup chicken, and 1 cup Monterey Jack cheese.
6. Top with 3 more noodles, half of remaining broccoli mixture, 1 cup ham, 1 cup chicken, and 1 cup Monterey Jack cheese.
7. For the last layer, use the remaining noodles, chicken, and cream-broccoli mixture.
8. Cover and bake until bubbly, about 50 minutes. Sprinkle with remaining cheese. Let stand for 15 minutes before cutting into squares to serve.

SERVES 12–14.

 Who Knew?

Want to know another great way to sanitize your cutting board? Use your microwave! Just wash the board thoroughly, rub it with the cut side of a lemon, then heat for 1 minute.

204 Barnyard Supper

5 boneless, skinless chicken breast halves
5 slices onion
5 potatoes, peeled, quartered
1 (10 ounce) can cream of celery soup
¼ cup water

1. Preheat oven to 325°.
2. Place chicken breasts in sprayed, 9 x 13-inch baking dish. Top chicken with onion slices, and place potatoes around chicken.
3. Heat soup with water in saucepan over medium heat for 5 minutes. Pour over chicken and vegetables.
4. Cover and bake for 1 hour 10 minutes.

SERVES 5.

 Who Knew? Light Switch

To make this recipe lower in fat, substitute 1¼ cup of our Low-Fat Cream of Celery Soup Base (Light Switch #4) for the can of cream of celery soup.

205 Walnut Chicken Casserole

Our kids love the crunchy topping on this dish, but we love that within 20 minutes, you'll have creamy chicken and vegetables ready to go in the oven.

3 tablespoons olive oil
6 boneless, skinless chicken breast halves, cubed
2 tablespoons vegetable or canola oil
2 cups sliced zucchini, ½ inch thick
1 (16 ounce) package baby carrots
½ medium to large onion, chopped
2 tablespoons water
2 (10 ounce) cans cream of chicken soup
1 cup milk or cream
½ teaspoon mustard
½ teaspoon dill weed
1 teaspoon dried basil
2 tablespoons butter
1½ cups fresh breadcrumbs or cracker crumbs
½ cup chopped walnuts

1. Preheat oven to 375°.
2. Heat oil over medium heat. When hot, add chicken and cook, stirring, for 5 minutes. Add zucchini, carrots, and onion, and water and continue to cook for 15 minutes. Drain.
3. Add soup, milk, mustard, dill weed, and basil; heat just enough to mix well, about 10–15 minutes. Pour into sprayed, 9 x 13-inch baking dish.
4. Combine butter, breadcrumbs, and walnuts in bowl; sprinkle over casserole.
5. Bake until topping browns lightly, about 35–40 minutes.

SERVES 6–8.

206 Chicken Medley Supreme

1 (6 ounce) package long-grain and wild rice mix
1 tablespoon olive oil
1 cup chopped onion
1 cup chopped celery
1 (10 ounce) can cream of chicken soup
1 (4 ounce) jar chopped pimentos
1 (15 ounce) can French-style green beans, drained
½ cup slivered almonds
1 cup mayonnaise
¼ teaspoon salt
⅛ teaspoon black pepper
3 cups lightly crushed potato chips

1. Preheat oven to 350°.
2. Prepare long-grain and wild rice mix according to package directions.
3. Add oil to skillet and heat over medium-high heat. When hot, add onion and celery and cook, stirring, until tender, about 5 minutes.
4. In large bowl, combine onion-celery mixture with rice, soup, pimentos, green beans, almonds, mayonnaise, salt, and pepper and mix well.
5. Spoon mixture into sprayed, 9 x 13-inch baking dish. Sprinkle crushed potato chips over top, and bake, uncovered, until chips are light brown, about 35 minutes.

SERVES 8.

207 Broccoli Chicken

We tried this recipe with both Worcestershire sauce and curry power, and couldn't decide which version we liked better! We'll let you pick which you prefer.

4 boneless, skinless chicken breast halves, cubed
1 tablespoon olive oil
2 (10 ounce) packages frozen broccoli
2 (10 ounce) cans cream of chicken soup
1 cup mayonnaise
1 teaspoon lemon juice
½ teaspoon curry powder or Worcestershire sauce
1½ cups shredded sharp Cheddar cheese, divided
½ cup seasoned breadcrumbs
1 teaspoon butter, melted

1. Preheat oven to 350°.
2. Cook chicken cubes in large skillet with oil, stirring occasionally, for 10 minutes.
3. Add broccoli and cook, stirring occasionally, until chicken is cooked through and broccoli is tender. Place chicken-broccoli mixture in sprayed, 9 x 13-inch baking dish.
4. Combine soup, mayonnaise, lemon juice, curry powder or Worcestershire sauce, and ¾ cup cheese in bowl. Spread mixture over chicken.
5. In separate bowl, combine breadcrumbs and butter. Layer breadcrumb mixture over chicken.
6. Sprinkle remaining cheese over top, and bake for 25–30 minutes.

SERVES 8.

208 Bob's Chicken Bake

This satisfying meat-and-potato dish is Bruce's brother's favorite. Chop up three vegetables and the rest is easy!

¼ cup (½ stick) butter
1 red bell pepper, seeded, chopped
1 medium onion, chopped
2 ribs celery, chopped
1 (8 ounce) carton sour cream
1½ cups cream
1 (7 ounce) can chopped green chilies, drained
1 teaspoon chicken bouillon granules
½ teaspoon salt
½ teaspoon black pepper
3–4 cups chopped rotisserie chicken
1 (16 ounce) package shredded Cheddar cheese, divided
1 (2 pound) package frozen hash-brown potatoes, thawed

1. Preheat oven to 350°.
2. Melt butter in large saucepan over medium-high heat and sauté bell pepper, onion, and celery until tender, about 5–10 minutes. Remove from heat.
3. Stir in sour cream, cream, green chilies, bouillon granules, salt, pepper, chicken, and half cheese. Fold in hash-brown potatoes.
4. Spoon into sprayed, 9 x 13-inch baking dish.
5. Bake until casserole is bubbly, about 45 minutes.
6. Remove from oven and sprinkle remaining cheese over top of casserole. Return to oven until cheese melts, about 5 minutes.

SERVES 12–14.

209 Chicken-Noodle Delight

The red and green bell peppers in this dish make it as colorful as it is delicious!

2 ribs celery, chopped
½ onion, chopped
½ green bell pepper, seeded, chopped
½ red bell pepper, seeded, chopped
6 tablespoons (¾ stick) butter, divided
5 boneless, skinless chicken breasts, cubed
3 cups cooked, cubed chicken breasts
1 (4 ounce) can sliced mushrooms, drained
1 (16 ounce) jar sun-dried tomato alfredo sauce
1½ teaspoons chicken bouillon granules
1 (8 ounce) package medium egg noodles, cooked, drained
1 cup bread crumbs
½ cup grated Parmesan cheese

1. Preheat oven to 325°.
2. Combine celery, onion, bell peppers, and 4 tablespoons butter in skillet or large saucepan over medium-high heat. Cook, stirring, for 5 minutes.
3. Reduce heat to medium and add chicken cubes. Continue to cook and stir until chicken is cooked through, about 8 minutes.
4. Remove from heat and add mushrooms, alfredo sauce, chicken bouillon, and noodles. Mix well. Pour into sprayed, 3-quart baking dish.
5. Combine bread crumbs and cheese in bowl, and sprinkle over top.
6. Bake until bubbly around edges, about 20 minutes.

SERVES 10.

210 Spiced-Spanish Chicken

2 cups instant rice
4 boneless, skinless, cooked chicken breast halves, cut into strips
1 (15 ounce) can Mexican stewed tomatoes with liquid
1 (8 ounce) can tomato sauce
1 (15 ounce) can whole kernel corn, drained
1 (4 ounce) jar diced pimentos, drained
1 teaspoon chili powder
1 teaspoon ground cumin
½ teaspoon salt
½ teaspoon black pepper

1. Preheat oven to 350°.
2. Spread rice evenly in sprayed, 3-quart baking dish.
3. Place chicken strips over top of rice.
4. Combine stewed tomatoes, tomato sauce, corn, pimentos, chili powder, cumin, salt, and pepper in large bowl and mix well.
5. Slowly pour mixture over chicken and rice.
6. Cover and bake for 1 hour.

SERVES 6.

 Who Knew?

Even though it's more convenient, instant rice should never be used in a dish that will be frozen, as it becomes mushy when reheated. Make sure you only stick this casserole in the fridge—not the freezer—for later.

211 Hearty Chicken-Noodle Casserole

1 (10 ounce) package frozen chopped onions and bell peppers
¼ cup (½ stick) butter
1 (10 ounce) can cream of chicken soup
1 (4 ounce) jar chopped pimentos
1 (8 ounce) package elbow macaroni (tube pasta), cooked
3 cups cooked, diced chicken
1 (15 ounce) carton ricotta cheese
1 (8 ounce) package shredded Mexican four-cheese blend
¾ cup crushed round buttery crackers

1. Preheat oven to 350°.
2. Sauté onions and bell peppers with butter in skillet over medium-high until tender, about 6 minutes. Stir in soup and pimentos.
3. Combine macaroni, chicken, and cheeses in large bowl. Mix until they blend well. Fold in soup-pimento mixture and mix well.
4. Spoon into sprayed, 9 x 13-inch baking dish. Bake for 40 minutes.
5. Remove from oven and sprinkle crushed crackers over top of casserole. Return to oven and cook for additional 15 minutes.

SERVES 10.

212 Chicken and Dumplings Casserole

¼ cup (1/2 stick) butter or margarine
4 boneless, skinless chicken breasts, chopped
2 garlic cloves, minced
½ cup chopped onion
½ cup chopped celery
½ cup all-purpose flour
1 teaspoon salt
¾ teaspoon pepper
1 (10 ounce) package frozen green peas
2 (14 ounce) cans chicken broth
2 teaspoons dried thyme
2 cups buttermilk biscuit mix
²/₃ cup milk, warmed

1. Preheat oven to 350°.
2. Melt butter in skillet over medium-high heat. Add chopped chicken and cook, stirring, for 3 minutes. Add garlic, onion, and celery, and garlic, and cook until onion and celery are tender, about 5 minutes more.
3. Add flour and mix into melted butter and juices. Add salt, pepper, peas, and broth. Bring to a boil, then reduce heat to low and cook, stirring constantly until thickened.
4. Pour into sprayed, 9 x 13-inch baking dish and set aside.
5. Combine biscuit mix and thyme in bowl and stir in milk until dough is moist. Dollop onto chicken mixture by the spoonful.
6. Bake, uncovered, for 30 minutes. Cover and bake until dumplings are completely baked, about 10 minutes more.

213 Chicken-Broccoli Deluxe

3 tablespoons olive oil
5 boneless, skinless chicken breast halves, sliced
¼ cup (1 stick) butter
½ cup flour
1 (14 ounce) can chicken broth
1 (1 pint) carton cream
1 (16 ounce) package shredded Cheddar cheese, divided
1 (5 ounce) package grated Parmesan cheese
2 tablespoons lemon juice
2 tablespoons dried parsley
1 teaspoon salt
½ teaspoon black pepper
¾ cup mayonnaise
2 (10 ounce) boxes frozen broccoli florets
1 (12 ounce) box vermicelli

1. Preheat oven to 325°.
2. Heat oil in very large saucepan over medium heat. When hot, add chicken slices and cook, stirring, until chicken is cooked through, about 8–12 minutes. Remove chicken from pan and reduce heat to medium-low. Add butter.
3. When butter is melted, add flour and mix until smooth.
4. Gradually add chicken broth and cream, stirring constantly until mixture thickens.
5. Add half Cheddar cheese, Parmesan cheese, lemon juice, dried parsley, salt, and pepper. Heat on low until cheeses melt.
6. Remove from heat and add mayonnaise.
7. Punch small holes in broccoli boxes and microwave for 4 minutes. Gently add broccoli and chicken slices to sauce.
8. Cook vermicelli according to package directions; drain and pour into sprayed, 10 x 15-inch baking dish. Spoon sauce-and-chicken mixture over vermicelli.
9. Cover and bake for 40 minutes. Uncover and sprinkle remaining cheese over top of casserole. Return to oven for additional 5 minutes.

SERVES 12.

214 Swiss Cheese Chicken

1 tablespoon olive oil
4 boneless, skinless chicken breasts, chopped
½ cup milk
²/₃ cup mayonnaise
1 small onion, chopped
4 ribs celery, chopped
2 cups croutons
1 cup shredded Swiss cheese

1. Preheat oven to 350°.
2. Heat oil in skillet over medium-high heat. Add chopped chicken and cook, stirring, until chicken is cooked through, about 8–12 minutes. Drain.
3. Combine chicken with remaining ingredients and pour into sprayed, 2-quart baking dish.
4. Cover and bake until heated through, about 40 minutes.

SERVES 4.

215 Family Night Spaghetti

This recipe offers a twist on the ever-popular chicken spaghetti. The mix of chicken, pasta, and colorful vegetables all in one dish make this a hearty meal full of flavor.

1 bunch fresh scallions with tops, chopped
1 cup chopped celery
1 red bell pepper, seeded, chopped
1 yellow or orange bell pepper, seeded, chopped
¼ cup (½ stick) butter
1 tablespoon dried cilantro leaves
1 teaspoon Italian seasoning
1 (8 ounce) package thin spaghetti, cooked, drained
4 cups cooked, chopped chicken or turkey
1 (8 ounce) carton sour cream
1 (16 ounce) jar Alfredo sauce
¼ teaspoon salt
⅛ teaspoon black pepper
1 (10 ounce) box frozen green peas, thawed
1 (8 ounce) package shredded mozzarella cheese, divided

1. Preheat oven to 350°.
2. Sauté onions, celery, and bell peppers with butter in large skillet over medium-high heat until vegetables are tender, about 8–10 minutes.
3. In large bowl, combine onion-pepper mixture, cilantro, Italian seasoning, spaghetti, chicken, sour cream, and Alfredo sauce and mix well.
4. Sprinkle salt and pepper into mixture. Fold in peas and half mozzarella cheese.
5. Spoon into sprayed, 10 x 15-inch deep baking dish. Cover and bake for 45 minutes.
6. Uncover and sprinkle remaining cheese over top of casserole. Return to oven until cheese melts, about 5 minutes.

SERVES 8–10.

216 Super Easy Turkey Treat

1 pound ground turkey
1 (10 ounce) can tomato soup
1 (10 ounce) can tomato bisque soup
1 cup chunky salsa
8 (6-inch) corn tortillas, cut into
　1-inch pieces
¼ cup water
1 cup shredded Mexican four-cheese
　blend, divided

1. Preheat oven to 375°.
2. Cook ground turkey in large skillet over medium-high heat, stirring often, until turkey is light brown. Drain.
3. Stir in soups, salsa, tortillas, water, and half cheese.
4. Spoon into sprayed, 7 x 11-inch glass baking dish.
5. Cover and bake for 35–40 minutes. Remove from oven and sprinkle with remaining cheese.

SERVES 4–6.

 Who Knew? Light Switch

To make this recipe lower in fat, try using our Super Healthy Salsa (Light Switch #7) and Low-Fat Four-Cheese Blend (Light Switch #5)!

---

217 Tasty Turkey Crunch

It doesn't get much easier than this yummy dish that's reminiscent of Thanksgiving. If you don't have any leftover turkey, ask at the deli counter for a slab of turkey (rather than slices).

1 (8 ounce) package noodles
2½ cups cooked, diced turkey
　(about 1 pound)
1 (1 ounce) packet chicken
　gravy, prepared
2 cups crushed round
　buttery crackers

1. Preheat oven to 350°.
2. Cook noodles according to package directions; drain.
3. Spread noodles into sprayed, 2-quart baking dish. Place turkey on top of noodles, cover with gravy, and top with cracker crumbs.
4. Bake for 35 minutes.

SERVES 6.

218 Chili Casserole

1 (40 ounce) can chili with beans
1 (4 ounce) can chopped
   green chilies
1 (2 ounce) can sliced ripe
   olives, drained
1 (8 ounce) package shredded
   Cheddar cheese
2 cups ranch-flavored tortilla
   chips, crushed

1. Preheat oven to 350°.
2. Combine all ingredients in bowl and transfer to sprayed, 3-quart baking dish.
3. Bake until bubbly, about 35 minutes.

SERVES 8.

 Who Knew? Light Switch

To make this recipe lower in fat, substitute 2 cups of our Low-Fat Four-Cheese Blend (Light Switch #5) for the package of Cheddar cheese.

219 Reuben Casserole

1 (18 ounce) package frozen
   hash-brown potatoes, thawed
¼ teaspoon salt
⅛ teaspoon black pepper
2 pounds deli corned beef, sliced
   ¼-inch thick
1 (8 ounce) bottle Russian salad
   dressing, divided
1 (15 ounce) can sauerkraut, drained
8 slices Swiss cheese

1. Preheat oven to 425°.
2. Place hash-brown potatoes in sprayed, 9 x 13-inch baking dish and sprinkle with salt and pepper. Bake for 25 minutes.
3. Place overlapping corned beef slices on top of potatoes.
4. Spoon half bottle of dressing over top of beef. Arrange sauerkraut on top. Cover with slices of cheese.
5. Reduce oven to 375° and bake for 20 minutes. Serve remaining Russian dressing on the side.

SERVES 8.

 Who Knew?

Never pay for aerosol cooking sprays. Instead, buy a giant jug of vegetable oil and add it to a clean spray bottle as needed. It's the same thing, and will cost you a fraction of the price.

220 Taco Pie

1 pound lean ground beef
½ of 1 bell pepper, chopped
2 jalapeno peppers, seeded, finely chopped
1 tablespoon vegetable or canola oil
½ teaspoon salt
1 (15 ounce) can Mexican stewed tomatoes
1 cup water
1 tablespoon chili powder
1 (8 ounce) package shredded sharp Cheddar cheese
1 (6 ounce) package corn muffin mix
1 egg
⅓ cup milk

1. Cook ground beef, bell pepper, and jalapeno peppers with oil in large skillet over medium heat, stirring occasionally, until beef is brown and peppers are tender; drain well.
2. Add salt, tomatoes, water, and chili powder. Cook on medium heat for 10 minutes.
3. Pour into sprayed, 9 x 13-inch glass baking dish. Sprinkle cheese on top.
4. When ready for baking, preheat oven to 375°.
5. In mixing bowl, combine corn muffin mix, egg, and milk. Beat well. Pour over top of cheese.
6. Bake until corn muffin mix is light brown, about 25 minutes. Remove from oven and set aside for 10 minutes before serving.

SERVES 8.

 ## Who Knew? Light Switch

To make this recipe lower in fat, substitute 2 cups of our Low-Fat Four-Cheese Blend (Light Switch #5) for the package of Cheddar cheese.

 ## Who Knew?

Do you have an iPhone? Use it to start saving! Download a free app at CouponSherpa.com, and while you shop it will look for coupons at the store you're in.

221 Beef and Noodles al Grande

You'll love the blend of flavors in this memorable casserole that is big enough for two dinners, and a lunch!

1 tablespoon olive oil	1. Preheat oven to 350°.
1½–2 pounds lean ground beef	2. Heat oil in skillet over medium heat. Add beef, onion, and bell pepper and cook, stirring, until beef is no longer pink and vegetables are tender, about 10–15 minutes. Drain.

1 tablespoon olive oil
1½–2 pounds lean ground beef
1 onion, chopped
1 green bell pepper, seeded, chopped
2 (8 ounce) packages Mexican Velveeta cheese, cubed
1 (10 ounce) can fiesta nacho cheese soup
1 (15 ounce) can stewed tomatoes
1 (10 ounce) can tomatoes and green chilies
1 (8 ounce) can whole kernel corn, drained
½ teaspoon chili powder
¼ teaspoon ground mustard
1½ teaspoons salt
½ teaspoon black pepper
1 (8 ounce) package medium egg noodles
¼ cup (½ stick) butter, cut into 4–5 slices
1 cup shredded Cheddar cheese

1. Preheat oven to 350°.
2. Heat oil in skillet over medium heat. Add beef, onion, and bell pepper and cook, stirring, until beef is no longer pink and vegetables are tender, about 10–15 minutes. Drain.
3. Reduce heat to low, add Velveeta cheese, and stir constantly until cheese is fully melted.
4. Combine soup, stewed tomatoes, tomatoes and green chilies, corn, chili powder, mustard, salt, and pepper in large bowl. Add beef mixture and mix well.
5. Cook egg noodles according to package directions and drain well.
6. While noodles are still very hot, add butter and stir until it melts.
7. Stir noodles in with tomato-beef mixture. Transfer to sprayed, 10 x 15-inch baking dish.
8. Cover and bake for 45 minutes.
9. Remove from oven and sprinkle Cheddar cheese over casserole. Return to oven and bake uncovered for 4–10 minutes.

SERVES 10–12.

Who Knew? Light Switch

To make this recipe lower in fat, substitute 3 cups of our Melty Cheese Sauce (Light Switch #6) for the 2 packages of Velveeta cheese.

Who Knew?

Never wrap foods that contain natural acids—like tomatoes, lemons, or onions—in aluminum foil. The combination of the foil and the acid in the foods produce a chemical reaction, which affects the taste of the food.

222 Simple Casserole Supper

½ tablespoon vegetable or olive oil
1 pound lean ground beef
¼ cup white rice
1 (10 ounce) can French onion soup
½ cup water
1 (6 ounce) can French-fried onion rings

1. Preheat oven to 325°.
2. Heat oil over medium heat in skillet. When hot, add beef and cook until beef is browned, about 8–10 minutes. Stir to break up beef throughout cooking time. Drain and spread into sprayed, 7 x 11-inch baking dish.
3. Combine rice, onion soup, and water. Add on top of beef.
4. Cover and bake for 40 minutes. Uncover, sprinkle onion rings over top, and return to oven for 10 minutes.

SERVES 6.

223 Super Spaghetti

1 (8 ounce) package thin spaghetti, broken in half
1 pound lean ground beef
1 (10 ounce) package frozen chopped bell peppers and onions
1 (10 ounce) can tomato soup
1 (10 ounce) can chopped tomatoes and green chilies
1 (15 ounce) can whole kernel corn, drained
½ cup water
1 (8 ounce) package Velveeta cheese, cubed, divided
¼ teaspoon salt
¼ teaspoon black pepper

1. Preheat oven to 375°.
2. Cook spaghetti according to package directions; drain.
3. Cook beef and bell pepper–onion mixture in large skillet over medium heat, stirring constantly, until beef is no longer pink and vegetables are heated through, about 10–15 minutes.
4. Stir in cooked spaghetti, soup, tomatoes and green chilies, corn, water, 1 cup cheese, salt, and pepper. Gently toss until they blend well. Spoon into sprayed, 9 x 13-inch glass baking dish.
5. Cover and bake for 1 hour. Uncover and continue baking until edges are hot and bubbly, about 20 minutes. Sprinkle remaining cheese over top.

SERVES 6–8.

 Who Knew? Light Switch

To make this recipe lower in fat, substitute 1½ cups of our Melty Cheese Sauce (Light Switch #6) for the package of Velveeta cheese.

224 Family-Favorite Casserole

1½ pounds lean ground beef
1 (15 ounce) can stewed tomatoes
1 (10 ounce) can tomatoes and green chilies
1 (12 ounce) package tagliatelle pasta (thin egg noodles)
1 (8 ounce) package cream cheese, softened
1 (8 ounce) carton sour cream
1 (16 ounce) package shredded mozzarella cheese, divided

1. Preheat oven to 350°.
2. Brown beef in large saucepan over medium heat, stirring to break up. Drain fat.
3. Add stewed tomatoes and tomatoes and green chilies. Reduce heat and simmer 20 minutes.
4. Cook pasta in saucepan according to package directions; drain.
5. Beat cream cheese in bowl until smooth; add sour cream and mix until they blend well.
6. Spread half pasta into sprayed, 9 x 13-inch baking pan. Cover with half cream cheese mixture, then half mozzarella cheese.
7. Spread meat-tomato mixture over cheese.
8. Layer remaining pasta, cream cheese mixture, and cheese.
9. Cover and bake for 35 minutes. Let stand for 10 minutes before serving.

SERVES 12.

225 Tator Tot Dinner

When our kids were little, they never got sick of tator tots. Here's a way to use them other than just as a side.

2 pounds lean ground beef
¼ teaspoon salt
⅛ teaspoon black pepper
1 medium onion, chopped
1 (2 pound) package frozen tator tots
1 (8 ounce) package shredded Cheddar cheese
2 (10 ounce) cans cream of mushroom soup
1 soup canful milk

1. Preheat oven to 350°.
2. Crumble ground beef into sprayed, 9 x 13-inch glass baking dish. Sprinkle with salt and pepper.
3. Cover with onion. Top with tator tots and shredded cheese.
4. Combine soup and milk in saucepan. Heat and stir just enough to mix in milk. Pour over casserole.
5. Bake covered for 1 hour. Uncover and bake for additional 15 minutes.

SERVES 8.

 Who Knew? Light Switch

To make this recipe lower in fat, substitute 2 cups of our Low-Fat Four-Cheese Blend (Light Switch #5) for the package of Cheddar cheese.

226 Beef and Mushroom Pie

1 (15 ounce) package refrigerated piecrust (2 crusts)
1 pound lean ground beef
1 (8 ounce) package fresh mushrooms, sliced
1 bunch scallions, sliced
3 tablespoons flour
1 (1 ounce) packet herb and garlic soup mix
1 teaspoon minced garlic
1 (5 ounce) can evaporated milk
1 (3 ounce) package cream cheese, softened
¾ cup shredded mozzarella cheese

1. Preheat oven to 350°.
2. Place 1 piecrust in 9-inch glass pie pan.
3. Combine beef, mushrooms, scallions, and flour in large skillet. Cook on medium heat, stirring often, until beef is cooked through, about 10 minutes.
4. Stir in soup mix, garlic, evaporated milk, and cream cheese. Cook until cream cheese melts and mixture blends well. Remove from heat and stir in mozzarella cheese.
5. Pour mixture into crust-lined pie pan and top with second crust; seal edges and crimp crust. Cut several slits in top crust.
6. Bake until crust is golden brown, about 40 minutes. Let stand for 10 minutes before cutting into wedges.

SERVES 6.

227 Enchilada Lasagna

1½ pounds lean ground beef
1 medium onion, chopped
1 teaspoon minced garlic
1 (15 ounce) can enchilada sauce
1 (15 ounce) can stewed tomatoes
1 teaspoon ground cumin
½ teaspoon salt
1 egg
1½ cups small curd cottage cheese
1 (12 ounce) package shredded four-cheese blend, divided
8 (8 inch) corn tortillas, torn into strips
1 cup shredded Cheddar cheese

1. Preheat oven to 325°.
2. Cook beef, onion, and garlic in large skillet over medium heat until meat is no longer pink. Drain.
3. Stir in enchilada sauce, tomatoes, cumin, and salt. Bring mixture to a boil over medium-high heat, then reduce heat to low and simmer for 20 minutes.
4. Combine egg and cottage cheese in small bowl.
5. Spread one-third of meat mixture into sprayed, 9 x 13-inch baking dish. Top with half four-cheese blend, half tortillas, and half cottage cheese mixture. Repeat layers.
6. Top with remaining meat mixture and sprinkle with Cheddar cheese.
7. Cover and bake for 25 minutes. Uncover and bake for additional 10 minutes.

SERVES 8.

 ### Who Knew? Light Switch

To make this recipe lower in fat, substitute 3 cups of our Low-Fat Four-Cheese Blend (Light Switch #5) for the package of four-cheese blend.

228 Aidan's Awesome Casserole

This casserole is named after our youngest. He didn't really help create it, but we let him think he did!

½ tablespoon vegetable or canola oil
1 pound lean ground beef
1 medium onion, chopped
¼ cup steak sauce
1 tablespoon flour
1 (15 ounce) can baked beans with liquid
1 (8 ounce) can whole kernel corn, drained
1½ cups garlic-flavored croutons, crushed

1. Preheat oven to 325°.
2. Heat oil over medium heat in skillet. When hot, add beef and onion. Cook, stirring, until beef is brown and onion is tender, about 10 minutes. Drain. Stir in steak sauce, flour, beans, and corn.
3. Pour into sprayed, 9 x 13-inch baking dish. Sprinkle crouton crumbs on top.
4. Bake until bubbly around edges, about 45 minutes.

SERVES 8.

229 Barbecued Beef Casserole

2 pounds ground beef
1 large onion, diced
1 red bell pepper, seeded and diced
1 (10 ounce) can whole kernel corn, drained
1 (15 ounce) can diced tomatoes, drained
½ cup barbecue sauce
1 teaspoon garlic powder
3 (8.5 ounce) packages cornbread mix

1. Preheat oven to 400°.
2. Cook ground beef, onion, and bell pepper in skillet over medium heat until vegetables are tender and beef is no longer pink, about 8–12 minutes. Drain.
3. Add corn, tomatoes, barbecue sauce, and garlic powder and stir to mix well. Pour into 9 x 13-inch baking dish.
4. Prepare cornbread batter according to package directions. Spread batter over beef mixture.
5. Bake, uncovered, until top is golden brown, about 20–25 minutes.

SERVES 8–10.

230 Sombrero Olé

This colorful casserole has a bit of kick, a bit of crunch, and lots of south-of-the-border taste.

1 cup rice, uncooked
1 (1½ pound) package lean ground beef
1 teaspoon salt
1 large onion, chopped
1 red bell pepper, seeded, chopped
1 yellow bell pepper, seeded, chopped
3 cups chopped zucchini
½ cup water
1 (1 ounce) packet taco seasoning
1 (16 ounce) jar chunky salsa
1½ cups shredded Cheddar cheese
2 cups lightly crushed tortilla chips

1. Preheat oven to 350°.
2. Cook rice according to package directions.
3. Brown ground beef in large skillet over medium heat; drain and add salt.
4. Add onion, bell peppers, zucchini, water, and taco seasoning. Cook, stirring occasionally, until vegetables are tender, about 10–12 minutes.
5. Spoon rice into sprayed, 9 x 13-inch baking dish; layer beef mixture, salsa, and cheese.
6. Bake for 20–25 minutes.
7. Remove from oven and sprinkle tortilla chips over top. Return to oven and bake for additional 10 minutes.

SERVES 6–8.

 Who Knew? Light Switch

To make this recipe lower in fat, use 2 cups of our Super Healthy Salsa (Light Switch #7) instead of the jar of salsa, and our Low-Fat Four-Cheese Blend (Light Switch #5) instead of the Cheddar cheese.

---

231 Potato-Beef Casserole

½ tablespoon vegetable or canola oil
1¼ pounds lean ground beef
4 medium potatoes, peeled, sliced
1 (10 ounce) can cream of mushroom soup
1 (10 ounce) can vegetable beef soup
¼ teaspoon salt
⅛ teaspoon black pepper

1. Preheat oven to 350°.
2. Heat oil over medium heat in skillet. When hot, add beef and cook until beef is browned, about 8–10 minutes. Stir to break up beef throughout cooking time. Drain.
3. Combine beef with remaining ingredients in large bowl.
4. Transfer to sprayed, 3-quart baking dish. Cover and bake until potatoes are tender, about 1 hour 30 minutes.

SERVES 4–6.

232 Beef and Broccoli Bake

1 cup rice, uncooked
1½ pounds lean ground beef
1 (16 ounce) package frozen broccoli florets, thawed
2 (10 ounce) cans broccoli cheese soup
¾ cup milk
1 teaspoon seasoned salt
⅛ teaspoon black pepper
1 cup crushed cheese crackers
2 tablespoon butter, melted

1. Preheat oven to 350°.
2. Cook rice according to package directions. While rice is cooking, place beef in large skillet and cook on medium heat, stirring occasionally until beef is no longer pink in color. Drain.
3. Stir in rice, broccoli, soup, milk, seasoned salt, and pepper. Spoon into 2½-quart glass baking dish.
4. Cover and bake for 25 minutes.
5. Combine cheese crackers and melted butter in bowl; sprinkle over casserole.
6. Bake uncovered until cheese crackers are light brown, about 15 minutes.

SERVES 6.

 Who Knew?

After finishing a stick of unsalted butter, hold on to the wrapper. It'll come in handy when you need to grease a pan: Simply wipe the pan with it. But don't use wrappers from salted butter, since they may cause foods to stick.

233 Crusty Beef Casserole

1 pound lean ground beef
1 (10 ounce) package frozen chopped bell peppers and onions, thawed
1 (10 ounce) can chopped tomatoes and green chilies
¾ teaspoon seasoned salt
1 (15 ounce) jar salsa con queso (spicy cheese dip), divided
2 cups biscuit mix
1 egg, slightly beaten
1 cup milk
½ teaspoon salt
3 fresh scallions, sliced

1. Preheat oven to 375°.
2. Place beef and bell pepper–onion mixture in skillet over medium heat and cook, stirring often, for 8–10 minutes; drain.
3. Stir in tomatoes and green chilies, seasoned salt, and 1 cup salsa con queso. Cook, stirring constantly, just until mixture is hot, about 3 minutes.
4. Combine biscuit mix, egg, milk, and salt in bowl and mix until they blend well. Spoon half batter into sprayed, 9 x 9-inch glass baking dish.
5. Top with beef mixture, then pour remaining batter evenly over top.
6. Bake uncovered until light golden brown and center is set, about 45 minutes. Let stand 5–10 minutes before cutting into squares to serve.
7. With large spoon, drizzle a little remaining salsa con queso over crust and sprinkle sliced scallion on top.

SERVES 6.

234 Pinto Bean Pie

Even though it's called "Pinto Bean Pie," you can really use black, kidney, or whatever kind of beans you find on sale.

½ tablespoon olive oil
1 pound lean ground beef
1 medium onion, chopped
2 (15 ounce) cans pinto beans with liquid, divided
1 (10 ounce) can tomatoes and green chilies with liquid, divided
1 (3 ounce) can French-fried onion rings

1. Preheat oven to 350°.
2. Heat oil over medium heat in skillet. When hot, add beef and onion. Cook, stirring, until beef is brown and onion is tender, about 10 minutes. Drain.
3. Spread 1 can beans into 2-quart baking dish. Layer half of beef-onion mixture on top, then half of tomatoes and green chilies. Repeat layers with remaining beans, remaining beef-onion mixture, and remaining tomatoes and green chilies.
4. Top with onion rings and bake for 30 minutes.

SERVES 6.

235 Hamburger Heaven

1 (8 ounce) package medium egg noodles
1¼ pounds lean ground beef
1 (8 ounce) package fresh mushrooms, halved
2 ribs celery, sliced
1 teaspoon minced garlic
2 (1 ounce) packets beef gravy mix
2½ cups water
1 (8 ounce) carton sour cream
1 (3 ounce) package fried onion rings

1. Preheat oven to 375°.
2. Cook noodles according to package directions; drain. Cover to keep warm.
3. Cook beef, mushrooms, celery, and garlic in sprayed skillet over medium heat, stirring often, until beef is cooked through, about 6 minutes. Drain and remove from skillet.
4. In same skillet, combine gravy mix and water; cook over medium heat, stirring constantly, until thickened, about 5 minutes. Remove from heat and stir in sour cream.
5. Add cooked noodles and beef mixture to gravy and mix well. Spoon mixture into sprayed, 3-quart baking dish.
6. Cover and bake for 25 minutes. Remove from oven and sprinkle onion rings over casserole. Return to oven and bake uncovered for additional 15 minutes.

SERVES 6.

 ## Who Knew? Light Switch

To make this recipe lower in fat, substitute 1 cup of our Low-Fat Sour Cream Substitute (Light Switch #8) for the carton of sour cream.

236 Cabbage Casserole

1½ pounds lean ground beef
½ cup chopped onion
½ cup chopped green bell pepper
1 can (15 ounces) diced tomatoes
1 teaspoon garlic powder
1 teaspoon salt
½ teaspoon black pepper
1 cabbage
1 cup four-cheese blend

1. Preheat oven to 350°.
2. Cook ground beef, onion, and pepper in skillet over medium heat until vegetables are tender and meat is no longer pink, about 8–12 minutes. Drain.
3. Stir in tomatoes, garlic powder, salt, and pepper. Reduce heat to low and simmer, uncovered, for 10 minutes, stirring ocassionaly.
4. Cut cabbage into 6 wedges. Cook in boiling water, covered, until cooked through, about 10 minutes. Drain. Line bottom and sides of sprayed, 9-inch square baking dish with cabbage leaves. Top with ground beef mixture.
5. Bake, uncovered, 25 minutes. Top with cheese and bake for additional 5 minutes.

 Who Knew? Light Switch

To make this recipe lower in fat, use our Low-Fat Four-Cheese Blend (Light Switch #5).

237 Meatballs and Orzo Casserole

1 (10 ounce) package frozen onions and bell peppers
2 ribs celery, sliced
2 tablespoons Italian salad dressing
1 (14 ounce) can beef broth
1 cup orzo (tiny pasta)
18 cooked, frozen Italian meatballs, thawed
2 tomatoes, chopped, drained
1 teaspoon dried parsley
⅓ cup grated Parmesan cheese

1. Stir-fry onions and bell peppers, celery, and dressing in large sprayed skillet over medium-high heat for 2 minutes.
2. Add broth and bring to a boil. Stir in orzo and meatballs and bring to a boil. Cover and cook for 10 minutes, stirring occasionally.
3. Stir in tomatoes and parsley. Cover and cook until most of liquid absorbs and orzo is tender, about 5 minutes.
4. Spoon into serving bowl and top with Parmesan cheese.

SERVES 6.

 Who Knew? Light Switch

To make this recipe lower in fat, substitute our Low-Fat Meatballs (Light Switch #12) for the package of frozen meatballs.

238 One-Dish Pork and Peas

Many of these recipes use chicken, but pork is also a delicious, tender meat that makes a great addition to casseroles.

1½ pounds pork tenderloin,
    cut into ½-inch cubes
  2 tablespoons vegetable or canola oil
  1 cup sliced celery
  1 onion, chopped
  1 red bell pepper, seeded, chopped
  1 (8 ounce) package small egg
    noodles, cooked, drained
  1 (10 ounce) can cream of chicken
    soup
  ½ cup half-and-half
  1 (10 ounce) package frozen green
    peas, thawed
  1 teaspoon salt
  ½ teaspoon black pepper
  1 cup seasoned breadcrumbs
  ⅓ cup chopped walnuts

1. Preheat oven to 350°.
2. Cook cubed pork with oil in large skillet over medium-high heat until brown on all sides, about 10 minutes. Reduce heat to low and cook, covered, for 20 minutes. Remove pork to separate dish.
3. In remaining oil, sauté celery, onion, and bell pepper over medium-high heat until tender, about 6–8 minutes. Add pork, noodles, soup, cream, peas, salt, and pepper and mix well.
4. Spoon into sprayed, 3-quart baking dish. Sprinkle with breadcrumbs and walnuts.
5. Bake until bubbly, about 25 minutes.

SERVES 8.

239 Pork Chop Casserole

  6 (¾-inch thick) boneless pork chops
  1 teaspoon salt, divided
  ½ teaspoon black pepper
  2 tablespoons canola oil
  1 green bell pepper
  1 yellow bell pepper, seeded, chopped
  1 (15 ounce) can tomato sauce
  1 (15 ounce) can Italian stewed
    tomatoes
  1 cup water
  1 teaspoon minced garlic
1½ cups long-grain rice

1. Preheat oven to 350°.
2. Sprinkle pork chops with ½ teaspoon salt and pepper.
3. Heat oil in skillet over medium-high heat. Cook chops in skillet, flipping once, until brown on both sides, about 3–5 minutes per side. Remove chops from skillet and set aside.
4. Cut top off green bell pepper and remove seeds. Cut 6 rings from pepper and set aside.
5. Combine yellow bell pepper, tomato sauce, stewed tomatoes, water, garlic, and ½ teaspoon salt in separate bowl; stir well.
6. Spread rice into sprayed, 9 x 13-inch baking dish. Slowly pour tomato mixture over rice.
7. Arrange pork chops over rice and place one pepper ring on top of each chop.
8. Cover and bake until chops and rice are heated through, about 1 hour.

SERVES 6.

240 Cheddar-Ham Bake

2 (10 ounce) cans cream of celery soup
1 tablespoon minced onions
½ teaspoon dried thyme
¾ cup milk
1 (8 ounce) carton sour cream
3 large potatoes, thinly sliced
4 cups cooked, cubed ham
1 (8 ounce) package shredded white Cheddar cheese

1. Preheat oven to 350°.
2. Combine soup, onions, thyme, and milk in saucepan and cook over medium heat, stirring constantly, just until mixture is warm. Remove from heat and stir in sour cream.
3. Combine potatoes and ham in large bowl.
4. Layer half potato-ham mixture, half cheese, then half soup mixture in sprayed, 9 x 13-inch glass baking dish. Spread evenly and repeat layers.
5. Cover and bake for 35 minutes. Uncover and continue baking for additional 45 minutes.

SERVES 6–8.

 Who Knew? Light Switch

To make this recipe lower in fat, substitute 2½ cups of our Low-Fat Cream of Celery Soup Base (Light Switch #4) for the cans of cream of celery soup, and 1 cup of our Low-Fat Sour Cream Substitute (Light Switch #8) for the carton of sour cream.

241 Ham with Balsamic-Roasted Vegetables

1 (16 ounce) package ziti or penne (tube) pasta
1 tablespoon balsamic vinegar
¾ teaspoon salt, divided
1 tablespoon olive oil
1 medium zucchini, halved lengthwise
1 small onion, quartered
2 cups cooked, chopped ham
1 cup spaghetti sauce
¾ cup (about 3 ounces) Feta cheese, crumbled
½ teaspoon red pepper flakes
2 cups shredded mozzarella cheese, divided

1. Preheat broiler.
2. Cook pasta according to package directions. Drain.
3. Combine vinegar, ½ teaspoon salt, and oil in small bowl and mix well.
4. Place zucchini and onion on baking sheet and coat with ⅔ of vinegar mixture. Reserve remaining vinegar mixture.
5. Place under broiler and cook until tender, flipping once, about 8 minutes per side.
6. Remove from broiler and preheat oven to 350°.
7. Chop roasted vegetables and combine with remaining vinegar mixture, pasta, ham, spaghetti sauce, Feta cheese, red pepper flakes, and half mozzarella cheese. Pour into sprayed, 9 x 13-inch baking dish.
8. Cover and bake for 35 minutes. Uncover, top with remaining mozzarella cheese, and bake for 15 additional minutes.

SERVES 5.

242 Chickpea Casserole with Ham

1½ cups cooked, chopped ham
1 (15 ounce) can chickpeas
1½ cups water
¾ cup minced onion
1 large sweet potato, peeled, diced
1 apple, diced
2 teaspoons curry powder
1 teaspoon cumin
¼ teaspoon minced ginger
⅛ teaspoon allspice
¼ teaspoon salt
⅛ teaspoon black pepper

1. Preheat oven to 375°.
2. In large bowl, combine all ingredients and mix well. Pour into a sprayed, 3-quart baking dish.
3. Cover and bake for 1 hour.

SERVES 4.

243 Tortellini-Ham Casserole

This dish is especially good when using our Low-Fat Alfredo Sauce!

2 (9 ounce) packages refrigerated tortellini pasta
1 (10 ounce) package frozen green peas, thawed
1 (8 ounce) jar sun-dried tomatoes with oil
1 red bell pepper, seeded, chopped
1 teaspoon minced garlic
1 (16 ounce) jar Alfredo sauce
½ tablespoon dried basil
2–3 cups cooked, cubed ham
½ cup grated Asiago or Parmesan cheese

1. Preheat oven to 350°.
2. Cook tortellini in saucepan according to package directions, except add green peas 5 minutes before end of cook time. Drain and set aside.
3. Add oil from sun-dried tomatoes to skillet; heat on medium-high. Add bell pepper and cook, stirring, for 3 minutes. Add garlic and cook until pepper and garlic are tender, about 2–4 minutes more.
4. Chop sun-dried tomatoes into bite-sized pieces and add to pepper-garlic mixture. Add Alfredo sauce, basil, and ham and mix well. Add tortellini-pea mixture and combine.
5. Pour into sprayed, 9 x 13-inch, baking dish. Cover and cook for 35 minutes. Sprinkle with cheese and cook uncovered for 8 minutes more.

SERVES 10.

 Who Knew? Light Switch

To make this recipe lower in fat, substitute 1¾ cups of our Low-Fat Alfredo Sauce (Light Switch #9) for the jar of Alfredo sauce.

244 Glowing Potatoes and Ham

²/₃ cup milk
1¾ cups water
½ cup (1 stick) butter, divided
¼ teaspoon salt
2²/₃ cups mashed potato flakes
1 (8 ounce) package cream cheese, cut into small chunks
1 (8 ounce) carton sour cream
1 (8 ounce) package Velveeta cheese, finely cubed, divided
2 cups cooked, shredded ham
¾ cup seasoned breadcrumbs

1. Preheat oven to 350°.
2. Combine milk, water, ¼ cup butter, and salt in large saucepan and bring to a boil over medium-high heat; remove from heat and stir in potato flakes.
3. Let stand 30 seconds for liquid to absorb, then add cream cheese chunks.
4. Whip with wire whisk until fluffy and cream cheese melts. Stir in sour cream and 1 cup Velveeta cheese.
5. Spoon half mixture into sprayed, 2-quart glass baking dish. Top with shredded ham, then remaining potato-cheese mixture. Sprinkle with remaining cheese.
6. Melt remaining ¼ cup butter and stir into breadcrumbs. Sprinkle over top of casserole.
7. Bake uncovered until top is light brown, about 35 minutes.

SERVES 4–6.

 Who Knew? Light Switch

To make this recipe lower in fat, substitute 1 cup of our Low-Fat Sour Cream Substitute (Light Switch #8) for the carton of sour cream, and 1½ cups of our Melty Cheese Sauce (Light Switch #6) for the package of Velveeta cheese.

---

245 Pretzel Casserole

1 (32 ounce) bag thin pretzels
¼ cup (½ stick) butter, melted
1 (10 ounce) can cream of chicken soup
1 cup chopped ham
1 medium onion, minced
1½ cups shredded Cheddar cheese, divided
½ teaspoon salt
¼ teaspoon black pepper

1. Preheat oven to 350°.
2. Combine pretzels, butter, soup, ham, onion, half cheese, salt, and pepper; mix well and pour into sprayed, 2-quart baking dish.
3. Bake, covered, for 35 minutes. Sprinkle with remaining cheese and bake uncovered until cheese melts, an additional 5–10 minutes.

SERVES 4.

246 Green Casserole

Believe it or not, pasta with sausage is much more commonplace in Italy than pasta with ground beef. But of course, the "green" in this casserole's name comes from the pesto and broccoli, not the meat!

1 (8 ounce) package multicolored rotini pasta
1 (10 ounce) package frozen broccoli florets, thawed
1 red bell pepper, seeded, chopped
1 (16 ounce) package Italian sausage links (kielbasa), cut into bite-sized pieces
1 (8 ounce) carton refrigerated pesto
¼ cup water
1 cup grated Parmesan cheese

1. Preheat oven to 325°.
2. Cook pasta according to package directions, but stir in broccoli and bell pepper during the last 10 minutes of cooking time. Drain and set aside.
3. Cook sausage in sprayed, large skillet over medium heat until brown, stirring often, about 6 minutes; drain.
4. Add pesto, water, and pasta-broccoli mixture and spoon into sprayed, 3-quart glass baking dish.
5. Cover and bake for 15 minutes. Uncover and sprinkle cheese over top of casserole.

SERVES 6.

 Who Knew?

To soften a piece of hardened (but not moldy) cheese like Parmesan, submerge it in a bowl of buttermilk for one minute. If it's still not soft, cover the dish and refrigerate it overnight.

247 Hawaiian Bake

3 tablespoons butter
1¼ cups water
1 (6 ounce) package long-grain and wild rice mix
½ cup pineapple preserves
1 (pound) Italian sausage (kielbasa), halved lengthwise, cut in ½-inch slices
1 (10 ounce) package frozen chopped bell peppers and onions, thawed
1 red bell pepper, seeded, chopped
2 ribs celery, thinly sliced
1 (8 ounce) can pineapple chunks with liquid
1 tablespoon soy sauce
¼ teaspoon dried ginger or ¾ teaspoon minced fresh ginger

1. Preheat oven to 375°.
2. Combine butter and water in large saucepan and bring to a boil over high heat.
3. Remove from heat and stir in rice, seasoning packet, preserves, sausage, bell pepper–onion mixture, red bell pepper, celery, pineapple chunks, soy sauce, and ginger. Transfer to 2½-quart glass baking dish.
4. Cover and bake until rice is tender, about 40–45 minutes. Let stand for 10 minutes before serving.

SERVES 6.

248 Pizza Topping Pie

If your family loves meaty pizza, they'll love this versatile pasta casserole that features both pepperoni and sausage.

2 cups tomato-spinach macaroni
(spiral pasta)
1 pound bulk Italian sausage
1 onion, chopped
1 green bell pepper, seeded, chopped
1 (15 ounce) can pizza sauce
1 (8 ounce) can tomato sauce
⅓ cup milk
1 (3 ounce) package sliced pepperoni, halved
1 (4 ounce) jar sliced mushrooms, drained
1 (2 ounce) can sliced ripe olives, drained
1 (8 ounce) package shredded mozzarella cheese, divided

1. Preheat oven to 350°.
2. Cook macaroni in saucepan according to package directions; drain.
3. Cook sausage, onion, and bell pepper in skillet over medium heat until sausage is no longer pink, about 10–12 minutes. Drain
4. Combine pizza sauce, tomato sauce, and milk in large bowl. Stir in sausage mixture, macaroni, pepperoni, mushrooms, olives, and half cheese. Mix well.
5. Spoon into sprayed, 9 x 13-inch baking dish. Cover and bake for 30 minutes.
6. Remove from oven and sprinkle remaining cheese over top of casserole. Return to oven and bake until cheese is melted, about 5–10 minutes.

SERVES 8.

249 Penne Pizzazz

1 (8 ounce) package penne pasta
1 pound bulk Italian sausage
1 teaspoon minced garlic
1 (4 ounce) can sliced mushrooms, drained
1 (10 ounce) can chopped tomatoes and green chilies
1 (28 ounce) jar spaghetti sauce
¼ teaspoon hot sauce (optional)
1 (8 ounce) package shredded mozzarella cheese, divided

1. Preheat oven to 350°.
2. Cook pasta according to package directions and drain.
3. Place sausage and garlic in skillet over medium-high heat and cook, stirring occasionally, until sausage is no longer pink; drain.
4. Combine pasta, sausage, mushrooms, tomatoes and green chilies, spaghetti sauce, hot sauce (if desired), and ½ cup cheese in large bowl; toss to mix well. Spoon into sprayed, 9 x 13-inch glass baking dish.
5. Cover and bake for 35 minutes. Uncover and sprinkle remaining cheese over casserole; return to oven for 5 minutes.

SERVES 6–8.

 Who Knew? Light Switch

To make this recipe lower in fat, substitute 2¾ cups of our Homemade Spaghetti Sauce (Light Switch #10) for the jar of spaghetti sauce.

250 Hot Cheese Squares

This is a great way to use refrigerated crescent rolls when you have one of those buy-one-get-one-free coupons.

1 (8 ounce) can refrigerated
   crescent rolls
1 (16 ounce) package refrigerated
   cocktail sausage links, halved
1 (10 ounce) package frozen
   chopped bell peppers and onions,
   thawed
1 (4 ounce) can pimentos, drained
1 (8 ounce) package shredded
   mozzarella cheese, divided
1 (10 ounce) can cream of celery soup
2 tablespoons cream
4 large eggs, slightly beaten

1. Preheat oven to 350°.
2. Unroll crescent rolls and place dough in sprayed, 7 x 11-inch glass baking dish. Press seams closed and push dough 1 inch up sides of pan.
3. Arrange sausage links evenly over dough and sprinkle with bell pepper–onion mixture, pimentos, and half cheese.
4. Combine soup, cream, and eggs in bowl. Beat with wire whisk and spoon over bell pepper–cheese mixture. Sprinkle with remaining cheese.
5. Bake uncovered until knife inserted in center comes out clean, about 35 minutes. Let stand for 5 minutes before cutting into squares to serve.

SERVES 8.

 Who Knew? Light Switch

To make this recipe lower in fat, substitute 1¼ cup of our Low-Fat Cream of Celery Soup Base (Light Switch #4) for the cans of cream of celery soup, and 2% milk for the cream.

251 Bacon-Potato Casserole

4 pounds new (red) potatoes with
   peels
2 teaspoons salt, divided
1 pound sliced bacon, cooked,
   drained, crumbled, divided
1 (8 ounce) package shredded
   Monterey Jack cheese, divided
1 (12 ounce) package Velveeta
   cheese, cubed
1 teaspoon black pepper
2 onions, chopped
1 (4 ounce) jar chopped pimentos,
   drained
1 cup mayonnaise
1 (8 ounce) carton sour cream
1 teaspoon basil

1. Preheat oven to 325°.
2. Cut potatoes in half and cook in boiling water with 1 teaspoon salt in saucepan until tender, about 20-25 minutes.
3. Combine potatoes, half crumbled bacon, half Jack cheese, and all other ingredients in large bowl; mix well.
4. Spoon into sprayed, 10 x 15-inch baking dish or 2 smaller dishes. (You may freeze one.)
5. Bake until edges bubble, about 40 minutes.
6. Remove from oven and sprinkle remaining Jack cheese over top of casserole. Return to oven and bake just until cheese melts, about 5 minutes.
7. Before serving, sprinkle remaining crumbled bacon over top of casserole.

SERVES 8–10.

252 Tuna Casserole

1 (8 ounce) package elbow macaroni (tube pasta)
1 (8 ounce) package Velveeta cheese, cubed
2 (6 ounce) cans tuna, drained
1 (10 ounce) can cream of celery soup
1 cup milk

1. Preheat oven to 350°.
2. Cook macaroni in saucepan according to package directions. Drain well, add cheese, and stir until cheese melts.
3. Add tuna, celery soup, and milk and continue stirring. Spoon into sprayed, 7 x 11-inch baking dish. Cover and bake until bubbly, about 35 minutes.

SERVES 6.

 Who Knew? Light Switch

To make this recipe lower in fat, substitute 1½ cups of our Melty Cheese Sauce (Light Switch #6) for the package of Velveeta cheese, and 1¼ cup of our Low-Fat Cream of Celery Soup Base (Light Switch #4) for the can of cream of celery soup.

253 Zesty Tuna Bake

Who knew a can of tuna and a box of mac 'n' cheese could be turned into such a delicious dish? (We did, of course!)

1 (16 ounce) package frozen mixed vegetables
1 (14 ounce) package macaroni and cheese dinner
¾ cup milk
¼ cup Italian salad dressing
½ teaspoon red pepper flakes
1 (12 ounce) can tuna in water, drained
1 cup shredded four-cheese blend, divided

1. Preheat oven to 375°F.
2. Cook macaroni as directed in package directions, except add vegetables 2 minutes before end of cook time. Drain and add ingredients for cheese sauce as directed. Add salad dressing, red pepper flakes, tuna, and half cheese and mix well.
3. Pour into 2-quart baking dish and bake, covered, for 35 minutes. Sprinkle remaining cheese on top and bake uncovered until melted, about 6–8 minutes.

SERVES 4.

 Who Knew? Light Switch

To make this recipe lower in fat, use our Low-Fat Four-Cheese Blend (Light Switch #5) instead of the four-cheese blend. Also try our Italian Salad Dressing (Light Switch #11)!

254 Savory Salmon Casserole

1 (6 ounce) package dried egg noodles
1 (10 ounce) can cream of celery soup
1 (5 ounce) can evaporated milk
1 tablespoon lemon juice
½ of 1 medium onion, chopped
1 (15 ounce) canned or fresh salmon, cooked, boned, skin removed
1 cup shredded Cheddar cheese
1 (8 ounce) can small green peas, drained
½ teaspoon seasoned salt
¼ teaspoon white pepper
½ teaspoon Creole seasoning
1 cup crushed cheese crackers
2 tablespoons butter, melted

1. Preheat oven to 350°.
2. Cook noodles according to package directions; drain.
3. Stir in soup, evaporated milk, lemon juice, onion, salmon, cheese, peas, seasoned salt, white pepper, and Creole seasoning.
4. Spoon into sprayed, 7 x 11-inch baking dish. Cover and bake for 25 minutes.
5. Combine cracker crumbs and butter in bowl and sprinkle over casserole. Return to oven until crumbs are light brown, about 10 minutes.

SERVES 8.

255 Shrimp Delight

1½ pounds raw shrimp
2 ounces shrimp boil
2 tablespoons butter
1 onion, chopped
1 red bell pepper, seeded, chopped
1 green bell pepper, seeded, chopped
1 teaspoon minced garlic
1 (10 ounce) can cream of shrimp soup
1 (10 ounce) can cream of celery soup
2 cups cooked rice
¾ teaspoon black pepper
1 teaspoon Creole seasoning
1 cup crushed potato chips

1. Preheat oven to 350°.
2. Boil a large pot of water and add shrimp and shrimp boil. Cook according to package directions. Cool, peel, and vein.
3. Melt butter over medium high-high heat. Add onion, bell peppers, and cook, stirring, until tender, about 5–8 minutes.
4. Combine shrimp, onion-pepper mixture, soups, rice, pepper, and Creole seasoning in large bowl and mix well.
5. Spoon into sprayed, 9 x 13-inch baking dish and sprinkle with potato chips. Bake for 30 minutes.

SERVES 6–8.

 Who Knew? Light Switch

To make this recipe lower in fat, substitute 1¼ cup of our Low-Fat Cream of Celery Soup Base (Light Switch #4) for the can of cream of celery soup.

256 Seafood Royale

- 1 cup rice (uncooked)
- 2 (10 ounce) cans cream of shrimp soup
- 1 cup milk
- 2/3 cup mayonnaise
- 3 pounds cooked, peeled shrimp
- 1 (6 ounce) can crabmeat, drained, flaked
- 1 medium onion, chopped
- 2 cups chopped celery
- 1/4 cup snipped parsley
- 1 (8 ounce) can sliced water chestnuts, drained
- 1 teaspoon Creole seasoning
- 1/2 teaspoon salt
- 1/2 teaspoon black pepper
- 1/2 cup slivered almonds

1. Preheat oven to 325°.
2. Cook rice according to package directions.
3. Combine soup, milk, and mayonnaise in large bowl and mix well.
4. Add shrimp, crabmeat, onion, celery, parsley, water chestnuts, Creole seasoning, salt, and pepper.
5. Fold in rice and mix well.
6. Spread into sprayed, 3-quart baking dish and sprinkle almonds over top.
7. Cover and bake for 25 minutes. Uncover and bake for additional 10 minutes.

SERVES 6.

257 Superior Seafood Casserole

If one of your favorite foods is stuffing, you don't have to wait until Thanksgiving to have it! Try this recipe that pairs stuffing with seafood.

- 1 (6 ounce) box herb-seasoned stuffing mix
- 1 (8 ounce) package frozen salad shrimp, thawed
- 1 (8 ounce) package refrigerated imitation crabmeat
- 2 ribs celery, sliced
- 1/2 cup chopped red bell pepper
- 1 (10 ounce) package frozen chopped bell peppers and onions, thawed
- 1 (10 ounce) can chicken broth
- 1/4 cup (1/2 stick) butter, melted

1. Preheat oven to 350°.
2. Combine stuffing mix, shrimp, imitation crabmeat, celery, red bell pepper, and bell pepper–onion mixture in bowl. Stir in broth and butter and spoon into sprayed, 2-quart baking dish.
3. Cover and bake until center is hot and bubbly, about 45 minutes.

SERVES 6.

258 Seafood-Pasta Casserole

- 1 (8 ounce) package bow-tie pasta
- 1 (16 ounce) package frozen broccoli florets, thawed
- 2 ribs celery, thinly sliced
- 1 red bell pepper, seeded, chopped
- 1 (16 ounce) jar Alfredo sauce
- 1 (8 ounce) package frozen salad shrimp, thawed
- 1 (8 ounce) package frozen imitation crabmeat, thawed
- ½ cup milk
- ½ cup shredded mozzarella cheese, divided
- 2 tablespoons butter, melted
- ⅔ cup Italian-style breadcrumbs

1. Preheat oven to 350°.
2. Cook pasta according to package directions, adding broccoli for last 2 minutes of cooking time. Drain.
3. Combine celery, bell pepper, and Alfredo sauce in large bowl. Stir in shrimp, imitation crabmeat, milk, and half cheese.
4. Add pasta-broccoli mixture and toss gently to mix well. Spoon into sprayed, 2-quart baking dish.
5. Cover and bake for 35 minutes.
6. Combine butter, breadcrumbs, and remaining cheese in bowl.
7. Remove casserole from oven and sprinkle breadcrumb mixture over casserole. Return to oven and bake uncovered until light golden brown, about 10–15 minutes.

SERVES 4–6.

 Who Knew? Light Switch

To make this recipe lower in fat, substitute 1¾ cups of our Low-Fat Alfredo Sauce (Light Switch #9) for the jar of Alfredo sauce.

259 Crab Casserole

- 2 (6 ounce) cans crabmeat, drained
- 1 (10 ounce) can cream of shrimp soup
- 1 (4 ounce) can chopped pimentos
- ¾ cup milk
- ⅔ cup mayonnaise
- ¾ cup shredded Cheddar cheese
- 2 cups tagliatelle pasta (thin egg noodles)
- ½ cup seasoned breadcrumbs

1. Preheat oven to 350°.
2. Combine crabmeat, soup, pimentos, milk, mayonnaise, cheese, and pasta in large bowl. Pour into sprayed, 3-quart baking dish.
3. Sprinkle breadcrumbs over top of casserole. Cover and bake for 45 minutes.

SERVES 6–8.

 Who Knew?

While you have the mayonnaise out, check your kitchen table for any water marks. Rubbing mayonnaise on marks on wood and leaving for several hours will make them vanish!

260 Spinach Casserole

This vegetarian creation is a casserole Popeye would be proud of!

3 (10 ounce) packages chopped spinach
½ cup (1 stick) plus 2 tablespoons butter, divided
1 (8 ounce) package cream cheese
1 (8 ounce) can sliced water chestnuts, drained
1 (4 ounce) can sliced pimentos
1 (14 ounce) can water-packed artichoke hearts, drained, quartered
¾ cup seasoned breadcrumbs

1. Preheat oven to 375°.
2. Cook spinach according to package directions. Drain and place in large bowl.
3. Combine ½ cup butter and cream cheese in saucepan; cook on medium heat, stirring constantly, until butter and cheese melt and blend together.
4. Stir mixture into spinach and add water chestnuts and pimentos.
5. Line sprayed, 7 x 11-inch glass baking dish with artichoke hearts and cover with spinach mixture.
6. Melt 2 tablespoons butter and combine with breadcrumbs in bowl. Sprinkle over casserole.
7. Bake uncovered for 25 minutes.

SERVES 6–8.

261 Serious Squash Casserole

This casserole is vegetarian, but it's also filling. Eating vegetarian one night a week is a great way to save money and calories!

1 cup biscuit mix
¾ cup shredded mozzarella cheese
1 tablespoon dried dill weed
¼ teaspoon salt
⅛ teaspoon black pepper
4 large eggs, beaten
½ cup (1 stick) butter, melted
2 cups finely chopped zucchini, drained
2 cups finely chopped yellow squash
1 (10 ounce) package frozen chopped bell peppers and onions, thawed

1. Preheat oven to 350°.
2. Combine biscuit mix, cheese, dill weed, salt, and pepper in large bowl. Add eggs and melted butter; mix well.
3. Stir in zucchini, yellow squash, and bell pepper–onion mixture.
4. Pour into sprayed, 7 x 11-inch glass baking dish.
5. Bake uncovered until golden brown, about 30–35 minutes.

SERVES 6–8.

262 Impromptu Cheese Casserole

1 (7 ounce) can chopped green chilies
1 (10 ounce) package frozen chopped
  bell peppers and onions, thawed
2 large tomatoes, seeded, chopped
1 (8 ounce) package Velveeta cheese,
  cubed
1 cup biscuit mix
½ teaspoon seasoned salt
½ cup sour cream
2 tablespoons mayonnaise
3 large eggs

1. Preheat oven to 350°.
2. Combine green chilies, bell pepper–onion mixture, and tomatoes in bowl. Sprinkle mixture into sprayed, 9 x 9-inch glass baking dish.
3. Combine cheese, biscuit mix, seasoned salt, sour cream, mayonnaise, and eggs in bowl. Beat with wire whisk until mixture is fairly smooth. Pour over green chilies–tomato mixture.
4. Bake uncovered until knife inserted in center comes out clean, about 40–45 minutes.

SERVES 6.

 ### Who Knew? Light Switch

To make this recipe lower in fat, substitute 1½ cups of our Melty Cheese Sauce (Light Switch #6) for the package of Velveeta cheese.

263 Buttered Noodle Casserole

2 (12 ounce) packages fettuccini
  (medium egg noodles)
1¼ cups (2½ sticks) butter, divided
¼ cup grated Parmesan cheese
½ cup grated Romano cheese
1 (16 ounce) package frozen green
  peas, thawed
¼ teaspoon salt
1 cup fresh breadcrumbs
½ teaspoon cayenne pepper

1. Preheat oven at 375°.
2. Cook noodles in large saucepan according to package directions; drain and return to saucepan.
3. In separate saucepan, melt 1 cup butter. Stir into noodles.
4. Add cheeses, peas, and salt. Stir until mixture combines well, then spoon into sprayed, 4-quart baking dish.
5. Melt remaining butter and toss with breadcrumbs and cayenne pepper; sprinkle over noodles.
6. Bake until edges are bubbly, about 15 minutes.

SERVES 10–12.

264 Cheesy Noodle Casserole

1 (8 ounce) package fettuccini
(medium egg noodles)
1 (16 ounce) package frozen broccoli
florets, thawed
1 red bell pepper, seeded, chopped
1 (8 ounce) package Velveeta cheese,
cubed
1 cup milk
¾ cup coarsely crushed cheese
crackers

1. Preheat oven to 350°.
2. Cook noodles in large saucepan according to package directions. Add broccoli and bell pepper for last 2 minutes of cooking time. Drain in colander.
3. In same saucepan, combine cheese and milk over low heat and stir until cheese melts.
4. Stir in noodle-broccoli mixture and spoon into sprayed, 3-quart baking dish.
5. Sprinkle with crushed crackers and bake until top is golden brown, about 25–30 minutes.

SERVES 10.

 Who Knew? Light Switch

To make this recipe lower in fat, substitute 1½ cups of our Melty Cheese Sauce (Light Switch #6) for the package of Velveeta cheese.

265 So-Easy Macaroni Bake

You'll love the taste of the feta cheese in this twist on macaroni and cheese.

1 (8 ounce) package elbow macaroni
(tube pasta)
2 tablespoons olive oil
4 large eggs
2¼ cups milk
1 cup crumbled feta cheese
1 cup low-fat small curd cottage
cheese
1 (4 ounce) jar chopped pimentos
½ teaspoon salt

1. Preheat oven to 375°.
2. Cook macaroni in saucepan according to package directions; drain and stir in olive oil. Transfer to sprayed, 9 x 13-inch baking dish.
3. Beat eggs in medium bowl, then stir in milk, feta cheese, cottage cheese, pimentos, and salt.
4. Pour cheese mixture over macaroni in baking dish. Cover and bake for 40 minutes.
5. Uncover dish and bake for 10 minutes more. Let stand for 10 minutes before serving.

SERVES 8.

266 Awesome Butternut Casserole

1 large butternut squash
½ cup (1 stick) butter, melted
¾ cup sugar
3 tablespoons brown sugar
3 eggs, beaten
1 (5 ounce) can evaporated milk
1 teaspoon vanilla
½ teaspoon ground cinnamon
1 cup crushed corn flakes
½ cup packed light brown sugar
½ cup chopped pecans

1. Preheat oven to 350°.
2. Cut the butternut squash in half and scoop out seeds and membranes.
3. Place cut-side down on plate and microwave on HIGH for 1–2 minutes.
4. Let stand in microwave for several minutes. If squash is not tender, microwave for additional 1 minute intervals until soft, letting sit for 1–2 minutes between microwaving.
5. Scoop out squash and place in bowl. Beat until fairly smooth.
6. Add butter, sugar, brown sugar, eggs, evaporated milk, vanilla, and cinnamon; mix well. (Mixture will be thin.)
7. Pour into sprayed, 3-quart baking dish.
8. Bake until almost set, about 45 minutes.
9. Combine corn flakes, light brown sugar, and pecans in bowl. Sprinkle over hot casserole and return to oven until top is crunchy, about 10–15 minutes.

SERVES 6–8.

 Who Knew?

To cook the butternut squash in the oven instead, simply prick it in several places with a fork and place on a foil-lined baking sheet or pizza pan. Cook on 300° for 1 hour.

267 Early-Morning Vegetable Lasagna

1 (14 ounce) can Italian stewed tomatoes
1½ cups pasta sauce
2 cups cottage cheese, drained
1 cup grated Parmesan cheese
¼ teaspoon salt
¼ teaspoon black pepper
9 lasagna noodles, divided
4 zucchini, shredded, divided
7 (1 ounce) slices provolone cheese, cut into strips, divided

1. Combine stewed tomatoes and pasta sauce in bowl and set aside.
2. In separate bowl, combine cottage cheese, Parmesan cheese, salt, and pepper.
3. In sprayed, 9 x 13-inch baking dish, layer one-third tomato mixture, 3 lasagna noodles, one-third zucchini, one-third cheese mixture, and one-third provolone cheese strips. Repeat layers twice more.
4. Cover and refrigerate for at least 8 hours.
5. When ready to bake, remove from refrigerator and let stand for 30 minutes. Preheat oven to 350°.
6. Cover and bake for 45 minutes.
7. Uncover and bake for additional 20 minutes. Let stand for 15 minutes before serving.

SERVES 8–10.

268 Vegetarian Pasta Bake

1 (12 ounce) package rotini (spirals) pasta
½ cup bottled balsamic vinaigrette salad dressing
1 (15 ounce) can cannellini beans, rinsed and drained
2 (15 ounce) cans diced tomatoes with garlic, drained
1 (8 ounce) package feta cheese, crumbled
1 cup coarsely chopped pitted Greek black olives
⅓ cup bread crumbs with Italian seasonings
1 (8 ounce) carton plain, low-fat yogurt
¾ cup milk
⅓ cup grated Parmesan cheese
1 tablespoon all-purpose flour

1. Preheat oven to 375°.
2. Cook pasta according to package directions. Drain. In sprayed, 3-quart baking dish, combine pasta, vinaigrette dressing, beans, tomatoes, feta cheese, and olives.
3. In bowl, combine milk, yogurt, Parmesan cheese, and flour and mix well. Pour evenly over pasta mixture. Sprinkle with bread crumbs. (If you don't have breadcrumbs with Italian seasonings, just use regular breadcrumbs and add a few pinches of garlic powder, black pepper, and dried oregano, basil, and/or thyme.)
4. Bake, covered, for 25 minutes. Uncover and bake 10–15 minutes more until heated through and top is lightly browned. Let stand 5 minutes before serving.

SERVES 4–5.

269 Green Bean Casserole

¼ cup (½ stick) butter, divided
½ cup chopped onion
½ cup chopped celery
1 tablespoon flour
1 teaspoon sugar
½ teaspoon salt
½ teaspoon black pepper
1 cup cream
3 (15 ounce) cans French-style green beans, drained
¾ cup crushed corn flakes
1 cup shredded Swiss cheese

1. Preheat oven to 325°.
2. Melt half butter in skillet over medium-high heat and sauté onion and celery until tender, about 6–8 minutes. Stir in flour, sugar, salt, and pepper. Cook, stirring constantly, for 1 minute over medium heat.
3. Reduce heat to low, slowly add cream, and stir until smooth. Cook, stirring constantly, until mixture thickens, about 2 minutes; do not boil.
4. Fold in green beans. Spread into sprayed, 9 x 13-inch baking dish.
5. Melt remaining butter in saucepan and toss with corn flake crumbs. Mix in cheese, then sprinkle over top of casserole.
6. Bake until hot, about 25 minutes.

SERVES 8–10.

270 Flavorful Veggie Bake

For a tasty kick, heat some spicy chunky salsa to spoon over the top of each serving of this appetizing dish.

2 tablespoons plus ¼ cup (½ stick) butter, divided
1 red bell pepper, seeded, chopped
1 medium zucchini, halved, sliced
1 small onion, chopped
1 (10 ounce) can cream of celery soup
1 cup shredded Cheddar cheese
1 (16 ounce) package frozen broccoli, cauliflower, and carrots, thawed
1½ cups crushed round cheese crackers

1. Preheat oven to 375°.
2. Melt 2 tablespoons butter in large skillet over medium-high heat and cook bell pepper, zucchini, and onion just until tender, about 5 minutes. Stir in soup, cheese, and vegetables.
3. Spoon into sprayed, 9 x 13-inch baking dish.
4. Combine cheese crackers and ¼ cup (½ stick) melted butter in bowl; sprinkle over casserole. Bake until mixture is bubbly hot, about 30 minutes.

SERVES 8–10.

271 Zucchini Casserole

4 eggs
2 cups shredded Monterey Jack cheese
4 cups grated zucchini
1 (4 ounce) jar green chilies, chopped
1 (4 ounce) jar sliced pimentos, drained
1 onion, finely minced
1 teaspoon Creole seasoning
½ teaspoon black pepper
1½ cups seasoned croutons, crushed
1 (3 ounce) package grated Parmesan cheese

1. Preheat oven to 350°.
2. Beat eggs well in large bowl. Stir in Jack cheese, zucchini, green chilies, pimentos, onion, Creole seasoning, and pepper and mix well.
3. Pour into sprayed, 2-quart baking dish.
4. Bake for 35 minutes.
5. Mix crushed croutons and Parmesan cheese in bowl and set aside.
6. After 35 minutes of baking, remove casserole from oven and sprinkle crouton mixture on top. Return to oven and bake for additional 10 minutes.

SERVES 4–6.

 ## Who Knew?

To grate the zucchini for this recipe, simply use a cheese grater. Grate the zucchini after the cheese the easily clean the cheese off of the grater.

272 Zucchini Bake

3 cups grated zucchini
1½ cups shredded Cheddar cheese
4 eggs, beaten
¼ teaspoon garlic powder
½ teaspoon salt
½ teaspoon black pepper
2 cups cheese cracker crumbs

1. Preheat oven to 350°.
2. Combine zucchini, cheese, eggs, garlic powder, salt, and pepper and mix well. Spoon into sprayed, 2-quart baking dish.
3. Sprinkle cracker crumbs over top.
4. Bake for 35–40 minutes.

SERVES 4–6.

 Who Knew? Light Switch

To make this recipe lower in fat, use our Low-Fat Four-Cheese Blend (Light Switch #5) instead of the Cheddar cheese.

273 Vegetable Frittata

This makes an elegant dish that works just as well for brunch as it does dinner.

¼ cup light olive oil
1 onion, chopped
¾ cup chopped green bell pepper
¾ cup chopped red bell pepper
2 cups chopped zucchini
2 cups chopped yellow squash
¼ cup cream
1 (8 ounce) package cream cheese, softened
6 eggs
1 cup shredded mozzarella cheese
¾ teaspoon garlic powder
2 teaspoons marinade for chicken
½ teaspoon salt
½ teaspoon black pepper
1 cup seasoned breadcrumbs
3 tablespoons butter, melted

1. Preheat oven to 350°.
2. Heat oil in large skillet. Sauté onion, bell peppers, zucchini, and squash just until tender-crisp. Remove from heat and set aside to cool.
3. Beat cream and cream cheese in bowl until creamy. Add eggs and beat until mixed well, about 4 minutes.
4. Add mozzarella cheese, garlic powder, marinade for chicken, salt, and pepper; mix with spoon.
5. Fold in breadcrumbs, butter, and vegetables. Pour into sprayed, 9-inch springform pan.
6. Bake until light brown and set in center, about 55–60 minutes.
7. Set aside for 10 minutes before slicing. Be sure to use a thin, sharp knife to cut around the edge of the springform pan before you open the pan.

SERVES 6–8.

Slow-Cooker Dinners

Set it and forget it! Using a slow-cooker is an easy way to make sure you have dinner waiting for you when you come home—just prepare one of these simple dinners in the morning, turn on the Crock Pot, and it will be done by the time you get back. Though slow cookers have gotten somewhat of a bad name in recent years due to concerns over bacteria, most bacteria die at 140°, well below the lowest heat setting on your slow-cooker. So try out one of the delicious dinners on the following pages, and enjoy!

274 Chicken and Risotto

2½ cups water
1 (6 ounce) box long-grain and wild rice mix
1 (16 ounce) jar Alfredo sauce
12–15 boneless, skinless, chicken breast halves
1 cup frozen petite green peas, thawed

1. Pour water, rice, and seasoning packet into sprayed, 5-quart slow cooker; stir well.
2. Spoon in Alfredo sauce and mix well.
3. Place chicken in slow cooker and cover with green peas.
4. Cover and cook on low heat for 4–5 hours.

SERVES 4.

 Who Knew? Light Switch

To make this recipe lower in fat, substitute 1¾ cups of our Low-Fat Alfredo Sauce (Light Switch #9) for the jar of Alfredo sauce.

---

275 Slow Cooker Meat Medley

You'll love this slow cooker meal that's based on our "Party Chicken Breasts."

1 (2.5 ounce) jar dried beef
6 boneless, skinless chicken breast halves
6 slices bacon
2 (10 ounce) cans golden mushroom soup
⅓ cup water

1. Place dried beef slices in sprayed, 5-quart slow cooker.
2. Wrap slice of bacon around each chicken breast half and place on top of dried beef.
3. Combine soup and water in saucepan over medium-high heat for 3 minutes; mix well.
4. Pour soup mixture over chicken. Cover and cook on low heat for 7–8 hours.
5. Serve over rice.

SERVES 4–6.

276 Oregano Chicken

½ cup (1 stick) butter, melted
1 (1 ounce) packet Italian salad dressing
1 tablespoon lemon juice
4–5 boneless, skinless chicken breast halves
2 tablespoons dried oregano

1. Combine butter, salad dressing, and lemon juice in bowl and mix well.
2. Place chicken breasts in sprayed, large slow cooker. Spoon butter mixture over chicken.
3. Cover and cook on low heat for 5–6 hours.
4. One hour before serving, baste chicken with pan juices and sprinkle oregano over top.

SERVES 4–6.

 Who Knew? Light Switch

Try our Italian Salad Dressing Mix (Light Switch #11) for this recipe!

277 Sweet-and-Spicy Chicken

2 pounds chicken thighs
¾ cup chili sauce
¾ cup packed brown sugar
1 (1 ounce) packet onion soup mix
⅛ teaspoon cayenne pepper
¼ cup water

1. Arrange chicken pieces in bottom of sprayed, 5-quart slow cooker.
2. Combine chili sauce, brown sugar, onion soup mix, cayenne pepper, and water in bowl and spoon over chicken.
3. Cover and cook on low heat for 6–7 hours. Serve over rice.

SERVES 6.

 Who Knew?

Here's an important safety tip when using slow cookers: Make sure that the slow cooker is at least half to two-thirds full or the food may not absorb enough heat to kill all of the bacteria from the meat.

278 Broccoli-Cheese Chicken

4 boneless, skinless chicken breast halves
2 tablespoons butter, melted
1 (10 ounce) can broccoli-cheese soup
¼ cup milk
1 (10 ounce) package frozen broccoli spears

1. Dry chicken breasts with paper towels and place in sprayed, oval slow cooker.
2. Combine melted butter, soup, and milk in bowl and spoon over chicken. Cover and cook on low heat for 4–6 hours.
3. Remove cooker lid and place broccoli over chicken. Cover and cook for additional 1 hour. Serve over rice.

SERVES 4.

279 Chicken and Vegetables

4–5 boneless, skinless chicken breast halves
2 teaspoons seasoned salt
1 (16 ounce) package frozen broccoli, cauliflower, and carrots, thawed
1 (10 ounce) can cream of celery soup
1 (8 ounce) package shredded Cheddar–Monterey Jack cheese, divided

1. Cut chicken into strips, sprinkle with seasoned salt, and place in sprayed slow cooker.
2. Combine vegetables, celery soup, and half cheese in large bowl and mix well. Spoon over chicken breasts.
3. Cover and cook on low heat for 4–5 hours.
4. About 10 minutes before serving, sprinkle remaining cheese on top of casserole.

SERVES 4–6.

 Who Knew? Light Switch

To make this recipe lower in fat, substitute 1¼ cup of our Low-Fat Cream of Celery Soup Base (Light Switch #4) for the can of cream of celery soup, and 2 cups of our Low-Fat Four-Cheese Blend (Light Switch #5) for the package of Cheddar–Monterey Jack cheese.

280 Chicken for the Gods

1¾ cups flour
2 tablespoons dry mustard
6 boneless, skinless chicken breast halves
2 tablespoons vegetable or canola oil
1 (10 ounce) can chicken-and-rice soup
¼ cup water

1. Place flour and mustard in shallow bowl and dredge chicken to coat all sides.
2. Add oil to skillet and cook over medium-high heat. When hot, add chicken breasts and cook until browned, about 3 minutes on each side. Place all breasts in sprayed, 6-quart oval slow cooker.
3. Pour chicken-and-rice soup over chicken and add water.
4. Cover and cook on low heat for 6–7 hours.

SERVES 4–6.

281 Chicken Curry over Rice

3 large boneless, skinless chicken breast halves
½ cup chicken broth
1 (10 ounce) can cream of chicken soup
1 onion, coarsely chopped
1 red bell pepper, seeded, julienned
¼ cup golden raisins
1½ teaspoons curry powder
¼ teaspoon ground ginger

1. Cut chicken into thin strips and place in sprayed, 5- or 6-quart slow cooker.
2. Combine broth, soup, onion, bell pepper, raisins, curry powder, and ginger in bowl and mix well. Pour over chicken.
3. Cover and cook on low heat for 3–4 hours. Serve over rice.

SERVES 4.

 Who Knew? Light Switch

To make this recipe lower in fat, substitute 1¼ cup of our Low-Fat Cream of Chicken Soup Base (Light Switch #3) for the can of cream of chicken soup.

282 Chicken Delight

¾ cup white rice
1 (14 ounce) can chicken broth
1 (1 ounce) packet onion soup mix
1 red bell pepper, seeded, chopped
2 (10 ounce) cans cream of
   celery soup
¾ cup water
¾ cup white cooking wine
¼ teaspoon black pepper
4–6 boneless, skinless chicken
   breast halves
1 (3 ounce) package grated fresh
   Parmesan cheese

1. Combine rice, broth, soup mix, bell pepper, celery soup, water, wine, and black pepper in bowl and mix well. (Make sure to mix soup well with liquids.)
2. Place chicken breasts in sprayed, 6-quart oval slow cooker.
3. Pour rice-soup mixture over chicken breasts.
4. Cover and cook on low heat for 4–6 hours.
5. One hour before serving, sprinkle Parmesan cheese over chicken.

SERVES 4–6.

 ## Who Knew? Light Switch

To make this recipe lower in fat, substitute 2½ cups of our Low-Fat Cream of Celery Soup Base (Light Switch #4) for the cans of cream of celery soup.

---

283 Russian Chicken

1 (8 ounce) bottle Russian salad
   dressing
1 (16 ounce) can whole-berry
   cranberry sauce
½ cup water
1 (1 ounce) packet onion soup mix
4 chicken quarters, skinned, or 6
   boneless, skinless chicken breasts

1. Combine salad dressing, cranberry sauce, water, and soup mix in bowl. Stir well to get all lumps out of soup mix.
2. Place 4 chicken pieces in sprayed, 6-quart oval slow cooker. Spoon dressing-cranberry mixture over chicken.
3. Cover and cook on low heat for 4–5 hours. Serve sauce and chicken over rice.

SERVES 4–6.

284 Chicken Delicious

Dig that old bottle of sherry out of your cabinet for this dish that's so delicious we had to include the word in its name!

5–6 boneless, skinless chicken breast halves
1 tablespoon olive oil
1 (16 ounce) package frozen broccoli florets, thawed
1 red bell pepper, seeded, julienned
1 (16 ounce) jar alfredo sauce
3 tablespoons sherry

1. Place chicken breast halves in skillet with oil and cook over medium-high heat until brown on both sides, about 3 minutes per side. Then place in sprayed, 5- or 6-quart oval slow cooker.
2. Place broccoli florets on plate, remove much of stems, and discard.
3. Combine broccoli florets, bell pepper, cheese sauce, and sherry in bowl and mix well. Spoon over chicken breasts.
4. Cover and cook on low heat for 4–5 hours. Serve over noodles.

SERVES 4–6.

 ### Who Knew? Light Switch

To make this recipe lower in fat, substitute 1¾ cups of our Low-Fat Alfredo Sauce (Light Switch #9) for the jar of Alfredo sauce.

285 Slow Cooker Cordon Bleu

4 boneless, skinless chicken breast halves
4 slices cooked ham
4 slices Swiss cheese, softened
1 (10 ounce) can cream of chicken soup
¼ cup milk
4 cups noodles, cooked

1. Place chicken breasts on cutting board and pound until breast halves are thin.
2. Place ham and cheese slices on chicken breasts; roll and secure with toothpicks.
3. Arrange chicken rolls in sprayed, 4-quart slow cooker.
4. Pour chicken soup and milk into saucepan, heat just enough to mix well, and pour over chicken rolls.
5. Cover and cook on low heat for 4–5 hours.
6. Serve over noodles and cover with sauce from soup.

SERVES 4.

 ### Who Knew? Light Switch

To make this recipe lower in fat, substitute 1¼ cup of our Low-Fat Cream of Chicken Soup Base (Light Switch #3) for the can of cream of chicken soup.

286 Chicken 'n' Stuffing Supper

1 tablespoon olive oil
3 boneless, skinless chicken breast halves, chopped
1 (6 ounce) package stuffing mix
3 cups chopped chicken breasts
1 (16 ounce) package frozen whole green beans, thawed
2 (12 ounce) jars chicken gravy

1. Heat oil in skillet over medium-high heat. When hot, add chicken pieces and cook, stirring, until brown on all sides, about 8–10 minutes.
2. Prepare stuffing mix according to package directions and place in sprayed, oval slow cooker.
3. Follow with layer of chopped chicken, then layer of green beans. Pour chicken gravy over green beans.
4. Cover and cook on low heat for 3 hours 30 minutes–4 hours.

SERVES 4–6.

 Who Knew?

Take a bit of that olive oil and rub it into your cuticles! Olive oil will help them stay moisturized at a fraction of the cost of cuticle creams.

287 Chicken Marseilles

4–5 boneless, skinless chicken breast halves
2 tablespoons butter
1 (2 ounce) packet leek soup and dip mix
½ teaspoon dill weed
1 cup milk
½ cup water
4 cups brown rice, cooked
¾ cup sour cream

1. Place chicken breasts in sprayed, large slow cooker.
2. Combine butter, leek soup mix, dill weed, milk, and water in saucepan and heat just enough for butter to melt and ingredients to mix well. Pour over chicken.
3. Cover and cook on low heat for 3–5 hours.
4. When ready to serve, remove chicken breasts to platter with hot, cooked brown rice. Cover to keep warm.
5. Add sour cream to cooker liquid and stir well. Pour sauce over chicken and rice.

SERVES 4–5.

 Who Knew? Light Switch

To make this recipe lower in fat, use our Low-Fat Sour Cream Substitute (Light Switch #8).

288 Chicken Breast Deluxe

4 slices bacon
5–6 boneless, skinless chicken breast halves
1 cup sliced celery
1 cup sliced red bell pepper
1 (10 ounce) can cream of chicken soup
2 tablespoons white wine or cooking wine
6 slices Swiss cheese
2 tablespoons dried parsley

1. Cook bacon in large skillet; drain, crumble, and reserve drippings.
2. Place chicken in skillet with bacon drippings and lightly brown on both sides, about 3 minutes per side.
3. Transfer chicken to sprayed oval slow cooker and place celery and bell pepper over chicken.
4. In same skillet, combine soup and wine; stir. Spoon over vegetables and chicken.
5. Cover and cook on low heat for 3–4 hours.
6. Place 1 slice of cheese over each chicken breast and sprinkle parsley on top. Cook for additional 10 minutes.
7. Sprinkle with crumbled bacon.

SERVES 4–6.

 Who Knew? Light Switch

To make this recipe lower in fat, substitute 1¼ cup of our Low-Fat Cream of Chicken Soup Base (Light Switch #3) for the can of cream of chicken soup.

289 Southwestern Chicken Pot

6 boneless, skinless chicken breast halves
1 teaspoon ground cumin
1 teaspoon chili powder
¼ teaspoon salt
⅛ teaspoon black pepper
1 (10 ounce) can cream of chicken soup
1 (10 ounce) can fiesta nacho cheese soup
1 cup salsa

1. Sprinkle chicken breasts with cumin, chili powder, salt, and pepper and place in sprayed, oval slow cooker.
2. Combine soups and salsa in saucepan and heat just enough to mix; pour over chicken breasts.
3. Cover and cook on low heat for 6–7 hours. Serve over rice or with warmed flour tortillas.

SERVES 4–6.

 Who Knew? Light Switch

To make this recipe lower in fat, substitute 1¼ cup of our Low-Fat Cream of Chicken Soup Base (Light Switch #3) for the can of cream of chicken soup, and use our Super Healthy Salsa (Light Switch #7).

290 American Chicken

4 large boneless, skinless chicken breast halves
1 tablespoon poultry seasoning
4 slices American cheese
1 (10 ounce) can cream of celery soup
½ cup sour cream
1 (6 ounce) box chicken stuffing mix
½ cup (1 stick) butter, melted

1. Wash chicken breasts and dry with paper towels. Place in sprayed, oval slow cooker. Sprinkle each breast with poultry seasoning.
2. Place 1 slice of cheese over each chicken breast.
3. Combine celery soup and sour cream in bowl, mix well, and spoon over chicken and cheese.
4. Sprinkle chicken stuffing mix over top of chicken. Drizzle melted butter over stuffing mix.
5. Cover and cook on low heat for 5–6 hours.

SERVES 4.

 Who Knew? Light Switch

To make this recipe lower in fat, substitute 1¼ cup of our Low-Fat Cream of Celery Soup Base (Light Switch #4) for the can of cream of celery soup, and use our Low-Fat Sour Cream Substitute (Light Switch #8).

291 Honey-Baked Chicken

2 small fryer chickens, quartered
¼ teaspoon salt
½ cup (1 stick) butter, melted
⅔ cup honey
¼ cup Dijon-style mustard
1 teaspoon curry powder

1. Place chicken pieces in sprayed, large slow cooker, skin-side up, and sprinkle salt over chicken.
2. Combine butter, honey, mustard, and curry powder in bowl and mix well.
3. Pour butter-honey mixture over chicken quarters.
4. Cover and cook on low heat for 6–8 hours. Baste chicken once during cooking.

SERVES 6–8.

 Who Knew?

While you have the salt out, throw a handful down your garbage disposal, turn on a small stream of hot water, and run it for 10 seconds. The salt will get rid of any build-up in your drain and help your disposal run more smoothly.

292 White Wine Chicken

4–5 carrots
6 medium new (red) potatoes with peels, cleaned, quartered
4–5 boneless, skinless chicken breast halves
1 tablespoon poultry seasoning
2 (10 ounce) cans cream of chicken soup
⅓ cup white wine
¼ cup water

1. Cut carrots into ½-inch pieces. Place potatoes and carrots in sprayed slow cooker.
2. Sprinkle chicken breasts with poultry seasoning and place chicken over vegetables.
3. Heat soup, wine, and water in saucepan just to mix, and pour over chicken and vegetables.
4. Cover and cook on low heat for 5–6 hours.

SERVES 4–5.

 Who Knew? Light Switch

To make this recipe lower in fat, substitute 2½ cups of our Low-Fat Cream of Chicken Soup Base (Light Switch #3) for the cans of cream of chicken soup.

293 Tasty Chicken and Veggies

1 (2½–3 pound) whole chicken, quartered
1 (16 ounce) package baby carrots
4 yukon gold potatoes, peeled, sliced
3 ribs celery, sliced
1 onion, peeled, sliced
1 cup Italian salad dressing
⅔ cup chicken broth

1. Rinse, dry, and place chicken quarters in sprayed, 6-quart slow cooker with carrots, sliced potatoes, celery, and onion.
2. Pour salad dressing and chicken broth over chicken and vegetables.
3. Cover and cook on low heat for 6–8 hours.

SERVES 4–6.

Who Knew? Light Switch

To save money and make this dish even more delicious, try using our Italian Salad Dressing Mix (Light Switch #11)!

294 Lemon Chicken

1 (2½–3 pound) chicken, quartered
1 teaspoon salt
½ teaspoon black pepper
1 teaspoon dried oregano
2 teaspoons minced garlic
2 tablespoons butter
⅓ cup water
¼ cup lemon juice

1. Sprinkle chicken quarters with salt, pepper, and oregano. Rub garlic on chicken.
2. Place butter in skillet and melt over medium-high heat. Add chicken quarters and cook until browned, about 3 minutes per side. Transfer to sprayed, oval slow cooker.
3. Add water to skillet, scrape bottom, and pour over chicken.
4. Cover and cook on low heat for 6–7 hours.
5. Pour lemon juice over chicken, then cook for additional 1 hour.

SERVES 4–6.

295 Alfredo's Chicken

5 boneless, skinless chicken breast halves
1 (16 ounce) jar Alfredo sauce
1 (16 ounce) package frozen green peas, thawed
1½ cups shredded mozzarella cheese
4 cups noodles, cooked

1. Cut chicken into strips and place in sprayed slow cooker.
2. Combine Alfredo sauce, peas, and cheese in bowl and mix well. Spoon over chicken strips.
3. Cover and cook on low heat for 5–6 hours.
4. When ready to serve, spoon over noodles.

SERVES 4–5.

 Who Knew? Light Switch

To make this recipe lower in fat, substitute 1¾ cups of our Low-Fat Alfredo Sauce (Light Switch #9) for the jar of Alfredo sauce.

296 Imperial Chicken

1 (6 ounce) box long-grain and wild rice mix
2½ cups water
2 teaspoons minced garlic
1 (16 ounce) jar Alfredo sauce
6 boneless, skinless chicken breast halves
1 (16 ounce) box frozen French-style green beans, thawed
½ cup slivered almonds, toasted

1. Combine rice, seasoning packet, water, and garlic in sprayed, oval slow cooker and stir well.
2. Spoon in Alfredo sauce and mix well.
3. Place chicken breasts in slow cooker and cover with green beans.
4. Cover and cook on low heat for 3–5 hours. When ready to serve, sprinkle with slivered almonds.

SERVES 4–6.

 Who Knew? Light Switch

To make this recipe lower in fat, substitute 1¾ cups of our Low-Fat Alfredo Sauce (Light Switch #9) for the jar of Alfredo sauce.

297 Chicken Fajitas

2 pounds boneless, skinless chicken breast halves
1 onion, thinly sliced
1 red bell pepper, cored, seeded, julienned
1 teaspoon ground cumin
1½ teaspoons chili powder
1 tablespoon lime juice
½ cup chicken broth
8–10 flour tortillas
Lettuce and tomatoes, chopped, for garnish

1. Cut chicken into diagonal strips and place in sprayed slow cooker. Top with onion and bell pepper.
2. Combine cumin, chili powder, lime juice, and chicken broth in bowl and pour over chicken and vegetables.
3. Cover and cook on low heat for 5–7 hours.
4. Warm tortillas by placing in microwave one at a time for 10 seconds.
5. Place several slices of chicken mixture with sauce in center of each warm tortilla; fold.
6. Garnish with lettuce and tomatoes and serve with guacamole or sour cream, if desired.

SERVES 4–6.

298 Arroz Con Pollo

3 pounds chicken thighs
2 (15 ounce) cans Italian stewed tomatoes
1 (16 ounce) package frozen green peas, thawed
2 cups long-grain rice (uncooked)
1 teaspoon poultry seasoning
2 (14 ounce) cans chicken broth
1 heaping teaspoon minced garlic
1 teaspoon dried oregano
¾ cup water

1. Combine all ingredients in sprayed large slow cooker and stir well.
2. Cover and cook on low heat for 7–8 hours or on high heat for 3 hours 30 minutes–4 hours.

SERVES 6–8.

 Who Knew?

Don't have any poultry seasoning on hand? Use some sage and a blend of any of these spices: thyme, marjoram, savory, black pepper, and rosemary.

299 Chicken Coq au Vin

1 large fryer chicken, quartered, skinned
1 tablespoon vegetable or canola oil
10–12 small white onions, peeled
½ pound whole mushrooms
1 teaspoon minced garlic
½ teaspoon dried thyme leaves
10–12 small new (red) potatoes with peels
1 (10 ounce) can chicken broth
¼ teaspoon salt
⅛ teaspoon black pepper
1 cup Burgundy wine
6 bacon slices, cooked, crumbled

1. Place quarters in skillet with oil and cook over medium-high heat until brown on all sides, about 3 minutes per side.
2. Place white onions, whole mushrooms, garlic, and thyme in sprayed, oval slow cooker.
3. Add chicken quarters, potatoes, chicken broth, salt, and pepper.
4. Cover and cook on low heat for 8–10 hours or on high heat for 3–4 hours.
5. During last hour, turn heat to high, add wine, and continue cooking.
6. Sprinkle crumbled bacon over chicken before serving.

SERVES 4–6.

300 Sweet and Spicy Chicken

2 pounds chicken thighs
¾ cup chili sauce
¾ cup packed brown sugar
1 (1 ounce) packet dry onion soup mix
¼ teaspoon cayenne pepper
¼ cup water

1. Arrange chicken pieces in sprayed, 5-quart slow cooker.
2. Combine chili sauce, brown sugar, dry onion soup mix, cayenne pepper, and water in bowl and spoon over chicken.
3. Cover and cook on low heat for 6–7 hours. Serve over rice.

SERVES 4–6.

301 Maple-Plum Glazed Turkey Breast

1 cup red plum jam
1 cup maple syrup
1 teaspoon dry mustard
¼ cup lemon juice
1 (3–5 pound) boneless turkey breast

1. Combine jam, syrup, mustard, and lemon juice in saucepan. Bring to a boil, reduce heat, and simmer until slightly thick, about 20 minutes. Reserve 1 cup.
2. Place turkey breast in sprayed slow cooker and pour remaining glaze over turkey.
3. Cover and cook on low heat for 5–7 hours.
4. When ready to serve, slice turkey and serve with heated reserved glaze.

SERVES 6–8.

302 Turkey Bake

1½ pounds turkey tenderloins
1 tablespoon olive oil
1 (6 ounce) package Asian rice and vermicelli
1 (10 ounce) package frozen green peas, thawed
1 cup sliced celery
¼ cup (½ stick) butter, melted
1 (14 ounce) can chicken broth
1 cup water
1½ cups fresh broccoli florets

1. Cut tenderloins into strips. Cook in skillet with oil over medium heat, stirring occasionally, until turkey is cooked through.
2. Combine turkey strips, rice-vermicelli mix plus seasoning packet, peas, celery, butter, chicken broth, and water in sprayed, large slow cooker; mix well.
3. Cover and cook on low heat for 4–5 hours. Turn heat to high, add broccoli, and cook for additional 20 minutes.

SERVES 4–6.

303 Turkey Cassoulet

This version of the French classic is great for leftover turkey.

½ pound smoked turkey sausage
2 cups cooked, cubed turkey
3 carrots, sliced
1 onion, halved, sliced
1 (15 ounce) can navy beans
1 (15 ounce) can white lima beans
1 (8 ounce) can tomato sauce
1 teaspoon dried thyme
¼ teaspoon ground allspice

1. Cut turkey sausage into ½-inch pieces.
2. Combine all ingredients in sprayed slow cooker.
3. Cover and cook on low heat for 4–5 hours.

SERVES 6.

304 Sausage and Rice

1 pound turkey sausage
1 (6 ounce) box flavored rice mix
1 cup water
2 (14 ounce) cans chicken broth
2 cups sliced celery
1 red bell pepper, cored, seeded, julienned
1 (15 ounce) can cut green beans, drained
⅓ cup slivered almonds, toasted

1. Break up turkey sausage and brown in skillet.
2. Place turkey in sprayed, 4- or 5-quart slow cooker.
3. Add rice, water, chicken broth, celery, bell pepper, and green beans and stir to mix.
4. Cover and cook on low heat for 3–4 hours.
5. When ready to serve, sprinkle almonds over top.

SERVES 4.

 Who Knew?

To easily remove the skin of almonds, soak them in hot water for 15–20 minutes.

305 Turkey Loaf

2 pounds ground turkey
1 onion, very finely chopped
½ red bell pepper, very finely chopped
2 teaspoons minced garlic
½ cup chili sauce
2 large eggs, beaten
¾ cup Italian seasoned breadcrumbs
1 teaspoon salt
½ teaspoon black pepper

1. Make foil handles by cutting 3 strips of heavy foil; place in bottom of slow cooker in crisscross strips (resembling spokes on a wheel) up and over sides.
2. Combine all ingredients in large bowl and mix well.
3. Shape into round loaf and place on top of foil. Fold extended strips over turkey loaf.
4. Cover and cook on low heat for 5–6 hours. Lift loaf out by handles.

SERVES 4–6.

 ### Who Knew?

If your plastic storage containers smell like garlic, onions, or another potent food, wash them thoroughly, then stuff crumpled newspaper inside before snapping on the lids. In a few days, the smell will be gone.

306 Mac 'n' Cheese Supper

1½ pounds lean ground beef
1 teaspoon salt
2 (7 ounce) packages macaroni-and-cheese dinners
1 (15 ounce) can whole kernel corn, drained
1½ cups shredded Monterey Jack cheese

1. Place ground beef in large skillet and sprinkle with salt. Heat, stirring, over medium heat until brown, about 8–10 minutes. Drain.
2. Prepare macaroni and cheese in saucepan according to package directions.
3. Spoon beef, macaroni, and corn into sprayed, 5-quart slow cooker; mix well.
4. Cover and cook on low heat for 4–5 hours.
5. When ready to serve, sprinkle Jack cheese over top and leave in cooker until cheese melts.

SERVES 4–6.

 ### Who Knew? Light Switch

To make this recipe lower in fat, use our Low-Fat Four-Cheese Blend (Light Switch #5) instead of the Monterey Jack cheese.

307 Enchilada Soup

1 pound lean ground beef, browned, drained
1 (15 ounce) can Mexican stewed tomatoes
1 (15 ounce) can pinto beans with liquid
1 (15 ounce) can whole kernel corn with liquid
1 onion, chopped
2 (10 ounce) cans enchilada sauce
1 cup water
1 (8 ounce) package shredded four-cheese blend
20 tortilla chips, crushed (optional)

1. Combine beef, tomatoes, beans, corn, onion, enchilada sauce, and water in sprayed, 5- or 6-quart slow cooker and mix well.
2. Cover and cook on low heat for 6–8 hours or on high heat for 3–4 hours.
3. Stir in shredded cheese. If desired, top each serving with a few crushed tortilla chips.

SERVES 6.

 Who Knew? Light Switch

To make this recipe lower in fat, substitute 2 cups of our Low-Fat Four-Cheese Blend (Light Switch #5) instead of the package of four-cheese blend.

308 Mushroom Meat and Potatoes

4 medium potatoes, peeled, sliced
1¼ pounds lean ground beef, browned
1 onion, sliced
1 (10 ounce) can cream of mushroom soup
1 (10 ounce) can vegetable beef soup
¼ teaspoon salt
⅛ teaspoon black pepper

1. Layer potatoes, beef, onion, soups, salt, and pepper in sprayed, large slow cooker.
2. Cover and cook on low heat for 5–6 hours.

SERVES 4–6.

 Who Knew?

Freezing causes russet or Idaho potatoes to fall apart; make sure to use potatoes with red skin or waxy flesh for this dish!

309 Cheeseburger Supper

1 (5 ounce) box bacon and Cheddar
   scalloped potatoes
2¼ cups boiling water
⅓ cup milk
¼ cup (½ stick) butter, melted
1½ pounds lean ground beef
1 onion, coarsely chopped
1 tablespoon vegetable or canola oil
1 (15 ounce) can whole kernel corn
   with liquid
1 (8 ounce) package shredded
   Cheddar cheese

1. Place scalloped potatoes in sprayed slow cooker.
2. Pour boiling water, milk, and butter over potatoes.
3. Brown ground beef and onion with oil in skillet; drain and spoon over potatoes. Top with corn.
4. Cover and cook on low heat for 6–7 hours.
5. When ready to serve, sprinkle cheese over corn.

SERVES 4–6.

 Who Knew? Light Switch

To make this recipe lower in fat, substitute 2 cups of our Low-Fat Four-Cheese Blend (Light Switch #5) for the package of Cheddar cheese.

310 Jack's Favorite Meat Loaf

This cheesy meat loaf is a favorite of our oldest son, Jack.

2 pounds lean ground beef
2 eggs
½ cup chili sauce
1¼ cups seasoned breadcrumbs
1 (8 ounce) package shredded
   Monterey Jack cheese, divided

1. Make foil handles by cutting 3 strips of heavy foil; place in bottom of slow cooker in crisscross strips (resembling spokes on a wheel) up and over sides.
2. Combine beef, eggs, chili sauce, and breadcrumbs in bowl and mix well.
3. Shape half beef mixture into flat loaf and place in sprayed slow cooker.
4. Sprinkle half cheese over meat loaf and press into meat.
5. Form remaining meat mixture into same shape. Place over cheese as top layer and seal seams.
6. Cover and cook on low heat for 6–7 hours.
7. When ready to serve, sprinkle remaining cheese over loaf and leave in cooker until cheese melts.
8. Carefully remove loaf with handles and place on serving plate.

SERVES 4–6.

311 Southwest Spaghetti

1½ pounds lean ground beef
2½ teaspoons chili powder
1 (15 ounce) can tomato sauce
1 (7 ounce) package spaghetti
2⅓ cups water
1 heaping tablespoon beef seasoning
1 (8 ounce) package shredded Cheddar-Jack cheese

1. Cook ground beef in skillet over medium heat, stirring occasionally to break up, until no longer pink. Place in sprayed, 4- or 5-quart slow cooker.
2. Add chili powder, tomato sauce, spaghetti, water, and beef seasoning and mix well.
3. Cover and cook on low heat for 6–7 hours.
4. When ready to serve, cover with shredded Cheddar-Jack cheese.

SERVES 4–6.

 Who Knew? Light Switch

To make this recipe lower in fat, substitute 2 cups of our Low-Fat Four-Cheese Blend (Light Switch #5) for the package of Cheddar-Jack cheese.

312 Sloppy Joes

Make a giant batch of this delicious mix and freeze any extra for a quick sloppy joe dinner.

3 pounds ground beef
1 tablespoon minced garlic
1 large onion, finely chopped
2 ribs celery, chopped
¼ cup packed brown sugar
3½ tablespoons mustard
1 tablespoon chili powder
1½ cups ketchup
3 tablespoons Worcestershire sauce
16–18 hamburger buns

1. Cook beef, garlic, and onion in large skillet over medium heat, stirring occasionally, until beef is brown and onion is tender, about 12–16 minutes. Drain.
2. Combine celery, brown sugar, mustard, chili powder, ketchup, and Worcestershire sauce in sprayed, 5-quart slow cooker. Stir in meat mixture.
3. Cover and cook on low heat for 6–7 hours.

SERVES 9–12.

 Who Knew?

Mustard isn't only great at providing a tangy kick to dinners, it's also good at removing stains from plastic! Place a dab on and leave overnight, then wipe clean.

313 Sweet-and-Sour Slow-Cooker Meatballs

These delicious meatballs are great served over rice or noodles. To make them for an appetizer, just insert toothpicks into each meatball for easy pickup.

1 (16 ounce) can whole-berry
   cranberry sauce
1 cup ketchup
⅔ cup packed brown sugar
½ cup beef broth
1 (18 ounce) package frozen
   meatballs, thawed

1. Combine cranberry sauce, ketchup, brown sugar, and broth in sprayed, large slow cooker.
2. Turn heat to high and boil for 30 minutes–1 hour. Place thawed meatballs in sauce.
3. Cover and cook on low heat for 2 hours.
4. Remove meatballs to serving dish using slotted spoon.

SERVES 4–6.

 Who Knew? Light Switch

To make this recipe lower in fat, substitute our Low-Fat Meatballs (Light Switch #12) for the package of frozen meatballs.

---

314 Beef Tips Over Pasta

2–2½ pounds lean beef stew meat
2 cups frozen, small whole onions,
   thawed
1 green bell pepper, seeded
1 (6 ounce) jar pitted Greek olives or
   ripe olives
½ cup sun-dried tomatoes in oil,
   drained, chopped
1 (28 ounce) jar spaghetti sauce
1 (8 ounce) package pasta twirls,
   cooked

1. Place beef and onions in sprayed, 4- or 5-quart slow cooker.
2. Cut bell pepper in 1-inch cubes and add to slow cooker.
3. Add olives and tomatoes and pour marinara sauce over top.
4. Cover and cook on low heat for 8–10 hours.
5. Prepare pasta twirls according to package directions. Serve beef and marinara sauce mixture over pasta.

SERVES 4–6.

315 Pot Roast with Veggies

1 (2 pound) chuck roast
2 tablespoons olive oil, divided
4–5 medium potatoes, peeled,
     quartered
4 large carrots, quartered
1 onion, quartered
1 (14 ounce) can beef broth, divided
2 tablespoons cornstarch

1. Trim fat from roast and cut roast into 2 equal pieces.
2. Place each piece in skillet with 1 tablespoon oil and brown on all sides over medium-high heat, about 3–5 minutes per side.
3. Place potatoes, carrots, and onion in sprayed, 4- or 5-quart slow cooker; mix well.
4. Place browned roast halves over vegetables.
5. Pour 1½ cups broth over beef and vegetables. Save remaining broth and refrigerate.
6. Cover and cook on low heat for 8–9 hours.
7. About 5 minutes before serving, remove beef and vegetables with slotted spoon and place on serving platter. Cover to keep warm.
8. Pour liquid from slow cooker into medium saucepan.
9. Blend remaining ½ cup broth and cornstarch in bowl until smooth; add to liquid in saucepan. Boil for 1 minute and stir constantly to make gravy.
10. Serve gravy with roast and veggies; season with salt and pepper to taste, if desired.

SERVES 4–6.

316 Sweet-and-Sour Beef

1 (2 pound) boneless chuck roast
½ cup flour
1 teaspoon salt
½ teaspoon black pepper
1 tablespoon vegetable or canola oil
1 onion, sliced
½ cup chili sauce
¾ cup packed brown sugar
¼ cup red wine vinegar
1 tablespoon Worcestershire sauce
1 cup water
1 (16 ounce) package baby carrots

1. Cut beef into 1-inch cubes and dredge in flour, salt, and pepper.
2. Heat oil in large skillet over medium-high heat. Add beef and cook, stirring, until brown on all sides, about 10–12 minutes. Place in sprayed slow cooker.
3. Add remaining ingredients, except carrots.
4. Cover and cook on low heat for 7–8 hours.
5. Add carrots and cook for additional 1 hour 30 minutes.

SERVES 4–6.

317 Savory Steak

Make some mashed potatoes to serve with this saucy steak for a perfect meal.

1½ **pounds lean round steak**
1 **teaspoon black pepper**
1 **onion, halved, sliced**
2 **(10 ounce) cans golden mushroom soup**
1½ **cups hot, chunky salsa**

1. Trim fat from steak and cut into serving-size pieces.
2. Sprinkle with pepper and place in sprayed, 5- or 6-quart slow cooker.
3. Place onion slices on top of steak.
4. Combine mushroom soup and salsa in bowl and mix well. Spoon over steak and onions.
5. Cover and cook on low heat for 7–8 hours.

SERVES 4–6.

 ## Who Knew? Light Switch

To save money and make this recipe even more delicious, use our Super Healthy Salsa (Light Switch #7) with a pinch of cayenne pepper added.

318 Mushroom Round Steak

1½–2 **pounds round steak**
1 **(1 ounce) packet onion soup mix**
½ **cup dry red wine**
1 **(8 ounce) carton fresh mushrooms, sliced**
1 **(10 ounce) can French onion soup**
½ **cup water**

1. Cut round steak in serving-size pieces and place in sprayed, oval slow cooker.
2. Combine soup mix, red wine, mushrooms, French onion soup, and water in bowl. Spoon over steak pieces.
3. Cover and cook on low heat for 7–8 hours.

SERVES 4–6.

319 Beefy Onion Supper

1–1½ pounds round steak
1 medium onion
2 cups fresh sliced mushrooms
1 (10 ounce) can French onion soup
1 (6 ounce) package herb stuffing mix
½ cup (1 stick) butter, melted

1. Cut beef into 5–6 serving-size pieces.
2. Slice onion and separate into rings.
3. Place steak pieces in sprayed, oval slow cooker and top with onions and mushrooms.
4. Pour soup over ingredients in cooker.
5. Cover and cook on low heat for 7–9 hours.
6. Just before serving, combine stuffing mix with seasoning packet, butter, and ½ cup liquid from cooker and toss to mix.
7. Place stuffing mixture on top of steak and increase heat to high.
8. Cover and cook until stuffing is fluffy, about 15 minutes.

SERVES 4–6.

320 Classic Slow-Cooker Stroganoff

2 pounds round steak
¾ cup flour, divided
½ teaspoon mustard
¼ teaspoon salt
⅛ teaspoon black pepper
2 medium onions, thinly sliced
½ pound fresh mushrooms, sliced
1 (10 ounce) can beef broth
¼ cup dry white wine or cooking wine
1 (8 ounce) carton sour cream

1. Trim excess fat from steak and cut into 3-inch strips about ½-inch wide.
2. Combine ½ cup flour, mustard, salt, and pepper in bowl and toss with steak strips.
3. Place strips in sprayed, oval slow cooker.
4. Cover with onions and mushrooms. Add beef broth and wine. Cover and cook on low heat for 8–10 hours.
5. Just before serving, combine sour cream and remaining ¼ cup flour in bowl.
6. Stir into cooker and cook until stroganoff thickens slightly, about 10–15 minutes.

SERVES 4–6.

321 Swiss Steak

1–1½ pounds boneless, round steak
½ teaspoon seasoned salt
½ teaspoon pepper
8–10 medium new (red) potatoes with peels, halved
1 cup baby carrots
1 onion, sliced
1 (15 ounce) can stewed tomatoes
1 (12 ounce) jar beef gravy

1. Cut steak into 6–8 serving-size pieces. Sprinkle with seasoned salt and pepper, then cook, stirring, over medium heat in skillet until browned on all sides, about 8–10 minutes.
2. Layer steak pieces, potatoes, carrots, and onion in sprayed slow cooker.
3. Combine tomatoes and beef gravy in bowl and spoon over vegetables.
4. Cover and cook on low heat for 7–8 hours.

SERVES 6–8.

 Who Knew?

Wine corks (the natural kind, not plastic) contain a chemical that, when heated, will help tenderize beef. Save one to throw into your slow cooker while making this or another beef dish!

322 Spicy Swiss Steak

1½ pounds boneless round steak
1 tablespoon olive oil
½ pound spicy bratwurst
2 small onions
2 tablespoons quick-cooking tapioca
1 teaspoon dried thyme
¼ teaspoon salt
⅛ teaspoon black pepper
2 (15 ounce) cans Mexican stewed tomatoes

1. Trim fat from steak and cut into 4 serving-size pieces.
2. Heat oil in skillet over medium-high heat. When hot, add steak and bratwurst. Cook, stirring occasionally, until browned on all sides, about 8–10 minutes. Drain and place in sprayed, 4- or 5-quart slow cooker.
3. Slice onions and separate into rings.
4. Cover meat with onions and sprinkle with tapioca, thyme, salt, and pepper. Pour stewed tomatoes over onion and seasonings.
5. Cover and cook on low heat for 5–8 hours.
6. Serve over noodles.

SERVES 4–6.

 Who Knew?

Don't spend money on store-bought breadcrumbs. Set aside a special jar and pour in the crumbs from the bottom of cracker boxes or low-sugar cereal boxes. Also add crumbs from dried-up garlic bread and a few dried herbs and you'll have seasoned bread crumbs!

323 Beef Roulades

1½ pounds beef flank steak
5 slices bacon
¾ cup finely chopped onion
1 (4 ounce) can mushroom pieces
1 tablespoon Worcestershire sauce
⅓ cup Italian-seasoned breadcrumbs
1 (12 ounce) jar beef gravy

1. Cut steak into 4–6 serving-size pieces.
2. Cut bacon into small pieces and combine with onion, mushrooms, Worcestershire sauce, and breadcrumbs in bowl. Place about ½ cup onion mixture on each piece of steak.
3. Roll each steak and secure ends with toothpicks. Dry steak rolls with paper towels.
4. Place steak rolls in skillet over medium-high heat and brown on all sides, about 6–10 minutes. Transfer to sprayed slow cooker.
5. Pour gravy evenly over steaks to thoroughly moisten. Cover and cook on low heat for 7–9 hours.
6. Serve over noodles, rice, or mashed potatoes.

SERVES 4–6.

 Who Knew? Light Switch

To make this recipe lower in fat, substitute 1¼ cup of our Low-Fat Cream of Chicken Soup Base (Light Switch #3) for the can of cream of chicken soup.

---

324 Herb-Crusted Beef Roast

1 (2–3 pound) rump roast
¼ teaspoon salt
⅛ teaspoon black pepper
¼ cup chopped fresh parsley
¼ cup chopped fresh oregano leaves
½ teaspoon dried rosemary leaves
1 teaspoon minced garlic
1 tablespoon oil
6 slices thick-cut bacon

1. Rub roast with salt and pepper.
2. Combine parsley, oregano, rosemary, garlic, and oil in small bowl; press mixture on top and sides of roast.
3. Place roast in sprayed slow cooker. Place bacon over top of roast and tuck ends under bottom.
4. Cover and cook on low heat for 6–8 hours.

SERVES 4–6.

325 Robust Beef Roast

1 (4 pound) boneless rump roast
½ cup flour, divided
1 (1 ounce) packet brown gravy mix
1 (1 ounce) packet beefy onion soup mix
2 cups water

1. Place roast in sprayed, 5- or 6-quart slow cooker. If needed, cut roast in half to fit into cooker.
2. Rub half of flour over roast.
3. Combine remaining flour, gravy mix, and soup mix in small bowl. Gradually add water, stirring until they mix well. Pour over roast.
4. Cover and cook on low heat until roast is cooked through, about 7–8 hours.

SERVES 6–8.

 Who Knew?

When storing a cooked roast in the fridge, place it back into its own juices whenever possible to make sure it doesn't get dehydrated.

326 O'Brian's Hash

This recipe from a dear friend of Irish and Mexican decent uses cooked beef roast. If you don't have any leftovers on hand, simply cook beef cubes in a skillet with 1 tablespoon olive oil over medium heat until cooked through.

3 cups cubed, cooked rump roast
1 (28 ounce) package frozen hash browns with onions and peppers, thawed
1 tablespoon vegetable or canola oil
1 (16 ounce) jar salsa
1 tablespoon beef bouillon
1 cup shredded Cheddar-Jack cheese

1. Place cubed beef in sprayed, large slow cooker.
2. Brown potatoes with oil in large skillet and transfer to slow cooker. Stir in salsa and beef bouillon.
3. Cover and cook on high heat for 4–5 hours.
4. When ready to serve, sprinkle cheese over hash.

SERVES 8.

 Who Knew? Light Switch

To make this recipe lower in fat, substitute 2 cups of our Super Healthy Salsa (Light Switch #7) for the jar of salsa, and our Low-Fat Four-Cheese Blend (Light Switch #5) for the Cheddar-Jack cheese.

327 Old-Time Pot Roast

1 (2–2½ pound) boneless rump roast
5 medium potatoes, peeled, quartered
1 (16 ounce) package peeled baby carrots
2 medium onions, quartered
1 (10 ounce) can golden mushroom soup
½ teaspoon dried basil
½ teaspoon salt

1. Brown roast on all sides in skillet.
2. Place potatoes, carrots, and onions in sprayed, 4- or 5-quart slow cooker.
3. Place browned roast on top of vegetables.
4. Combine soup, basil, and salt in bowl and pour mixture over meat and vegetables.
5. Cover and cook on low heat for 9–11 hours.
6. To serve, transfer roast and vegetables to serving plate. Stir juices remaining in slow cooker and spoon over roast and vegetables.

SERVES 8.

 Who Knew?

Here's a simple tip to make this dish even more tender. When your roast is ready to slice, make sure to cut it against the grain (look for slight lines on the surface). Meat cut across the grain will be more tender.

328 Smoked Brisket

1 (4–6 pound) trimmed brisket
1 (4 ounce) bottle liquid smoke
½ tablespoon garlic salt
1 teaspoon celery salt
    Worcestershire sauce
1 onion, chopped
1 (6 ounce) bottle barbecue sauce

1. Place brisket in large shallow dish and pour liquid smoke over top.
2. Sprinkle with garlic salt and celery salt. Cover and refrigerate overnight.
3. Before cooking, drain liquid smoke and douse brisket with Worcestershire sauce.
4. Place chopped onion in slow cooker and place brisket on top of onion.
5. Cover and cook on low heat for 7–8 hours.
6. Pour barbecue sauce over brisket and cook for additional 1 hour.

SERVES 6–8.

329 Shredded Brisket Sandwiches

2 teaspoons onion powder
1 teaspoon minced garlic
1 tablespoon liquid smoke
1 (3–4 pound) beef brisket
⅓ cup water
1 (16 ounce) bottle barbecue sauce
6–8 kaiser rolls or hamburger buns

1. Combine onion powder, minced garlic, and liquid smoke in bowl and rub over brisket.
2. Place brisket in sprayed, large slow cooker. Add water to cooker.
3. Cover and cook on low heat until brisket is tender, about 6–8 hours.
4. Remove brisket, cool, and reserve ½ cup cooking juices.
5. Shred brisket with 2 forks and place in large saucepan. Add ½ cup cooking juices and barbecue sauce and heat thoroughly.
6. Make sandwiches with kaiser rolls or hamburger buns.

SERVES 6–8.

 Who Knew?

If you're reheating this brisket in the microwave, place it in a casserole dish between lettuce leaves. The lettuce provides just the right amount of moisture to keep the beef from drying out.

330 Beef Ribs and Gravy

Ribs take awhile to tenderize in a slow cooker (9–11 hours), but the results are delicious and the recipe is simple!

4 pounds beef short ribs
1 onion, sliced
1 teaspoon pepper
1 (12 ounce) jar beef gravy
1 (1 ounce) packet beef gravy mix

1. Place beef ribs in sprayed, 6-quart slow cooker. Cover with onion and sprinkle with pepper.
2. Combine beef gravy and dry gravy mix in small bowl and pour over ribs and onion.
3. Cover and cook on low heat for 9–11 hours.

SERVES 4–6.

331 Terrific Pork Tenderloin

2–3 (1 pound) pork tenderloins
1 teaspoon seasoned salt
1 teaspoon garlic powder
1 (4 ounce) can chopped green chilies
2 (10 ounce) cans cream of celery soup

1. Place tenderloins in sprayed, oval slow cooker. Sprinkle with seasoned salt and garlic powder.
2. Combine green chilies and celery soup in bowl. Spoon over tenderloins, covering completely.
3. Cover and cook on low heat for 8 hours. Serve over rice.

SERVES 4–5.

 Who Knew? Light Switch

To make this recipe lower in fat, substitute 2½ cups of our Low-Fat Cream of Celery Soup Base (Light Switch #4) for the cans of cream of celery soup.

332 Spinach-Stuffed Pork Roast

1 (2–2½ pound) pork tenderloin
1 (10 ounce) package frozen chopped spinach, thawed
⅓ cup seasoned breadcrumbs
⅓ cup grated Parmesan cheese
2 tablespoons vegetable or canola oil
½ teaspoon seasoned salt

1. Cut tenderloin horizontally lengthwise about ½ inch from top to within ¾ inch of opposite end; open flat.
2. Turn pork to cut other side, from inside edge to outer edge, and open flat. If one side is thicker than other side, cover with plastic wrap and pound until both sides are ¾-inch thick.
3. Squeeze spinach between paper towels to completely remove excess moisture.
4. Combine spinach, breadcrumbs, and cheese in bowl and mix well.
5. Spread mixture on inside surfaces of pork and press down. Roll pork and tie with kitchen twine.
6. Heat oil in large skillet over medium-high heat; cook pork until browned on all sides, about 3 minutes per side.
7. Place in sprayed oval slow cooker and sprinkle with salt. Cover and cook on low heat for 6–8 hours.

SERVES 4–6.

 Who Knew?

If you don't have kitchen twine, the perfect substitute is dental floss!

333 Roasted Red Pepper Tenderloin

2 tablespoon olive oil
2 pounds pork tenderloin
1 (1 ounce) packet ranch dressing mix
1 cup roasted red bell peppers, rinsed, chopped
½ cup water
1 (8 ounce) carton sour cream

1. Heat oil in skillet over medium-high heat. Add tenderloins and brown on all sides, about 3–5 minutes per side. Place in sprayed, 6-quart oval slow cooker.
2. Combine ranch dressing mix, red bell peppers, and water in bowl and spoon over tenderloins.
3. Cover and cook on low heat for 4–5 hours.
4. Remove tenderloins from slow cooker and reserve sauce.
5. Stir sour cream into remaining sauce. Serve over tenderloin slices.

SERVES 4–6.

 Who Knew? Light Switch

To make this recipe lower in fat, substitute 1 cup of our Low-Fat Sour Cream Substitute (Light Switch #8) for the carton of sour cream.

334 Western Pork Supper

6 (¾ inch thick) pork loin chops
1 (15 ounce) can pinto beans with jalapenos
1½ cups salsa
1 (16 ounce) package frozen seasoned corn with black beans, tomatoes, bell peppers, and onions, thawed
1 (4 ounce) can sliced ripe olives
1½–2 cups instant brown rice
2 tablespoons butter, melted

1. Arrange pork chops in sprayed, oval slow cooker and cover with chili beans and salsa.
2. Cover and cook on low heat for 5 hours or on high heat for 2 hours 30 minutes. Increase heat to high (if cooking on low) and stir in seasoned corn and olives. Cover and cook for additional 30 minutes.
3. Cook brown rice according to package directions and stir in melted butter.
4. Place on serving platter. Spoon pork chops and vegetables over rice.

SERVES 6–8.

 Who Knew? Light Switch

To make this recipe even healthier, use our Super Healthy Salsa (Light Switch #7) instead of jarred salsa.

335 Tender Pork Loin

It might be hard to find a small (3–4 pound) pork loin, but they are commonly available in larger (8–9 pound) sizes. Because pork loin is such a good cut of pork—no bones, no fat—you can buy a whole loin, cut it into 2 or 3 pieces, and freeze the pieces not used for later.

1 (3–4 pound) pork loin
2 teaspoons minced garlic
½ teaspoon rosemary
1 teaspoon sage
1½ teaspoons marjoram
¼ cup water

1. Place pork loin in sprayed slow cooker, rub with minced garlic, and sprinkle with rosemary, sage, and marjoram. Add water to slow cooker.
2. Cover and cook on low heat for 4–5 hours.

SERVES 6–8.

 Who Knew?

Want to wake up the flavor of dried herbs before using them in a recipe? Just toast them in a pan for a minute or two, and their flavors will be revived.

336 Good-Time Chops, Tators, and Peas

1 (10 ounce) can cream of mushroom soup
1 (4 ounce) can sliced mushrooms
¼ cup water
5–6 boneless pork chops
1 tablespoon lemon pepper
2 (15 ounce) cans whole new potatoes, drained
1 (10 ounce) package frozen green peas, thawed

1. Spoon soup and mushrooms into sprayed slow cooker and stir in water to thin soup slightly.
2. Sprinkle each pork chop with lemon pepper and place in slow cooker.
3. Cover and cook on low heat for 6–8 hours.
4. Remove lid and place potatoes and peas around pork chops. Turn heat to high and cook for additional 1 hour 30 minutes.

SERVES 5.

337 Ranch Pork Chops

6 (¾ inch thick) bone-in pork chops
1 (1 ounce) packet ranch dressing mix
½ teaspoon pepper
2 pounds new (red) potatoes, cleaned, quartered
1 (10 ounce) can French onion soup
½ cup water

1. Place pork chops in sprayed, 6-quart oval slow cooker.
2. Sprinkle pork chops with ranch dressing mix and pepper.
3. Place potatoes around pork chops and pour French onion soup and water around potatoes and chops.
4. Cover and cook on low heat for 4–5 hours.

SERVES 4–6.

338 Pork Chops and Gravy

6 (½-inch thick) pork chops
1 tablespoon salt
1 tablespoon black pepper
1 tablespoon olive oil
8–10 new (red) potatoes with peels, quartered
1 (16 ounce) package baby carrots
2 (10 ounce) cans cream of mushroom soup with roasted garlic
½ cup water

1. Sprinkle pork chops with salt and pepper.
2. Heat oil over medium-high heat in skillet. When hot, add pork chops and brown on each side, about 3–5 minutes per side.
3. Place pork chops in 5- or 6-quart slow cooker. Place potatoes and carrots around pork chops.
4. Heat mushroom soup with water in saucepan and pour over chops and vegetables.
5. Cover and cook on low heat for 6–7 hours.

SERVES 6.

 Who Knew?

Whether you're pan frying or deep-frying, it's important to heat the oil above 350° before tossing in your ingredients. Otherwise, your food can absorb too much oil and become heavy and greasy. A good test is to toss a hunk of bread in the oil, and if it browns in 10 seconds or less, you're ready to cook!

339 Honey-Mustard Pork Chops

1 (10 ounce) can golden mushroom soup
1/3 cup white wine
1/4 cup honey mustard
1 teaspoon minced garlic
1 teaspoon salt
4–5 (3/4 inch thick) pork chops
1/8 teaspoon black pepper

1. Combine soup, wine, honey mustard, minced garlic, and salt in large bowl and mix well.
2. Sprinkle pork chops with pepper and place in sprayed, 5-quart slow cooker. Spoon soup mixture over chops.
3. Cover and cook on low heat for 5–6 hours.
4. When ready to serve, lift pork chops out of sauce and place on serving plate. Stir sauce to mix well and serve with chops.

SERVES 4–5.

 Who Knew?

For a "meat-and-potatoes meal," just slice 3 potatoes and place in slow cooker before adding pork chops.

340 Easy Slow Cooker Pork Chops

1 3/4 cups flour
2 tablespoons dry mustard
8 boneless, thick pork chops
1 tablespoon vegetable or canola oil
1 (10 ounce) can chicken-and-rice soup
1/4 cup water

1. Place flour and mustard in shallow bowl. Dredge pork chops in flour-mustard mixture.
2. Heat oil over medium-high heat in skillet. When hot, add pork chops and brown on each side, about 3–5 minutes per side. Place all chops in sprayed, 6-quart oval slow cooker.
3. Pour soup over pork and add water. Cover and cook on low heat for 6–8 hours.

SERVES 6–8.

341 Country Pork Chops

7–8 new (red) potatoes with peels, sliced
2 onions, sliced
1 (10 ounce) can cream of celery soup
1/3 cup chicken broth
3 tablespoons Dijon-style mustard
1 (4 ounce) can sliced mushrooms, drained
1 teaspoon minced garlic
3/4 teaspoon dried basil
8 boneless pork chops
1/4 teaspoon salt
1/8 teaspoon black pepper
1 tablespoon vegetable or canola oil

1. Place potatoes and onions in sprayed, large slow cooker.
2. Combine soup, broth, mustard, mushrooms, garlic, and basil in bowl; mix well and pour over potatoes and onions. Stir to coat vegetables.
3. Sprinkle pork chops with salt and pepper. Heat oil over medium-high heat in skillet. When hot, add pork chops and brown on each side, about 3–5 minutes per side.
4. Place chops over vegetables.
5. Cover and cook on low heat for 6–7 hours.

SERVES 6–8.

 Who Knew? Light Switch

To make this recipe lower in fat, substitute 1 1/4 cup of our Low-Fat Cream of Celery Soup Base (Light Switch #4) for the can of cream of celery soup.

---

342 Deconstructed Pork Chop Pizza

This recipe came about after one of our kids requested pizza on slow-cooker night. The pizza sauce gives it the taste of pizza without the shape!

6 (1 inch thick) boneless pork chops
1/4 teaspoon salt
1/8 teaspoon black pepper
1 medium onion, finely chopped
1 green bell pepper, seeded, finely chopped
1 (8 ounce) jar pizza sauce
1 (10 ounce) box plain couscous
2 tablespoons butter
1 cup shredded mozzarella cheese

1. Trim fat from pork chops and sprinkle with salt and pepper. Place in skillet and cook over medium-high heat until browned, about 3 minutes per side. Transfer chops to sprayed, oval slow cooker.
2. Spoon onion and bell pepper over chops and pour pizza sauce over top.
3. Cover and cook on low heat for 4–6 hours.
4. Cook couscous according to package directions, except add 2 tablespoons butter instead of 1 tablespoon.
5. Place couscous on serving platter. Spoon chops and sauce over couscous and sprinkle cheese over chops.

SERVES 4–6.

343 Cranberry-Glazed Pork

2 tablespoons vegetable or
canola oil
1 (3–4 pound) pork shoulder roast
1 (16 ounce) package frozen stew
vegetables, thawed
1 (16 ounce) can whole
cranberry sauce
1 (4 ounce) can chopped
green chilies
¾ cup chili sauce
1 teaspoon Dijon-style mustard
2 tablespoons brown sugar

1. Heat oil in large skillet over medium heat. Add roast
and brown on all sides, about 5–8 minutes per side.
2. Place roast in sprayed slow cooker and top with stew
vegetables.
3. Combine cranberry sauce, green chilies, chili sauce,
mustard, and brown sugar in saucepan; heat just
enough to blend ingredients. Pour mixture over roast and
vegetables.
4. Cover and cook on low heat for 8–9 hours or on high
heat for 4 hours–4 hours 30 minutes. Transfer roast and
vegetables to serving platter and keep warm.
5. Strain cooking juices and skim off fat. Bring juices to
a boil in medium saucepan; reduce heat and simmer until
mixture thickens, about 25 minutes.
6. Serve sauce with sliced pork roast.

SERVES 6–8.

344 Barbecue Pork Roast

Recycle any leftovers for tasty next-day pork sandwiches. Just shred the pork and place in slow cooker until
heated through and it's ready for buns!

1 onion, thinly sliced
2 tablespoons flour
1 (2–3 pound) pork shoulder roast
1 (8 ounce) bottle barbecue sauce
1 tablespoon chili powder
1 teaspoon ground cumin

1. Separate onion slices into rings and place in sprayed,
4- or 5-quart slow cooker. Sprinkle flour over onions.
2. If necessary, cut roast to fit cooker; place roast over
onions.
3. Combine barbecue sauce, chili powder, and cumin in
bowl and pour over roast.
4. Cover and cook on low heat for 8–10 hours.
5. Remove roast from cooker and slice. Serve remaining
sauce over sliced roast.

SERVES 6–8.

345 Pork and Cabbage Supper

1 (16 ounce) package baby carrots
1 cup chicken broth
1 cup water
1 (1 ounce) packet golden onion soup mix
½ tablespoon black pepper
1 (3–4 pound) pork shoulder roast
1 medium head cabbage

1. Place carrots in sprayed, 5-quart slow cooker.
2. Add chicken broth and water. Sprinkle dry soup mix and pepper over carrots.
3. If roast is too large to fit in cooker, cut it in half. Place over carrot mixture.
4. Cover and cook on low heat for 6–7 hours.
5. Cut cabbage in small-size chunks and place over roast. Cover and cook until cabbage cooks through, about 1–2 hours.

SERVES 6–8.

 ### Who Knew? Light Switch

Try using our Healthy Chicken Broth (Light Switch #1) in this recipe!

346 Home-Style Ribs

4–6 pounds boneless pork spareribs
1 tablespoon salt
1 tablespoon black pepper
½ cup water
1 cup chili sauce
1 cup packed brown sugar
2 tablespoons vinegar
2 tablespoons Worcestershire sauce

1. Sprinkle ribs liberally with salt and pepper. Place ribs in sprayed slow cooker.
2. Combine water, chili sauce, brown sugar, vinegar, and Worcestershire sauce in bowl. Pour over ribs.
3. Cover and cook on low heat for 5–6 hours.

SERVES 6–8.

Who Knew?

Wet some washcloths and place them in bowls next to each plate for easy cleaning of messy fingers!

347 Zesty Ham Supper

1 (28 ounce) package frozen hash-
  brown potatoes with onions and
  peppers, thawed
3 cups cooked, diced ham
1 (10 ounce) box frozen green peas,
  thawed
2 (10 ounce) cans fiesta nacho
  cheese soup
1 cup milk
1 bunch fresh scallions, chopped

1. Place potatoes, ham, and peas in sprayed, 6-quart slow cooker; stir to mix.
2. Combine soup and milk in bowl and mix well. Pour over potato mixture and mix well.
3. Cover and cook on low heat for 6–8 hours.
4. Sprinkle scallions over top when ready to serve.

SERVES 6–8.

348 Creamy Potatoes and Ham

5 medium potatoes, peeled, sliced,
  divided
1 teaspoon seasoned salt, divided
1 onion, chopped, divided
2 cups cooked, cubed ham, divided
1 (8 ounce) package Velveeta cheese,
  cubed, divided
1 (10 ounce) can broccoli cheese
  soup
¼ cup milk

1. Layer half each of potatoes, seasoned salt, onion, ham, and cheese in slow cooker; repeat second layer.
2. Combine soup and milk in bowl, stirring until fairly smooth, and pour over potato mixture.
3. Cover and cook on high heat for 1 hour. Reduce heat to low and cook for 6–7 hours.

SERVES 6.

 Who Knew? Light Switch

To make this recipe lower in fat, substitute 1½ cups of our Melty Cheese Sauce (Light Switch #6) for the package of Velveeta cheese.

349 Mushroom Ham and Rice

1 (6.7 ounce) box Uncle Ben's Brown
and Wild Rice Mushroom Recipe
rice
3–4 cups cooked, chopped or cubed
ham
1 (4 ounce) can sliced mushrooms,
drained
1 (10 ounce) package frozen green
peas
2 cups chopped celery
2²/₃ cups water

1. Combine rice, seasoning packet, ham, mushrooms, peas, celery, and water in sprayed, 4- or 5-quart slow cooker. Stir to mix well.
2. Cover and cook on low heat for 2–4 hours.

SERVES 4–6.

 ## Who Knew?

Keep celery lasting even longer in your refrigerator by wrapping it in aluminum foil!

350 Saucy Ham Loaf

This ham loaf is super-tasty with our sweet-and-hot mustard sauce. The mustard should be prepared one day before serving, and you might want to make extra—it's also delicious on ham sandwiches.

4 ounces dry mustard
1 cup vinegar
5 eggs, beaten, divided
1 cup sugar
1 pound ground ham
½ pound ground beef
½ pound ground pork
2 eggs, slightly beaten
1 cup Italian-seasoned breadcrumbs
1 (5 ounce) can evaporated milk
¼ cup chili sauce
1 teaspoon seasoned salt

1. Mix mustard and vinegar in bowl until smooth and let stand overnight.
2. Add 3 beaten eggs and sugar to mustard mixture. Cook in double boiler over medium heat until mixture coats the spoon, about 8–10 minutes. Cool and store in covered jars in refrigerator until ready to serve with ham loaf.
3. Combine ham, beef, pork, 2 beaten eggs, breadcrumbs, evaporated milk, chili sauce, and seasoned salt in bowl. Form into loaf in sprayed, oval slow cooker; shape loaf so that neither end touches sides of cooker.
4. Cover and cook on low heat for 6–7 hours.

SERVES 4–6.

351 Tator Talk Soup

5 medium potatoes, peeled, cubed
2 cups cooked, cubed ham
1 cup fresh broccoli florets, cut very fine
1 (10 ounce) can Cheddar cheese soup
1 (10 ounce) can fiesta nacho cheese soup
1 (14 ounce) can chicken broth
2½ soup canfuls milk
Paprika for garnish (optional)

1. Place potatoes, ham, and broccoli in sprayed slow cooker.
2. Combine soups, broth, and milk in saucepan. Heat just enough to mix until smooth. Stir into slow cooker.
3. Cover and cook on low heat for 7–9 hours.
4. When ready to eat, sprinkle paprika over each serving, if desired.

SERVES 6.

 Who Knew?

Want to know the easiest way to peel a raw potato? Simply insert a corkscrew into one end, then peel as usual with a peeler. The cork screw will keep the peeler clear of your holding hand.

352 Black Bean Soup

2 (14 ounce) cans chicken broth
3 (15 ounce) cans black beans, rinsed and drained
2 (10 ounce) cans tomatoes and green chilies
1 onion, chopped
1 teaspoon ground cumin
½ teaspoon dried thyme
½ teaspoon dried oregano
2–3 cups cooked, finely diced ham
¾ cup water

1. Combine chicken broth and black beans in slow cooker and cook on high heat just long enough for ingredients to get hot, about 20–30 minutes.
2. With potato masher, mash about half beans in slow cooker.
3. Reduce heat to low and add tomatoes and green chilies, onion, cumin, thyme, oregano, ham, and water.
4. Cover and cook for 5–6 hours.

SERVES 4–6.

353 Corn-Ham Chowder

In this ingenious recipe, potato flakes are used to thicken up the soup without using flour.

1 (14 ounce) can chicken broth
1 cup milk
1 (10 ounce) can cream of celery soup
1 (15 ounce) can cream-style corn
1 (15 ounce) can whole kernel corn
½ cup dry potato flakes
1 onion, chopped
2–3 cups cooked, chopped, ham
Salt and black pepper to taste

1. Combine broth, milk, soup, cream-style corn, whole kernel corn, potato flakes, onion, and ham in 6-quart slow cooker.
2. Cover and cook on low heat for 4–5 hours.
3. When ready to serve, sprinkle with salt and pepper to taste.

SERVES 6.

 Who Knew? Light Switch

Make this recipe low fat by substituting 1¾ cups of our Healthy Chicken Broth (Light Switch #1) for the can of chicken broth, and 1¼ cups of our Low-Fat Cream of Celery Soup Base (Light Switch #4) for the can of soup.

354 Sauerkraut and Bratwurst Supper

1 (28 ounce) jar refrigerated sauerkraut
¾ cup beer
1 tablespoon Worcestershire sauce
1 (1 ounce) packet onion soup mix
2 pounds bratwurst

1. Combine sauerkraut, beer, Worcestershire sauce, and onion soup mix in sprayed, 4- or 5-quart slow cooker; mix well.
2. Cut bratwurst in diagonal slices and place on top of sauerkraut-beer mixture.
3. Cover and cook on low heat for 5–6 hours or on high heat for 2 hours 30 minutes–3 hours.

SERVES 4–6.

355 Sausage and Beans

1 (1 pound) fully cooked smoked link sausage
2 (15 ounce) cans baked beans
1 (15 ounce) can great northern beans, drained
1 (15 ounce) can pinto beans, drained
½ cup chili sauce
⅔ cup packed brown sugar
⅛ teaspoon black pepper
1 tablespoon Worcestershire sauce

1. Cut link sausage into 1-inch slices. Place sausage in slow cooker, then layer baked beans, great northern beans, and pinto beans on top.
2. Combine chili sauce, brown sugar, pepper, and Worcestershire sauce in bowl and pour over beans and sausage.
3. Cover and cook on low heat for 4 hours. Stir before serving.

SERVES 8.

356 Spicy Sausage Soup

1 pound mild bulk sausage
1 pound hot bulk sausage
2 (15 ounce) cans Mexican stewed tomatoes
3 cups chopped celery
1 cup sliced carrots
1 (15 ounce) can cut green beans, drained
1 (14 ounce) can chicken broth
1 teaspoon seasoned salt
1 teaspoon salt
1 cup water

1. Combine mild and hot sausage, shape into small balls, and place in nonstick skillet. Cook over medium-high heat until brown on all sides, about 2–3 minutes per side. Drain and place in large slow cooker.
2. Add remaining ingredients and stir gently, making sure to keep meatballs intact.
3. Cover and cook on low heat for 6–7 hours.

SERVES 6.

357 Sweet-and-Sour Sausage Links

Your kids will love these mini sausage links for dinner, but this recipe also makes a great appetizer when served on its own (without rice).

2 (16 ounce) packages miniature smoked sausage links
¾ cup chili sauce
1 cup packed brown sugar
¼ cup horseradish

1. Place sausages in sprayed, 4-quart slow cooker.
2. Combine chili sauce, brown sugar, and horseradish in bowl and pour over sausages.
3. Cover and cook on low heat for 4 hours. Serve over hot rice.

SERVES 4–6.

358 Navy Bean Soup

8 slices thick-cut bacon, divided
1 carrot
3 (15 ounce) cans navy beans with liquid
3 ribs celery, chopped
1 onion, chopped
2 (14 ounce) cans chicken broth
1 teaspoon Italian herb seasoning
1 cup water
1 (10 ounce) can cream of chicken soup

1. Cook bacon in skillet, drain, and crumble. Reserve 2 crumbled slices for garnish.
2. Cut carrot in half lengthwise and slice.
3. Combine most of crumbled bacon, carrot, beans, celery, onion, broth, seasoning, and water in 5- or 6-quart slow cooker; stir to mix.
4. Cover and cook on low heat for 5–6 hours.
5. Ladle 2 cups soup mixture into food processor or blender and process until smooth.
6. Return to cooker, add cream of chicken soup, and stir to mix.
7. Turn heat to high and cook for additional 10–15 minutes.

SERVES 4–6.

 Who Knew? Light Switch

To make this recipe lower in fat, substitute 1¼ cup of our Low-Fat Cream of Chicken Soup Base (Light Switch #3) for the can of cream of chicken soup.

---

359 Tasty Tuna Bake

2 (6 ounce) cans white tuna, drained, flaked
1 (10 ounce) can cream of chicken soup
3 eggs, hard-boiled, chopped
3 ribs celery, thinly sliced
1 red bell pepper, seeded, chopped
½ cup coarsely chopped pecans
½ cup mayonnaise
1 teaspoon white pepper
2 cups crushed potato chips, divided
¼ teaspoon salt

1. Combine tuna, soup, eggs, celery, bell pepper, pecans, mayonnaise, white pepper, 1 cup potato chips, and salt in bowl; mix well. Transfer to sprayed slow cooker.
2. Cover and cook on low heat for 5–7 hours. When ready to serve, sprinkle remaining potato chips on top.

SERVES 4–5.

360 Tammy's Seafood Bake

Thanks to reader Tammy Sherwood of Oak Park, Illinois, for this delicious recipe!

2 tablespoons olive oil
1 medium onion, sliced
1 green pepper, sliced
1 (15 ounce) can Italian stewed tomatoes
¼ cup white wine
½ teaspoon dried basil
⅛ teaspoon garlic powder
½ teaspoon salt
¼ teaspoon black pepper
3 frozen flounder fillets, cubed (thawed or frozen)

1. In large bowl, combine olive oil, garlic, onion, green pepper, tomatoes, wine, basil, garlic, salt, and pepper. Fold in flounder cubes.
2. Pour into slow cooker. Cover and cook on high for 4–6 hours.

SERVES 4.

361 St. Pat's Noodles

1 (12 ounce) package fettuccini (medium noodles)
1 cup cream
1 (10 ounce) package frozen chopped spinach, thawed
6 tablespoons (¾ stick) butter, melted
2 teaspoons seasoned salt
1½ cups shredded Cheddar–Monterey Jack cheese blend

1. Cook noodles in saucepan according to package directions; drain. Place in 5- or 6-quart slow cooker.
2. Add cream, spinach, butter, and seasoned salt and stir until they blend well.
3. Cover and cook on low heat for 2–3 hours.
4. When ready to serve, fold in cheese.

SERVES 4.

 Who Knew? Light Switch

To make this recipe lower in fat, substitute our Low-Fat Four-Cheese Blend (Light Switch #5) for the Cheddar-Monterey Jack cheese blend.

362 Vegetarian Chili

1 (15 ounce) can pinto beans, drained
1 (15 ounce) can black beans, drained
1 (15 ounce) can kidney beans, drained
1 (15 ounce) can whole kernel corn, drained
2 (15 ounce) cans diced tomatoes with green chilies
1 (6 ounce) can tomato paste
1 green, red, or yellow bell pepper, seeded, chopped
1 medium onion, diced
2 garlic cloves, minced
½ tablespoon ground cumin
2 teaspoons chili powder
  Dash cayenne pepper
½ teaspoon salt
¼ teaspoon black pepper

1. Place all ingredients in slow cooker; stir to mix well. Cook on low for 5–6 hours.

SERVES 5.

363 Cheese-Spaghetti and Spinach

1 (7 ounce) box spaghetti
2 tablespoons butter
1 (8 ounce) carton sour cream
1 cup shredded Cheddar cheese
1 (8 ounce) package shredded Monterey Jack cheese, divided
1 (12 ounce) package frozen, chopped spinach, thawed, well-drained
1 (6 ounce) can Cheddar French-fried onions, divided

1. Cook spaghetti according to package directions, drain, and stir in butter until it melts.
2. Combine sour cream, Cheddar cheese, half Monterey Jack cheese, spinach, and half can fried onions in large bowl.
3. Fold cheese mixture into spaghetti and spoon into sprayed slow cooker.
4. Cover and cook on low heat for 2–4 hours.
5. When ready to serve, sprinkle remaining Jack cheese and fried onions over top.

SERVES 4.

 ## Who Knew?

Before cooking spinach or other greens, it's important to squeeze the leaves between paper towels to remove excess moisture. The excess water on leaves in a hot pan creates steam, leaving greens that are stewed and mushy rather than bright and tender.

364 Vegetarian Coconut Curry

This Thai-inspired dish will definitely break up your normal dinner routine! Look for cans of coconut milk in the ethnic aisle of your grocery store or at Mexican and Asian markets.

3 cups chopped cauliflower
1 (15 ounce) can garbanzo beans (chickpeas), drained
1 cup frozen cut green beans, thawed
1 small to medium onion, chopped
½ cup chopped peanuts or cashews
1 (14 ounce) can vegetable broth
2½ teaspoons curry powder
1 (14 ounce) can light coconut milk
¼ cup fresh basil leaves, finely chopped

1. Combine cauliflower, garbanzo beans, green beans, onion, and peanuts in a 3½ - or 4-quart slow cooker. Stir in broth and curry powder.
2. Cover and cook on low for 5–6 hours, or on high heat for 2½–3 hours. Stir in coconut milk and basil before serving.

SERVES 4–6.

 Who Knew?

If you're chopping nuts in a food processor, more oil is released than when you chop by hand, and you'll wind up with a sticky mess. To avoid this, simply add a bit of flour to the nuts before chopping.

365 Harvest Vegetable Casserole

3–4 medium new (red) potatoes with peels, sliced
2 onions, sliced
3 carrots, sliced
2 cups chopped green cabbage
¼ cup Italian dressing
1 (1 pound) kielbasa sausage
1 (15 ounce) can Italian stewed tomatoes

1. Place potatoes, onions, carrots, cabbage, and Italian dressing in sprayed, large slow cooker.
2. Cut sausage into 1-inch pieces and place on top of vegetables.
3. Drizzle stewed tomatoes over vegetables in even layers.
4. Cover and cook on low heat until vegetables are tender, about 6–8 hours.

SERVES 4–6.

 Who Knew? Light Switch

To save money, try using our Italian Salad Dressing Mix (Light Switch #11)!

Index

Note: Numbers refer to recipe number, not page number.

Note: Numbers refer to recipe number, not page number.

Note: Numbers refer to recipe number, not page number.

Note: Numbers refer to recipe number, not page number.

Note: Numbers refer to recipe number, not page number.

Note: Numbers refer to recipe number, not page number.

Note: Numbers refer to recipe number, not page number.

Note: Numbers refer to recipe number, not page number.

Alphabetical List of Recipes

Note: Numbers refer to recipe numbers (not page numbers). "LS" denotes Light Switch recipes.

Note: Numbers refer to recipe numbers (not page numbers). "LS" denotes Light Switch recipes.

Note: Numbers refer to recipe numbers (not page numbers). "LS" denotes Light Switch recipes.

Note: Numbers refer to recipe numbers (not page numbers). "LS" denotes Light Switch recipes.

The Who Knew?
Guide to Refrigeration, Freezing, and Thawing

It's great having food in your refrigerator at the ready, but what's even better is wondering what you're going to eat for dinner, and then remembering that you have a casserole in the freezer! Freezing food is a great way to keep it for later, but how do you know if it's safe? The following guide gives you information on how to properly freeze and refrigerate your food, how to safely thaw it, and how long it will keep.

How to Prepare Foods for Refrigerating or Freezing

Hot food can be placed directly in the refrigerator or it can be rapidly chilled in an ice or cold water bath before refrigerating. Cover foods to retain moisture and prevent them from picking up odors from other foods.

- A large pot of food like soup or stew should be divided into small portions and put in shallow containers before being refrigerated. A large cut of meat or whole poultry should be divided into smaller pieces or placed in shallow containers before refrigerating.

- Raw meat, poultry, and seafood should be in a sealed container or wrapped securely to prevent raw juices from contaminating other foods. To be extra careful, place raw meats under other food in the fridge to decrease the risk of contamination by dripping liquids. An adjustable temperature meat drawer maximizes the storage time of meats and cheeses. Additional cool air is directed into the drawer to keep items very cold without freezing.

- When storing foods in the freezer, proper packaging helps maintain quality and prevent freezer burn. It is safe to freeze meat or poultry directly in its original packaging, however this type of wrap is permeable to air and quality may diminish over time. For prolonged storage, overwrap these packages as you would any food for long-term storage. It is not necessary to rinse meat and poultry. Freeze unopened vacuum packages as is. If you notice that a package has accidentally been torn or has opened while food is in the freezer, the food is still safe to use; merely overwrap or rewrap it.

- In the refrigerator, sealed crisper drawers provide an optimal storage environment for fruits and vegetables. Vegetables require higher humidity conditions while fruits require lower humidity conditions. Some crispers are equipped with controls to allow the consumer to customize each drawer's humidity level.

- The one storage area of your fridge you should avoid is on the door. Don't store perishable foods in the door. Eggs should be stored in the carton on a shelf (upside-down for longer life!).

Keeping Your Refrigerator Clean

One very important step in keeping your food safe is keeping your refrigerator clean. Wipe up spills immediately—clean surfaces thoroughly with hot, soapy water; then rinse.

- Once a week, make it a habit to throw out perishable foods that should no longer be eaten. To keep the refrigerator smelling fresh and help eliminate odors, place an opened box of baking soda on a shelf. Avoid using solvent cleaning agents, abrasives, and all cleansers that may impart a chemical taste to food or ice cubes, or cause damage to the interior finish of your refrigerator.

- The exterior may be cleaned with a soft cloth and mild liquid dishwashing detergent as well as cleansers and polishes that are made for appliance use. The front grill should be kept free of dust and lint to permit free air flow to the condenser. Several times a year the condenser coil should be cleaned with a brush or vacuum cleaner to remove dirt, lint, or other accumulations. This will ensure efficiency and top performance.

Safe Refrigerator Temperature

- Refrigeration slows bacterial growth. Bacteria exist everywhere in nature. They are in the soil, air, water, and the foods we eat. When they have nutrients (food), moisture, and favorable temperatures, they grow rapidly, increasing in numbers to the point where some types of bacteria can cause illness. Bacteria grow most rapidly in the range of temperatures between 40° and 140° F, the "Danger Zone," some doubling in number in as little as 20 minutes. A refrigerator set at 40° F or below will protect most foods.

- For safety, it is important to verify the temperature of your refrigerator. Refrigerators should be set to maintain a temperature of 40° F or below. Some refrigerators have built-in thermometers to measure their internal temperature. For those refrigerators without this feature, keep an appliance thermometer (which is specifically made to work in cold temperatures) in the refrigerator to monitor the temperature. This can be critical in the event of a power outage. When the power goes back on, if the refrigerator is still 40°, your is still safe. Foods held at temperatures above 40° for more than 2 hours should not be consumed. Be sure refrigerator/freezer doors are closed tightly at all times. Don't open refrigerator/freezer doors more often than necessary and close them as soon as possible.

What Can I Freeze?

You can freeze almost any food. Some exceptions are canned food or eggs in shells. However, once the food (such as a ham) is out of the can, you may freeze it. Being able to freeze food and being pleased with the quality after defrosting are two different things. Some foods simply don't freeze well. Examples are mayonnaise, cream sauce, and lettuce. Raw meat and poultry maintain their quality longer than their cooked counterparts because moisture is lost during cooking.

Is Frozen Food Safe?

Food stored constantly at 0° F will always be safe. Only the quality suffers with lengthy freezer storage. Freezing keeps food safe by slowing the movement of molecules, causing microbes to enter a dormant stage. Freezing preserves food for extended periods because it prevents the growth of microorganisms that cause both food spoilage and foodborne illness.

- Freezing to 0° F inactivates any microbes—bacteria, yeasts, and molds—present in food. Once thawed, however, these microbes can again become active, multiplying under the right conditions to levels that can lead to foodborne illness. Since they will then grow at about the same rate as microorganisms on fresh food, you must handle thawed items as you would any perishable food. Thorough cooking, however, will destroy all parasites.

Freshness & Quality of Frozen Food

Freshness and quality at the time of freezing affect the condition of frozen foods. If frozen at peak quality, thawed foods emerge tasting better than foods frozen near the end of their useful life. So freeze items you won't use quickly sooner rather than later. Store all foods at 0° F or lower to retain vitamin content, color, flavor and texture. However, the freezing process itself does not destroy nutrients. In meat and poultry products, there is little change in nutrient value during freezer storage.

- Freeze food as fast as possible to maintain its quality. Rapid freezing prevents undesirable large ice crystals from forming throughout the product because the molecules don't have time to form into the characteristic six-sided snowflake. Slow freezing creates large, disruptive ice crystals. During thawing, they damage the cells and dissolve emulsions. This causes meat to "drip" and lose juiciness. Emulsions such as mayonnaise or cream will separate and appear curdled.

- Ideally, a food 2-inches thick should freeze completely in about 2 hours. If your home freezer has a "quick-freeze" shelf, use it. Never stack packages to be frozen. Instead, spread them out in one layer on various shelves, stacking them only after frozen solid.

Freezer Burn and Color Changes in Frozen Food

Freezer burn does not make food unsafe, merely dry in spots. It appears as grayish-brown leathery spots and is caused by air coming in contact with the surface of the food. Cut freezer-burned portions away either before or after cooking the food. Heavily freezer-burned foods may have to be discarded for quality reasons.

- Color changes can also occur in frozen foods. The bright red color of meat as purchased usually turns dark or pale brown depending on its variety. This may be due to lack of oxygen, freezer burn or abnormally long storage.

- Freezing doesn't usually cause color changes in poultry. However, the bones and the meat near them can become dark. Bone darkening results when pigment seeps through the porous bones of young poultry into the surrounding tissues when the poultry meat is frozen and thawed.

- The dulling of color in frozen vegetables and cooked foods is usually the result of excessive drying due to improper packaging or over-lengthy storage.

What if There's a Power Outage in My Freezer?

If there is a power outage, the freezer fails, or if the freezer door has been left ajar by mistake, your food may still be safe to use if ice crystals remain. If the freezer has failed and a repairman is on the way, or it appears the power will be on soon, don't open the freezer door. If the freezer door was left ajar and the freezer continued to keep the food cold, the food should stay safe.

- A freezer full of food will usually keep about 2 days if the door is kept shut; a half-full freezer will last about a day. The freezing compartment in a refrigerator may not keep foods frozen as long. If the freezer is not full, quickly group packages together so they will retain the cold more effectively. Separate meat and poultry items from other foods so if they begin to thaw, their juices won't drip onto other foods.

- When the power is off, you may want to put dry ice, block ice, or bags of ice in the freezer or transfer foods to a friend's freezer until power is restored. When it is freezing outside and there is snow on the ground, the outdoors may seem like a good place to keep food until the power comes on; however, frozen food can thaw if it is exposed to the sun's rays even when the temperature is very cold. Refrigerated food may become too warm and foodborne bacteria could grow. The outside temperature could vary hour by hour and the temperature outside will not protect refrigerated and frozen food. Additionally, perishable items could be exposed to unsanitary conditions or to animals, which may harbor bacteria or disease.

- To determine the safety of foods once the power is back on, check their condition and temperature. If food is partly frozen, still has ice crystals, or is as cold as if it were in a refrigerator (40 °F), it is safe to refreeze or use. It's not necessary to cook raw foods before refreezing. Throw way foods that have been warmer than 40° for more than 2 hours, and any foods that have been contaminated by raw meat juices. You also may want to throw away soft or melted ice cream for quality's sake.

How Long Will Food Last in The Refrigerator or Freezer?

This chart gives you the optimal storage time of foods kept at 40° (refrigerator) and 0° (freezer). Note: the freezer storage times are for quality only. Frozen foods remain safe to eat indefinitely.

Refrigerator & Freezer Storage Chart

Since product dates aren't a guide for safe use of a product, consult this chart and follow these tips. These short but safe time limits will help keep refrigerated food 40° F (4° C) from spoiling or becoming dangerous.

- Purchase the product before "sell-by" or expiration dates.
- Follow handling recommendations on product.
- Keep meat and poultry in its package until just before using.
- If freezing meat and poultry in its original package longer than 2 months, overwrap these packages with airtight heavy-duty foil, plastic wrap, or freezer paper, or place the package inside a plastic bag.

Because freezing 0° F (-18° C) keeps food safe indefinitely, the following recommended storage times are for quality only.

Product	Refrigerator	Freezer
Eggs		
Fresh, in shell	4 to 5 weeks	Don't freeze
Raw yolks, whites	2 to 4 days	1 year
Hard cooked	1 week	Don't freeze well
Liquid pasteurized eggs or egg substitutes,		
opened	3 days	Don't freeze
unopened	10 days	1 year
Mayonnaise, commercial Refrigerate after opening	2 months	Don't freeze
TV Dinners, Frozen Casseroles		
Keep frozen until ready to heat		3 to 4 months
Deli & Vacuum-Packed Products		
Store-prepared (or homemade) egg, chicken, tuna, ham, macaroni salads	3 to 5 days	Don't freeze well
Pre-stuffed pork & lamb chops, chicken breasts stuffed w/dressing	1 day	Don't freeze well
Store-cooked convenience meals	3 to 4 days	Don't freeze well
Commercial brand vacuum-packed dinners with USDA seal, unopened	2 weeks	Don't freeze well
Raw Hamburger, Ground & Stew Meat		
Hamburger & stew meats	1 to 2 days	3 to 4 months
Ground turkey, veal, pork, lamb	1 to 2 days	3 to 4 months
Ham, Corned Beef		
Corned beef in pouch with pickling juices	5 to 7 days	Drained, 1 month
Ham, canned, labeled "Keep Refrigerated,"		
unopened	6 to 9 months	Don't freeze
opened	3 to 5 days	1 to 2 months
Ham, fully cooked, whole	7 days	1 to 2 months
Ham, fully cooked, half	3 to 5 days	1 to 2 months
Ham, fully cooked, slices	3 to 4 days	1 to 2 months
Hot Dogs & Lunch Meats		**(in freezer wrap)**
Hot dogs,		
opened package	1 week	1 to 2 months
unopened package	2 weeks	1 to 2 months
Lunch meats,		
opened package	3 to 5 days	1 to 2 months
unopened package	2 weeks	1 to 2 months

Product	Refrigerator	Freezer
Soups & Stews		
Vegetable or meat-added & mixtures of them	3 to 4 days	2 to 3 months
Bacon & Sausage		
Bacon	7 days	1 month
Sausage, raw from pork, beef, chicken or turkey	1 to 2 days	1 to 2 months
Smoked breakfast links, patties	7 days	1 to 2 months
Summer sausage labeled "Keep Refrigerated,"		
unopened	3 months	1 to 2 months
opened	3 weeks	1 to 2 months
Fresh Meat (Beef, Veal, Lamb, & Pork)		
Steaks	3 to 5 days	6 to 12 months
Chops	3 to 5 days	4 to 6 months
Roasts	3 to 5 days	4 to 12 months
Variety meats (tongue, kidneys, liver, heart, chitterlings)	1 to 2 days	3 to 4 months
Meat Leftovers		
Cooked meat & meat dishes	3 to 4 days	2 to 3 months
Gravy & meat broth	1 to 2 days	2 to 3 months
Fresh Poultry		
Chicken or turkey, whole	1 to 2 days	1 year
Chicken or turkey, parts	1 to 2 days	9 months
Giblets	1 to 2 days	3 to 4 months
Cooked Poultry, Leftover		
Fried chicken	3 to 4 days	4 months
Cooked poultry dishes	3 to 4 days	4 to 6 months
Pieces, plain	3 to 4 days	4 months
Pieces covered with broth, gravy	1 to 2 days	6 months
Chicken nuggets, patties	1 to 2 days	1 to 3 months
Fish & Shellfish		
Lean fish	1 to 2 days	6 months
Fatty fish	1 to 2 days	2 to 3 months
Cooked fish	3 to 4 days	4 to 6 months
Smoked fish	14 days	2 months
Fresh shrimp, scallops, crawfish, squid	1 to 2 days	3 to 6 months
Canned seafood	after opening	out of can
Pantry, 5 years	3 to 4 days	2 months

Safe Thawing

The best way to thaw foods is in the refrigerator, however, thawing in cold water or in the microwave are also safe.

- Never thaw foods in a garage, basement, car, dishwasher, hot water, or plastic garbage bag. Thawing foods on the kitchen counter, outdoors, or on the porch is also not safe. Even though the center of the package may still be frozen as it thaws on the counter, the outer layer of the food could be in the "Danger Zone," between 40 and 140° F—temperatures where bacteria multiply rapidly.

- If you have time to plan ahead for slow, safe thawing in the refrigerator, you should know that small items may defrost overnight, but most foods require a day or two. And large items like turkeys may take longer, approximately one day for each 5 pounds of weight.

- After thawing in the refrigerator, items such as ground meat, stew meat, poultry, seafood, should remain safe and of good quality for an additional day or two before cooking; red meat cuts (such as beef, pork or lamb roasts, chops and steaks) 3 to 5 days. Food thawed in the refrigerator can be refrozen without cooking, although there may be some loss of quality.

- For faster thawing, place food in a leak-proof plastic bag and immerse it in cold water. (If the bag leaks, bacteria from the air or surrounding environment could be introduced into the food. Tissues can also absorb water like a sponge, resulting in a watery product.) Check the water frequently to be sure it stays cold. Change the water every 30 minutes.

- Small packages of meat, poultry or seafood—about a pound—may thaw in an hour or less. A 3-to 4-pound package may take 2–3 hours. For whole turkeys, estimate about 30 minutes per pound. If thawed completely, the food must be cooked immediately. Foods thawed by the cold water method should be cooked before refreezing.

- When microwave-defrosting food, plan to cook it immediately after thawing because some areas of the food may become warm and begin to cook during microwaving. For more information on microwaving food, see the Who Knew? Guide to Microwaving Anything in *365 Everyday Dinners*.

Cooking Frozen Foods

For best results, thaw frozen foods in the refrigerator before cooking. However, when there is not enough time to thaw frozen foods, or you're simply in a hurry, raw or cooked meat, poultry or casseroles can be cooked or reheated from the frozen state. Just be sure to remember that it will take approximately one and a half times as long to cook.

Refreezing

Unlike microwave and cold-water thawing, food thawed in the refrigerator is safe to refreeze without cooking, although there may be a loss of quality due to the moisture lost through thawing. After cooking raw foods which were previously frozen, it is safe to freeze the cooked foods. If previously cooked foods are thawed in the refrigerator, you may refreeze the unused portion. Freeze leftovers within 3–4 days. Do not refreeze any foods left outside the refrigerator longer than 2 hours; 1 hour in temperatures above 90° F.

- If you purchase previously frozen meat, poultry or fish at a retail store, you can refreeze if it has been handled properly.

Measurement Equivalents

Doubling up a recipe, or using metric measuring utensils? Use these helpful measurement equivalents to make cooking easier.

Measurement Conversions

3 teaspoons = 1 tablespoon

4 tablespoons = ¼ cup

2 cups = 1 pint

4 cups = 1 quart

1 gallon = 4 quarts

½ fluid ounce = 1 tablespoon

8 fluid ounces = 1 cup

Metric Equivalents

1 teaspoon = 5 milliliters

1 tablespoon = 15 milliliters

1 cup = 240 milliliters

1 quart (4 cups) = .95 liter

1 ounce = 28 grams

½ pound = 227 grams

1 pound = 454 grams

Oven Temperature Equivalents

225° F = 110° C = Gas mark ¼

250° F = 125° C = Gas mark ½

275° F = 140° C = Gas mark 1

300° F = 150° C = Gas mark 2

325° F = 165° C = Gas mark 3

350° F = 180° C = Gas mark 4

375° F = 190° C = Gas mark 5

400° F = 200° C = Gas mark 6

425° F = 220° C = Gas mark 7

450° F = 230° C = Gas mark 8

475° F = 240° C = Gas mark 9

Common Substitutions

Preparing a recipe and realize you forgot one essential ingredient? Use the chart on the following pages to find a proper substitution. Unless otherwise noted, use the substitution in equal measure to the ingredient called for in the recipe.

Ingredient Called for	Substitute
Active dry yeast (one ¼-ounce envelope)	1 cake compressed yeast
Allspice (for baking only)	1 part ground cinnamon + 2 parts ground cloves or ground nutmeg
Anise seed	fennel seed
Apples (1 cup chopped)	1 cup firm chopped pears + 1 tablespoon lemon juice
Arrowroot	use 2 tablespoons flour for every 4 teaspoons arrowroot
Baking powder (1 teaspoon, double-acting)	⅝ teaspoon cream of tartar + ¼ teaspoon baking soda or ¼ teaspoon baking soda + ¼ cup sour milk or buttermilk (lessen other liquid in recipe)
Basil (dried)	tarragon or summer savory or thyme or oregano
Bay leaf	thyme
Black pepper	cayenne pepper (use much less; start with a pinch)
Brandy	cognac or rum
Broth, 1 cup	1 cup hot water + 1 cube or teaspoon bouillon
Bulgur	cracked wheat or kasha or brown rice or couscous or quinoa
Butter	hard margarine or shortening; or oil if it is not a baked good
Buttermilk (1 cup)	1 cup milk + 1¾ tablespoons cream of tartar or 1 tablespoon lemon juice + milk to make 1 cup (let stand 5 minutes) or sour cream
Cake flour (1 cup)	1 cup minus 2 tablespoons unsifted all-purpose flour
Capers	chopped green olives
Caraway seed	fennel seed or cumin
Cardamom	cinnamon or mace
Chervil	parsley or tarragon or ground anise seed (use a bit less)
Chives	onion powder (small amount) or finely chopped leeks or shallots (small amount) or scallion greens
Chocolate, baking, unsweetened	3 tablespoons unsweetened cocoa powder + 1 tablespoon (one ounce or square) butter or 3 tablespoons carob powder + 2 tablespoons water
Chocolate, semisweet (6 ounces)	9 tablespoons unsweetened cocoa powder or squares + 7 tablespoons sugar + 3 tablespoons butter
Cilantro	parsley and lemon juice
Cinnamon	allspice (use less) or cardamom
Cloves (ground)	allspice or nutmeg or mace
Club soda	sparkling mineral water or seltzer

Cornmeal	polenta
Cornstarch	flour, as thickener
Corn syrup, light (1 cup)	1¾ cup granulated sugar + ¼ cup more of the liquid called for in recipe
Crème fraîche	sour cream in most recipes or ½ sour cream + ½ heavy cream in sauces. Note that crème fraîche can be boiled but sour cream cannot.
Creole seasoning	mixture of salt, black pepper, paprika, garlic powder, and a pinch of cayenne pepper
Cumin	1 part anise + 2 parts caraway or fennel seed (grind if necessary)
Dill seed	caraway or celery seed
Egg (1)	1 tablespoon cornstarch + 3 tablespoons water or 3 tablespoons mayonnaise or ½ of a mashed banana + ¼ teaspoon baking powder
Evaporated milk	half-and-half or cream
Flour	cornstarch or instant potato flakes or pancake mix
Garlic (1 medium clove)	¼ teaspoon minced dried garlic or ⅛ teaspoon garlic powder or ½ teaspoon garlic salt (omitting ½ teaspoon salt from recipe)
Ghee	clarified butter
Herbs, fresh (1 tablespoon)	1 teaspoon dried herbs
Honey (1 cup, in baked goods)	1¼ cups granulated sugar + ¼ cup more of the liquid called for in recipe
Italian seasoning	a blend of any of the following: oregano, basil, and rosemary
Lemongrass	lemon juice or lemon zest or finely chopped lemon verbena or lime zest
Lovage	celery leaves
Marjoram	oregano (use small amount) or thyme or savory
Masa harina	cornmeal
Mascarpone	8 ounces cream cheese whipped with 3 tablespoons sour cream and 2 tablespoons milk
Milk (in baked goods)	fruit juice + ½ teaspoon baking soda mixed in with the flour
Milk (1 cup)	½ cup evaporated milk + ½ cup water or ¼ cup powdered milk + ⅞ cup of water
Milk, whole	same as above + 2 ½ teaspoons melted and cooled butter
Milk, evaporated	half-and-half or cream

Molasses	honey
Mustard, dry (1 teaspoon)	I tablespoon prepared mustard
Nutmeg	allspice or cloves or mace
Oregano	marjoram or thyme
Pancetta	lean bacon (cooked) or very thinly sliced ham
Polenta	cornmeal or corn grits
Poultry seasoning	sage + a blend of any of these: thyme, marjoram, savory, black pepper, rosemary
Rosemary	thyme
Saffron (1/8 teaspoon)	1 teaspoon dried yellow marigold petals or 1 teaspoon safflower petals
Sage	poultry seasoning or savory or marjoram
Scallions	white or Spanish onions, use 1/3 of amount listed
Self-rising flour (1 cup)	1 cup all-purpose flour + 1½ teaspoons baking powder + 1/8 teaspoon salt
Shallots	scallions or leeks or yellow onions
Shortening (baked goods only)	butter or margarine
Sour cream	1 tablespoon white vinegar + milk (let stand 5 minutes before using) or 1 tablespoon lemon juice + evaporated milk or plain yogurt
Tahini	peanut butter
Tarragon	anise (use small amount) or chervil (use larger amount) or parsley (use larger amount) or a pinch of fennel seed
Tomato paste (1 tablespoon)	1 tablespoon ketchup or ½ cup tomato sauce (reduce some of the liquid in recipe)
Tomato sauce (2 cups)	¾ cup tomato paste + 1 cup water
Turmeric	mustard powder
Vanilla extract (baked goods only)	almond extract or any other extract
Vinegar	lemon juice for cooking and salads or wine in marinades
Yogurt	sour cream or crème fraîche or buttermilk or mayonnaise (in small amounts)

Your Recipes

Your Recipes

Your Recipes

Your Recipes

Your Recipes

Your Recipes

Your Recipes

Your Recipes

who knew?

Don't forget to find us on the web!

Visit WhoKnewTips.com, or follow us on Facebook or Twitter at www.Facebook.com/whoknewtips and www.Twitter.com/whoknewhome.

- Submit your tips and recipes

- Find out more about our products

- Get our latest household tips and deals from around the web